T0327970

"With characteristic lucidity and ins ⌐ ⌐ ⌐⌐⌐⌐ in this text an accessible yet contoured presentation of Christian teaching on the death of Jesus Christ. The volume explores the variety that exists among classic theological accounts of the atonement, explaining and critiquing their particularities while setting aside certain popular misreadings. Yet the volume also sets forth the outlines of a richly constructive account of the doctrine of the atonement that is highly creative while remaining attentive to the Scriptures and sensitive to tradition. This book will inform and challenge students of theology in welcome ways."

Paul T. Nimmo, King's Chair of Systematic Theology, University of Aberdeen

"*Approaching the Atonement* does many things very well. It provides a surefooted, historically and theologically informed survey of the doctrine of the atonement. It does so while engaging both creatively and critically with the classic models of the atonement. Moreover, it advances new and helpful frameworks for understanding the atonement and for addressing important objections raised in connection with the doctrine. Throughout, Professor Crisp displays a combination of clarity and rigor that is as characteristic of his work as it is generally rare in academic writing."

Steven R. Guthrie, professor of theology/religion and the arts, Belmont University

"There is more to this deceitfully little treatise on atonement than meets the eye, a superb reflection on the central theme of our faith and theology. This is vintage Oliver Crisp: wide learning, sharp analysis, careful consideration of options, and a thoughtful tentative solution. Oliver moves effortlessly between biblical, historical, philosophical, dogmatic, and contemporary contextual issues. This is retrieval theology at its best, an effort to rediscover the best of the tradition for the sake of the contemporary world. Highly recommended for both the newly initiated and the masters in the guild—everyone will benefit greatly!"

Veli-Matti Kärkkäinen, professor of systematic theology, Fuller Theological Seminary and docent of ecumenics, University of Helsinki

"Oliver Crisp's eagerly anticipated interpretation of the various options on atonement theology does not disappoint. Written in his usual clear style, Crisp distills the various options to their clear and distinct essence, while he identifies their respective tension points. His constructive account stresses the idea of union and participation with Christ, while collecting the best insights from the other views."

Adonis Vidu, professor of theology, Gordon-Conwell Theological Seminary

"Everything Oliver Crisp writes is worth reading. Readers will find here the fruits of his extensive contemplation of the mystery of Christ's reconciling work. He skillfully sifts and evaluates a number of ways of depicting the atonement before presenting his own constructive proposal. For readers, this book is a chance to join one of the most important contemporary laborers in the vineyard of 'faith seeking understanding.'"

Matthew Levering, James N. and Mary D. Perry Jr. Chair of Theology, Mundelein Seminary

APPROACHING THE ATONEMENT

✝

THE RECONCILING WORK OF CHRIST

OLIVER D. CRISP

Academic

An imprint of InterVarsity Press
Downers Grove, Illinois

InterVarsity Press
P.O. Box 1400, Downers Grove, IL 60515-1426
ivpress.com
email@ivpress.com

InterVarsity Press® is the book-publishing division of InterVarsity Christian Fellowship/USA®, a movement of
students and faculty active on campus at hundreds of universities, colleges, and schools of nursing in the United
States of America, and a member movement of the International Fellowship of Evangelical Students. For
information about local and regional activities, visit intervarsity.org.

Cover design: David Fassett
Interior design: Jeanna Wiggins
Images: red paint swashes: © zoom-zoom / iStock / Getty Images Plus
        cloud image: photograph by David Fassett

ISBN 978-0-8308-5197-3 (print)
ISBN 978-0-8308-8854-2 (digital)

Printed in the United States of America ∞

InterVarsity Press is committed to ecological stewardship and to the conservation of natural resources
in all our operations. This book was printed using sustainably sourced paper.

Library of Congress Cataloging-in-Publication Data

A catalog record for this book is available from the Library of Congress.

| **P** | 25 | 24 | 23 | 22 | 21 | 20 | 19 | 18 | 17 | 16 | 15 | 14 | 13 | 12 | 11 | 10 | 9 | 8 | 7 | 6 | 5 | 4 | 3 | 2 | 1 |
| **Y** | 37 | 36 | 35 | 34 | 33 | 32 | 31 | 30 | 29 | 28 | 27 | 26 | 25 | 24 | 23 | 22 | 21 | 20 |

TO FRED SANDERS,

THEOLOGIAN OF THE HOLY TRINITY

CONTENTS

ACKNOWLEDGMENTS

I wish to record grateful thanks to Dr. David Congdon, who saw the potential in this project early on, and to Rev. Dr. David McNutt, my editor at IVP Academic, who shepherded it through the press (with great patience and forbearance). Thanks are also due to several of my classes on the doctrine of atonement at Fuller Theological Seminary whose members read through early drafts of much of this book in the summer term of 2016 and the winter and fall terms of 2018. Particular thanks are due to Christopher Date, Robert Dryer, Zach Maldonado, and David Mitchell, whose comments on particular chapters were invaluable. Conversations with Dr. Jordan Wessling were very helpful in thinking about the moral exemplar view of atonement. He and Rev. Dr. James Arcadi both gave me feedback on a draft of the first chapter, and I am grateful to them for their help. My doctoral student at the University of St. Andrews, Jared Michelson, read through a whole draft and offered comments, which were a great help. My wife, Claire, herself a writer, has been a great source of encouragement and criticism of my prose in just the right measures. This book is dedicated to my friend and collaborator in the Los Angeles Theology Conferences, Fred Sanders, who is the epitome of a generous, winsome theologian.

INTRODUCTION

Atonement. It is a word we often use in Christian churches. It has even made its way into popular culture—witness British novelist Ian McEwan's book *Atonement,* which was made into a feature film in 2007. We are often told from the pulpit, and in popular books on spirituality, that atonement means "at-one-ment." In other words, it is about how God makes us one with himself, reconciling us by means of Christ's death. On the face of it this seems like a good rough-and-ready definition of the doctrine. But a moment's reflection will make us wonder whether it is entirely satisfactory. What is this *at-one-ment*? How are we made one with God by Christ's death on the cross? What sort of union with God is envisaged here? The simple description of atonement as reconciliation with God doesn't really provide any explanation of these things.

Often Christians do not have very clear ideas about key doctrines of the faith. That is not surprising. Most people lack a clear understanding of many important things in life they take for granted, such as how gravity works, or the way smartphones wirelessly connect one person with another across great distances via satellite relays. The Trinity is perhaps the most notorious example of a misunderstood Christian doctrine, and many a Bible study leader has found herself tongue-tied in trying to give some account of it. Yet often Christians think they have a pretty good grip on what the atonement is about. It seems intuitive, somehow, largely because of the familiarity of the Gospel narratives. Most Christians have read the biblical accounts of the life, death, and resurrection of Christ. They have heard sermon after sermon on the atoning work of Christ. That it is by his death that fallen human beings are healed is a mantra that has been drummed into church goers over many years of formation, from Sunday School to Sunday worship.

Once, when he was asked to give a summary statement of the gospel, the great Swiss theologian Karl Barth retorted with the words of the well-known children's hymn, "Jesus loves me this I know, for the Bible tells me so."

Somehow, we understand there to be a connection between these two things, even if we can't always articulate it. God's love is expressed in bringing about our salvation via the death of Christ. What connects God's love and our salvation in Christ is something like this claim: *Jesus dies on the cross to save us from our sins.* Or, as the writer of the pastoral epistles puts it, "Christ Jesus came into the world to save sinners" (1 Tim 1:15). The author of Colossians expands upon this theme when he writes, "Once you were alienated from God and were enemies in your minds because of your evil behavior. But now he has reconciled you by Christ's physical body through death to present you holy in his sight, without blemish and free from accusation—if you continue in your faith, established and firm, and do not move from the hope held out in the gospel" (Col 1:21-23).

Yet, how is it that the crucifixion of one person can somehow save other, fallen human beings? What is it about Christ's death on the cross—the death of a criminal in the Roman world—that makes it the means by which God is able to bring about human reconciliation as these New Testament epistles suggest?

Some Christians, particularly those from evangelical churches, have a ready response to this question. The meaning of the cross, they say, is that by Christ's death on it we are reconciled to God. What is more, this act of reconciliation is made possible by the crucifixion because Christ's death is a punishment for our sins. Christ stands in our place and takes upon himself the punishment due to us as sinners, so that God does not have to punish us. Christ has taken upon himself our debt, releasing us from it in his death. This, in a nutshell, is the doctrine of penal substitution. It is called penal substitution because the central idea is that someone stands in the place of another (that is, becomes a substitute) taking upon himself some punishment due to the other (that is, takes a penalty, the word "penal" having to do with punishment being meted out according to some code of law, in this case, God's moral law).

This is one popular way in which many Christians respond to the question about the meaning of the cross, but it is not the only way Christians have thought about the atonement. Today, it is also a doctrine under fire, and many Christian thinkers, even those within evangelicalism, are moving away from this way of thinking because there appear to be serious problems with it as an account of how Christ's crucifixion reconciles us to God.

Yet even if we set aside recent worries about penal substitution for the present, it is not clear how this account of the atonement provides the meaning for which we were searching. At the very least, much more would need to be said in order to give a complete account of the cross as an atonement. For instance, why is death necessary to atone for sin? Why the death of this particular person, why not someone else? And how does the death of this particular individual bring about an atonement for others? How, in other words, does the action of this individual apply to other individuals, or to a whole group of people? Is it part of the very fabric of atonement that it involves some vicarious action, that is, some circumstance where one person acts on behalf of another, standing in their place?

At the heart of these questions, which are about the meaning of the atonement, is an issue that we will return to in each of the subsequent chapters. This issue has to do with the *mechanism* by means of which Christ reconciles us to God. Put slightly differently, if the atonement is that work of Christ that removes obstacles to communion with God (particularly with respect to human sin) and somehow makes it possible to be united with God in Christ by the power of the Holy Spirit, then how is that achieved? What has to happen in order for this goal to be brought about?

OVERVIEW OF THE CHAPTERS

The first chapter of this book sets up the discussion of different responses to this question about the mechanism of the atonement that follows in chapters two through ten. In approaching the atonement, a number of different issues need to be addressed so that we have a clearer picture of what a doctrine of atonement should look like. First we need to consider why we need a doctrine of the atonement at all. Then we need to distinguish between the nature of atonement (how it is that Christ's work brings about human reconciliation) from the extent of atonement (how many are reconciled to God by means of this saving act). We also need to consider what it is about Christ's work that reconciles us to God, whether it is just the cross, or whether Christ's life and ministry are also relevant factors that bear upon the work of salvation. After that, we need to consider what we mean by a doctrine of atonement. Is it a theory about Christ's work, or a model, or a metaphor, or motif—or something else? All of these different terms are used on a regular basis in the literature on the atonement, but they aren't synonyms. We need to have a clearer idea about what they entail. Without some idea of the difference between these terms confusion about what a doctrine of atonement is supposed to achieve will result.

Having done that, we can consider some different typologies of atonement that have been offered by past writers on the topic. By a typology, I mean a classification of different accounts of the meaning of the atonement. There are a number of distinct doctrines of atonement. Often these are set out and compared against one another to see whether one or more of these accounts is better, or more comprehensive, or closer to the New Testament pictures of Christ's saving work, than the others. In recent times it has become popular to think of three or more types or families of views of the atonement into which different doctrines are sorted rather like sorting different sizes of shoes into different shoe boxes, or different sizes of apples into different barrels. It is important at the outset of a work like this one to give some account of such attempts at classification, as well as the value-judgments that are usually offered in light of such categorization. We need to ask whether there is a particular doctrine of atonement that best captures the meaning of this aspect of Christ's work, or whether no single account of Christ's work is able to do that.

After considering some methodological issues in the first chapter, we turn in the subsequent chapters to set out and evaluate a number of important accounts of the atonement. There are a number of historic works of theology that do the same job. However, the spirited recent debates about the nature of atonement and the development of important atonement-related themes in New Testament scholarship and in systematic theology, including new versions of old doctrines, put some of the particular explanations of atonement in rather a different light. (This is particularly true of penal substitution, though, as we shall see, it is true of other doctrines of atonement as well—and interested readers can begin to chase this up in the Further Reading sections provided at the end of the chapters of the book.) In each of these chapters one or two of these accounts of the atonement is set out. Then some of the most important objections to that particular formulation of the meaning of atonement are tackled. Finally, in an evaluative section, counter arguments are considered in favor of the doctrine. The objective is to interrogate each understanding of the atonement as thoroughly as possible through some of the most important and influential accounts of the doctrine. Imagine a law court in which witnesses are cross-examined in order to establish whether their testimony is trustworthy or not. Like a legal team, we shall be concerned to build a cumulative case on the basis of cross-examining the different "witnesses" before us. In this case, the witnesses are the particular doctrines of atonement, and they witness to the meaning of the atonement as it is explained to us in the different writings of Scripture and in subsequent Christian tradition. We want to establish the extent to which their testimony is, as it were, reliable. That is our task.

We shall see that not all atonement doctrines are equal, and that some are more satisfactory or more comprehensive than others. We shall even find that such cross-examination enables us to see that several traditional accounts of the cross of Christ do not amount to a doctrine of atonement at all, which is an important and unexpected result.

Chapters two and three consider several of the ways in which the theologians of the first millennia after Christ contributed to the doctrine of atonement. Chapter two looks at the work of Athanasius and Irenaeus in particular. Both these theologians have a rather different account of the work of Christ than most Protestant and evangelical Christians today. They think of Christ's life, death, and resurrection as parts or phases of one whole work of reconciliation. Although they think there are important things that the cross of Christ achieves, this is but one phase of the atonement, not the whole of it. In the course of setting out their views, they have some rather strange things to say about Christ's work, and about the way in which by assuming human nature he is (somehow) capable of healing fallen human beings.

Often this sort of view is conflated with what has become known as the Ransom account of the atonement, the subject of chapter three. This view was made popular in the 1930s by the work of the Swedish theologian Gustaf Aulén in his work *Christus Victor*. In the course of setting out a threefold typology of different approaches to the atonement, Aulén sought to reestablish what he thought of as the "classic" view of the atonement. This is the view according to which Christ buys back fallen human beings by his death, paying the ransom for our sin. His vicarious action is a victory over the powers of sin and death—hence, Christ the Victor (*Christus Victor*). In the last decade, the ransom account has become popular once more. However, in this chapter we shall see (a) that the ransom view is not the same as current *Christus Victor* views, (b) that the ransom view and *Christus Victor* motif are not necessarily the same as the Patristic view of atonement, and (c) that the ransom view is not, in fact, a complete doctrine of atonement at all but more like a theological motif. It may play a role as part of a more complete account of the reconciling work of Christ, but it cannot stand alone as a distinct doctrine of the atonement as has sometimes been suggested.

Chapter four deals with the satisfaction doctrine of atonement. This was first set forth in a systematic way by the great medieval theologian Anselm of Canterbury. It was developed in several ways in later medieval theology by the sublime Thomas Aquinas, and it is still the subject of theological debate today. We will set out the Anselmian version of the doctrine before considering some of the standard objections to it. Although there are potential shortcomings to this doctrine, it is in fact a lot more defensible than many modern critics think it is.

Chapter five sets out the moral exemplar view of the redemptive work of Christ. Often it is said that the medieval French theologian Abelard was the first to articulate this doctrine, which was in abeyance until it became popular as a way of thinking about the work of Christ in the European Enlightenment of the eighteenth century. However, in point of fact Abelard does not defend a mere moral exemplarist view of Christ's reconciling work. Probably the first theologians to attempt such a thing in a systematic way were the sixteenth century Socinians, a family of Italian theologians displaced to Poland, who were infamous for denying the doctrine of the Trinity. Their most famous son was Faustus Socinus, who wrote a treatise on the work of Christ in which he expounded a version of the exemplarist view of Christ's work. This did indeed become more popular around the time of Enlightenment, when the love of God expressed in the example of his Son became a favored way of thinking about Christ's work. The heirs of Enlightenment versions of moral exemplarism can be found today in the work of thinkers like the late John Hick, amongst others.

We shall see that there are, in fact, two versions of moral exemplarism. One version of this account does not, in fact, constitute a doctrine of atonement because no act of reconciliation is required. Instead, Christ's work displays divine love that we should emulate. All Christian thinkers have this much in common when they think about the atonement, though most have not thought that this is what makes Christ's work a work of reconciliation with God. But it may be that a thin account of reconciliation can be had on moral exemplarist grounds that go beyond the claim that Christ is an example of divine love we should emulate to provide some sort of act of reconciliation. Even though this too seems inadequate (for it is, as we shall see, an account that is arguably still too theologically anemic), it does mean that some versions of the doctrine do constitute an account of atonement, not just a way of conceiving the work of Christ as a moral example.

Chapter six concerns penal substitution, which we have already mentioned. Having set out the doctrine, we shall consider some of the criticisms that have been leveled against it. Almost all of these have been rehearsed in recent theological debates about the atonement, though very few of these objections are new. Almost all of them were anticipated by the Socinians hundreds of years ago. What is more, some of these recent objections, particularly the objections originally voiced by certain feminist theologians, are not always on target. Although there are indeed problems with penal substitution, these do not have to do with the oft-repeated objection that the doctrine amounts to "cosmic child abuse" of the Father towards the Son in punishing him for human sin. The real problems have to do with the transference of human sin and guilt from us to Christ, who is innocent of these things—a concern first raised by the Socinians.

Chapter seven focuses on two variations on a penal theme, so to speak. Some theologians in the aftermath of the Reformation turned to penal substitution, and the objections raised against the views of Reformers like Calvin and Luther by the likes of the Socinians attempted to provide alternative accounts of Christ's work that addressed the concerns of the objectors to penal substitution, yet without entirely giving up on the sort of view of divine justice and atonement that inform the penal substitutionary account. One of these views is the Governmental account, the beginnings of which are often thought to be found in the work of the Dutch jurist, Hugo Grotius. (Sometimes this view is referred to as the Grotian doctrine for this reason.) At the heart of this view is the notion that Christ is a penal example, rather than a penal substitute. God displays his wrath for sin in Christ, whose death acts a sort of deterrent, showing us what would happen if God were to punish us for our sin. This view became important in two very different strands of subsequent theology. The first was American Wesleyan theology of the nineteenth century, where theologians like John Miley took up the governmental view in part because it was consistent with a Wesleyan account of the scope of atonement. The second is the American New Divinity and New England Theology that developed out of the thought of Jonathan Edwards (1703–1758), which yielded a Calvinist version of the doctrine. We shall consider the conceptual core of this account, rather than the different versions it has spawned, and address ourselves to potential problems raised by these core-commitments.

A second variation on a penal theme comes from a rather different direction: nineteenth century Scotland. John McLeod Campbell is largely responsible for this view, which is often called vicarious penitence. It is a kind of non-penal substitutionary doctrine. For on this view, Christ, like the high priest in Hebrews, offers up "prayers and petitions with fervent cries and tears to the one who could save him from death," who hears Christ "because of his reverent submission" (Heb 5:7). Christ's life and ministry, and his death, are a kind of penitential act, by means of which he in the place of fallen human beings provided atonement for sin. This view has had some popularity in more recent times since it has been championed in later twentieth century theology by the Torrance brothers, James B. Torrance and Thomas F. Torrance, and a number of other theologians they have influenced. Although it has some important shortcomings, it remains a powerful alternative to penal versions of a substitutionary understanding of Christ's redeeming work.

Chapter eight concerns a serious theological problem with much traditional atonement language. A number of theologians from various quarters such as feminist theology, liberation theology, and Mennonite traditions, amongst others, have addressed themselves to the question of violence that seems embedded in many of the doctrines of atonement surveyed in the previous chapters. All of which raises the question, Must the reconciling work of Christ be a violent work? Does this really reflect the divine nature, that is, the God of love that we encounter in the Old and New Testaments? Some defenders of penal substitution have been quick to dismiss these concerns, saying that only by the death of Christ can sin be atoned for—something that is clear from the Old Testament temple cult, according to which "the life . . .

is in the blood" (Lev 17:11), which must be spilt in order to atone for human sin. However, this is too quick. At the heart of this problem raised by atoning violence is a real concern about God's relation to his creatures that is not easily deflected, as well as a worry about our human conception of Godself.

In this chapter we shall consider several ways in which these important criticisms of traditional atonement doctrines may be harnessed in order to provide more satisfactory ways of thinking about the reconciliation of Christ—ways that do not fall foul of the worries these critics raise. The first involves a controversial concept of redemptive violence, which attempts to make conceptual room for some understanding of violence consistent with the message of the gospel. A second, and more adequate response ensures that God is not implicated in violence in bringing about atonement. Like the doctrine of double effect in medical ethics, God may foresee and intend the crucifixion of Christ without also intending the violence that contributes to his death—violence intended by other humans, rather than by God.

This brings us to chapter nine. Can one, and only one, of these doctrines surveyed in previous chapters yield a complete understanding of the nature of the atonement—or as complete an understanding as we are capable of this side of the grave? Or is it that no single account of the atonement is capable of providing all we need to know about the work of Christ? This chapter considers two related recent developments in atonement theology that reflect such concerns. These are the mashup and kaleidoscopic approaches to the doctrine, respectively. Mashup views cannibalize historic doctrines, models, and metaphors of atonement to construct new composite doctrines of Christ's reconciling work. Kaleidoscopic views of atonement offer a theory about how to construe the different existing doctrines of the atonement—what we might call a theory about the different models of atonement and their explanatory power.

Chapter ten offers a view of the atonement that reflects my own theological sensibilities. It goes beyond the typology of different mechanisms presented in the earlier parts of the book to defend a particular view of Christ's work that draws deeply on the Pauline notion of participation in Christ's death and resurrection. This addresses problems we encountered with the substitutionary accounts in earlier chapters having to do with the punishment of an innocent and the transfer of sin and guilt to another. It also addresses the worry about redemptive violence present in much recent atonement theology. Drawing on recent work in New Testament studies as well as in systematic-theological reflection upon this, an account of the atonement can be provided that shares much in common with the Patristic authors with whom we began, even if the particular mechanism of atonement is different.

The atonement is a rich and complex topic, perhaps too rich and complex for any one doctrine of atonement to fully encompass. It is, after all, one of the central *mysteries* of the Christian faith. If this book helps provide a guide to those thinking through the difficult issues the atonement raises, some of which we have mentioned in this introduction, then it will have fulfilled its purpose. Often when tackling conceptually difficult material we want quick answers to hard questions. There are no such quick answers to be found in this volume, though there are plenty of hard questions that are asked along the way. Hopefully, there is also food for thought to be found in these pages, and tools with which to tackle some of these problems for ourselves as we seek to better understand the faith with which we have been entrusted.

FURTHER READING

Anselm of Canterbury. *Cur Deus Homo*. In *Anselm: Basic Writing*, translated by Thomas Williams. Indianapolis: Hackett, 2007.

Athanasius. *On the Incarnation*. Translated by John Behr. Crestwood, NY: St. Vladimir's Seminary Press, 2006.

Aulén, Gustaf. *Christus Victor: An Historical Study of the Three Main Types of the Idea of Atonement*. London: SPCK, 1931.

Beilby, James K., and Paul R. Eddy, eds. *The Nature of Atonement: Four Views*. Downers Grove, IL: IVP Academic, 2006.

Boersma, Hans. *Violence, Hospitality, and the Cross: Reappropriating the Atonement Tradition*. Grand Rapids: Baker Academic, 2004.

Finlan, Stephen. *Options on Atonement in Christian Theology*. Collegeville, MN: Liturgical Press, 2007.

Franks, R. S. *The Work of Christ*. 2nd ed. London: Thomas Nelson, 1962.

Grensted, L. W. *A Short History of the Doctrine of Atonement*. Manchester: University of Manchester Press, 1920.

Johnson, Adam. *Atonement: A Guide for the Perplexed*. London: T&T Clark, 2015.

Peacore, Linda. *The Role of Women's Experience in Feminist Theologies of Atonement*. Eugene, OR: Pickwick Publications, 2010.

Rashdall, Hastings. *The Idea of Atonement in Christian Theology, Being the Bampton Lectures for 1915*. London: Macmillan and Co., 1919.

Rutledge, Fleming. *The Crucifixion: Understanding the Death of Jesus Christ*. Grand Rapids: Eerdmans, 2015.

Tidball, Derek, David Hilborn, and Justin Thaker, eds. *The Atonement Debate*. Grand Rapids: Zondervan, 2008.

APPROACHING
THE ATONEMENT

> I believe in Jesus Christ, his only Son, our Lord,
> who was conceived by the Holy Spirit,
> born of the Virgin Mary,
> suffered under Pontius Pilate,
> was crucified, died, and was buried;
> he descended to the dead.
> On the third day he rose again;
> he ascended into heaven,
> he is seated at the right hand of the Father,
> and he will come to judge the living and the dead.
> *Apostles' Creed* (trans. used in the Church of England)

One of the oldest summaries of Christian doctrine is the Apostles' Creed. It is used today in many churches throughout the world, where it is recited as part of the liturgy. Even if it isn't a part of regular church worship, most Christians are familiar with it as an important summary of the faith. However, if we are to approach it with the idea of trying to see what it says about the doctrine of the atonement, that is, Christ's work of reconciliation, we will be disappointed. It does give us certain information about events in the life of Christ: his conception; his birth; his suffering; his death and descent to the dead; and his resurrection and ascension. But which of these events constitute the atonement? Which of these things brought about human salvation? We are not told.

This ambiguity in the Apostles' Creed reflects the fact that there is no single view of the atonement that is universally agreed upon by all Christians. Instead, there are a number of different views of the matter, which have grown up over time and represent the contributions of particular theologians or church communities to our greater understanding of how it is that Christ's work atones for human sin. We might say that there is no canonical definition of the atonement, no official church doctrine on the matter that is shared across different churches and denominations, though there are views expressed by particular church bodies and denominations. This is strange because the same is not true of other central teachings of Christianity, such as the Trinity or the incarnation, where there is ecumenical agreement on a conceptual or doctrinal core that all Christians confess.

In the case of the Trinity, theological battles were fought in the early church over what was the right way to express this central and defining Christian mystery. It was not until the formulation of the Nicene-Constantinopolitan creed at the First Council of Constantinople in AD 381 that the churches had a clear doctrine of the Trinity. But with the decision reached by that council, the theological landscape changed. Thereafter, there was a form of words that could be used to express something of this mystery of the Godhead in a way that could be grasped by all Christians. As a result, we now confess that God is one in essence, and yet three persons: Father, Son, and Holy Spirit. This is the central and defining doctrine of the Christian faith.

The incarnation is like the doctrine of the Trinity in that it too was a matter of dispute in the early church, and it too received attention by several great ecumenical councils of church leaders. At the Council of Chalcedon in AD 451 the familiar two natures doctrine was promulgated. Even if most Christians aren't acquainted with the term "two natures doctrine," what it conveys is probably familiar in some respect. The idea was that Christ is one divine person, with a divine nature, who takes on a human nature in addition to his divine one in order to become incarnate. Hence, "two natures," one divine and one human, possessed by one person who is the Second Person of the Trinity. Like the doctrine of the Trinity, this is now part of the very fabric of Christian faith. But it was not always so. It took time, controversy, and reflection on what Scripture and the apostles taught to come to this view.

The same is not true of the atonement, despite the fact that this too is a central theological commitment of Christianity. Instead, over time different ways of understanding this doctrine have grown up and been embraced by different groups of Christians. Today, there are a plethora of different views about the reconciling work of Christ, and precisely how we should understand this doctrine remains a source of dispute among Christians of different denominations and affiliations. For this reason, if for no other, it is worth spending time considering the doctrine of the atonement and the different accounts that have been put forward by Christian thinkers down through the ages.

SOME THEOLOGICAL DISTINCTIONS

Before attempting to grasp some of these different accounts of the atonement, we need to do some ground-clearing. Just as one must clear a parcel of land, and then level the ground out before beginning the task of construction that leads to the erection of a new house, so we must clear the ground of any conceptual obstacles and misunderstanding before embarking on the construction of particular doctrines of atonement. That is the task of the present chapter.

To begin, we should ask what a doctrine of atonement is, and why such a doctrine is important. In the introduction, I said that atonement is an English word that means "at-one-ment."[1] It is about the reconciling of two parties that are estranged, especially God and human beings. But there is more to it than that. It also has the connotation of reparation, that is, the repairing of some breach, the restitution of some wrong done. The missing element here is a doctrine of sin. It is because human beings are estranged from God, alienated from him on account of their sin, that Christ must make amends through an act of reconciliation. So, at the outset, it is important to see that atonement is about God's initiative in bringing about the restoration of the broken relationship between Godself and fallen humans. It is about God providing a means of removing the obstacles to that restitution, especially the obstacle of sin. And it is about God doing this on our behalf in the person of Christ. In speaking of this aspect of Christ's reconciling work, theologians often talk about Christ's *expiation*. This just means his atonement does away with the power of sin in our lives.

For many Christians this divine action of reconciliation also includes notions such as payment, propitiation, or sacrifice of atonement. Thus 1 John 2:2 says, "He is the atoning sacrifice [*hilasmos*] for our sins, and not only for ours but also for the sins of the whole world." Similarly, in Romans 3:23-26, the apostle Paul says this:

---

[1]This is the point of departure for Eleonore Stump's monumental study, *Atonement*. Oxford Studies in Analytic Theology (Oxford: Oxford University Press, 2018).

For all have sinned and fall short of the glory of God, and all are justified freely
by his grace through the redemption that came by Christ Jesus. God presented
Christ as a sacrifice of atonement [*hilastērion*], through the shedding of his
blood—to be received by faith. He did this to demonstrate his righteousness,
because in his forbearance he had left the sins committed beforehand unpunished—he did it to demonstrate his righteousness at the present time, so as to
be just and the one who justifies those who have faith in Jesus.

In contemporary biblical studies, a connection is often drawn between the
way in which Christ's redemptive work is thought of as a sacrifice of atonement
(*hilastērion* in Greek) and the mercy seat or lid on the ark of the covenant in
the Old Testament (this relationship is made particularly clear in Hebrews 9).
The ark was a gold-covered wooden box containing the tablets of the Mosaic
Law. It was traditionally thought to be the place where God's grace was
received on the basis of the blood of sacrifice sprinkled upon it by the high
priest once a year on the Day of Atonement (see Lev 16:2, 13-15; compare
Heb 9:5). So, in addition to the ideas of reconciliation and restitution, the
biblical basis for the notion of atonement is rooted in cultic imagery of blood
sacrifice and the judgment seat of God on the ark of the covenant, which was
placed in the holy of holies in the temple, and represented the presence of
God to his people. We might say that Christ, as God incarnate, is the true
representation of God to his people, the true mercy seat, the one in whom
God's grace and judgment meet in atonement. It is by his redemptive work
that our sin is atoned for, and we are reconciled to God.

The nature and scope of atonement. With this in mind, we may turn to
some important distinctions that serve to demarcate the aspect of Christ's
saving work that is the focus of this book. The first of these has to do with the
difference between the *nature* of the atonement and its *scope*. The nature of
the atonement has to do with what the atonement is about, that is, how it is
that by means of Christ's saving work fallen human beings are reconciled
to Godself.

Suppose a lifeguard saves a drowning child. We may ask, How did the
lifeguard actually rescue the child from the pool? What did she do to save
the boy who was drowning? There are a number of different possibilities.
Perhaps she threw the child a lifebelt or buoyancy aid. Alternatively, she may
have fished him out of the pool with the help of a pole or rod. She may even

have jumped into the pool in order to perform the rescue. These are different ways to achieve the same result. In a similar manner, Christians affirm that Christ's work of salvation reconciles fallen human beings with God. Yet there are a number of different ways in which this could have been achieved. Down through the ages different theologians have offered various accounts of how Christ's work brings this about. These different views provide the basis for the different doctrines of atonement we have before us today. Each of these accounts constitutes a way of thinking about how it is that Christ's work is saving in nature.

By contrast, the scope of atonement has to do with how many people are actually saved by means of Christ's action. Return to the case of the lifeguard saving the drowning child. Suppose several children have fallen into the pool and are drowning, instead of the one previously mentioned. In this second scenario, the lifeguard is able to save them all, and does so, working efficiently and effectively. Now suppose this second lifeguard-rescue story was related to a group of parents. "How many of the children did she manage to save?" they ask, anxious to know the answer. "All of them," is the response the relieved parents receive. The parents are not concerned about how the children were saved. In other words, they are not focused on the manner in which the lifeguard saved the children. Instead, they are worried about whether all the children were rescued. We might say they are concerned about the scope of the rescue. Was the lifeguard able to save *all* the children, or only *some* of them? Did some drown because she was unable to reach them in time? And so on.

In this book we are primarily concerned with questions arising from the nature of the atonement, not its scope. More particularly, our focus is on the means by which Christ brings about human salvation and reconciliation with God. We want to get a clearer picture of the mechanism of atonement. Although the question of the scope of Christ's saving work is an important one, it is not the principal focus of attention in what follows. The majority of Christians have agreed that Christ's saving work is in principle sufficient to save all human beings, just as the lifeguard may be sufficiently competent to save all the drowning children. The more controversial question for the scope of atonement is whether in fact Christ's atonement brings about the salvation of all human beings, or only some human beings. This distinction between the sufficiency and effectiveness of the atonement has a long history and continues to be debated today. However, it will only feature in passing in what follows.[2]

What is the atonement? This brings us to a further distinction, which touches upon the question we began with in relation to the atonement in the Apostles' Creed. If the focus of our attention in this work is upon the nature of the atonement, then what is it that constitutes the reconciling work of Christ? Some theologians have distinguished between different aspects of Christ's work. The French Reformer John Calvin famously differentiated between the prophetic, priestly, and royal work of Christ in his influential work *Institutes of the Christian Religion* (1559). Others have teased out the atoning work of Christ on the cross, which they call his passive work because he passively and obediently suffers in accordance to the Father's will, as distinct from his active work of obedience to the Father's will in his incarnate life and ministry. In each case, the intention is to conceptually separate that aspect of Christ's work that pertains to the atonement from other aspects of his work. To this extent, such distinctions are illuminating. However, when this becomes a way of sectioning off one event in Christ's life as the act of atonement, such distinctions may be less helpful.

We can see an example of the "sectioning off" I have in mind in the case of the medieval theologian Anselm of Canterbury. In his great work *Cur deus homo* (*Why the God-Man*) he maintained that the life and ministry of Christ were the precondition for his atonement, but not part of it. Atonement, according to Anselm, is reserved for the events of the crucifixion. By contrast, an older theological tradition, which can be found in the works of some of the early church fathers like Athanasius, Cyril of Alexandria, and Irenaeus, maintains that the life and ministry of Christ are integral to his atonement. They are, as it were, different phases in one divine work of salvation, not merely a prerequisite to the cross. This seems to me to be a much more promising approach to thinking about Christ's atoning work.

---

[2]Interested readers are directed to the discussion of the scope of the atonement in my previous work, Oliver D. Crisp, *Saving Calvinism: Expanding the Reformed Tradition* (Downers Grove, IL: IVP Academic, 2016). Those who think Christ's work saves only some human beings are said to believe in a "limited" atonement. Those who think Christ's work is in principle for all humanity, though it saves only those who have faith in Christ are said to believe the scope of atonement is "hypothetically universalist." Those who think it definitely saves all human beings are universalists. Those who think Christ dies to make atonement available to all who have faith are said to think the atonement is "unlimited" in scope.

In popular Christianity, the atonement is often associated with one particular event, namely, the crucifixion. Like Anselm, many Christians think that the life and ministry of Christ are preconditions for the atonement, not part of the atonement. The approach such Christians take to the atonement is akin to thinking of the work of Christ in terms of the performance of a great stage actor. All the work, discipline, practice, and rehearsal are, on this way of thinking, merely preliminaries necessary for the final performance. They are not themselves part of that performance; they are prerequisites for the performance. Just so with the life and ministry of Christ and his crucifixion. However, this is not the only way to think of the story of the stage actor. It could be argued that the disciplined formation and rehearsal taken together with the different professional performances are parts of one entire vocation, the vocation of acting. Rehearsal and practice are just as much acting as the different performances; they are just as much part of the one vocation. Similarly, it may be that the different aspects of the life and work of Christ can be regarded, from a certain point of view, as phases or stages in one divine action of human reconciliation in which the crucifixion is one (but only one) critical element. We shall see that different accounts of the atonement take different views on this question of what constitutes the reconciling work of Christ. In this respect, my own view, which is outlined in chapter ten, is much closer to the patristic view than to the Anselmian.

Forgiveness, reparation, and punishment. Let us turn to a third cluster of conceptual distinctions that will be of help in approaching the atonement. It is sometimes said that God must punish sin. However, this can appear to be a rather strange claim to make. Are we saying that God cannot forgive our sin without some act of atonement? That seems problematic. For one thing, it suggests that God cannot do a morally virtuous action that humans beings can do. Suppose Jones catches her child with his hand in the cookie jar. Jones could punish her child. Yet she could also forgive him without punishment; sometimes that may be the appropriate response. Are we saying God *cannot* forgive us without punishment as Jones can forgive her son? Additionally, there seem to be biblical grounds for thinking God can forgive sin without punishment. For instance, see the parable of the unjust servant (Mt 18:21-35) or the way Jesus forgives and heals the paralyzed man in Matthew 9:1-8. In this latter passage, Jesus says, "'Which is easier: to say,

"Your sins are forgiven," or to say, "Get up and walk"? But I want you to know that the Son of Man has authority on earth to forgive sins.' So he said to the paralyzed man, 'Get up, take your mat and go home.' Then the man got up and went home" (Mt 9:5-7). On the face of it, this certainly looks like Jesus forgives sin without punishment.

There are broadly two sorts of responses to this issue in the theological literature. The first, which can be found in the work of Anselm and Jonathan Edwards, amongst others, reasons that God cannot, in fact, forgive sin without punishment. It is not merely that he *may* forgive us our sin without punishment; he *cannot* do so. The idea is that to forgive sin in this way would be to fail to treat it with sufficient moral seriousness, which God cannot do. To see this, let us take a different example. Imagine that instead of catching her son with his hand in the cookie jar, Jones catches her son savagely beating his sister. Offering forgiveness for this action without some kind of punishment would be entirely inappropriate. Such a crime requires substantial reparation. Those who follow Anselm and Edwards in this matter think that the same is true of our sin. If God simply forgave human sin without reparation he would be failing to treat it with sufficient moral seriousness; God cannot fail to treat such things with sufficient moral seriousness because he is morally perfect; so he cannot forgive human sin without reparation.

A second response to the question of whether God can forgive sin without punishment involves acknowledging that God can, in fact, forgive our sin in this way, whilst also recognizing that there may be very good moral reasons for punishing our sin. One such line of reasoning goes like this: God may forgive our sin as Jones forgives her son without reparation, but in order for us to understand the moral seriousness of our sin, God often punishes us. This is also a response that seems appropriate in some mundane circumstances. Suppose Jones catches her son carving his initials into the kitchen countertop with a pocket knife. It may be that Jones realizes she can forgive her son, but knows that punishment will help him to see that what he has done is not a trivial infraction; he has defaced and vandalized someone else's property, and he needs to understand the moral seriousness of his action. Reparation also seems appropriate in such circumstances, in the form of some punishment. We shall see that much depends on which of these two views (if either) is adopted by the theologian approaching the atonement.[3]

This distinction between whether God may or must punish sin raises a deeper issue, to which we shall return later in the book when considering the problem of atoning violence. This deeper issue has to do with the difference between forgiveness, reparation, and punishment. To forgive someone is to forego reparation, including punishment. Reparation is some way of making amends for a wrong committed. Punishment is one way in which reparation can be made. So, to forgive someone is to lay aside the prospect of having a penalty meted out to the person who has sinned, in order to provide a space to excuse and exonerate the person who has committed wrong instead. Return to the child and the cookie jar example. Jones can forgive her child for this misdemeanor, or punish him. But Jones cannot forgive the child *by* exacting reparation from him by means of punishment. That makes no sense. We have the intuition that forgiveness is one sort of moral action, and reparation and punishment are different sorts of moral action, and that these moral actions are not commensurate, any more than embracing a person and pushing that person away are commensurate actions. You cannot embrace someone by pushing them away, and you cannot forgive someone by exacting reparation from them in the form of punishment.

Occasionally, theologians speak of forgiveness *through* the atonement.[4] I think they mean by this that it is through the atoning work of Christ that our debt of sin is cancelled. (We sometimes speak of a debt being "forgiven" in this way.) If we think that Christ somehow acts on our behalf in the atonement, making reparation for our sin, then we are not forgiven through the atonement in the sense of reparation being set aside; rather, we are pardoned by means of his reparative action. To see this, consider the example of a friend who pays my parking fine. It would be mistaken for me to report this as being forgiven by my friend's action. I am not forgiven the fine, it is just that I did not pay the fine. Nevertheless, it *was* paid—by my friend on my behalf! However, if by forgiveness we mean the cancellation of a debt,

---

[3]These are what we might call two "live options" in the Christian tradition for thinking about the atonement. But they are not the only possible ones.

[4]For instance, P. T. Forsyth in *The Cruciality of the Cross* (London: Hodder and Stoughton, 1910), 1. Perhaps biblical passages like Is 53:5 and 1 Pet 2:24 are in the conceptual background here.

then we can say that, from a certain point of view, it is through atonement that we are forgiven.

This distinction between forgiveness on the one hand, and reparation and punishment on the other, is important and plays an important and under-valued role in different doctrines of the atonement. We shall see that some doctrines of atonement maintain that reparation for sin must be made either in the person of the sinner or in the person of some suitable substitute—which is Christ. Other doctrines state that God may forgive us our sins and that attending to Christ's work helps us to see how that plays out. But note that these two ideas of forgiveness and reparation, respectively, yield different ways of thinking about the work of Christ. Those views that include a notion of reparation as a requirement for human reconciliation with God presume that some act of atonement is needed to reconcile us to God. By contrast, those views that place the notion of forgiveness as the setting aside of repa-ration at the center of the explanation of the work of Christ cannot require some act of reparation in order for us to be reconciled with God through Christ. As we shall see in due course when thinking about the moral exemplar view, the idea that Christ's work has to do with forgiveness understood in terms of the setting aside of reparation does not amount to a doctrine of atonement at all, for, as we have seen, atonement is about reparation whereas forgiveness (understood in terms of the setting aside reparation) is not. That, it need hardly be said, is a theologically significant outcome.

Objective and subjective accounts of atonement. A fourth distinction often found in the recent literature concerns objective and subjective views of the saving work of Christ. An objective work of Christ is an account of the atonement that emphasizes something that happens independent of any per-sonal response or experience I might have. It often has to do with some trans-action between God and Christ in the atonement that is then applied to fallen human beings like you and me. Imagine that a distant relative leaves you a large fortune upon her death. You inherit the material benefits of that fortune, which transforms your life. Yet the transaction between lawyers and your distant relative that produced the will that provides for your new wealth happened entirely independent of you. This is like an objective account of the atonement.

By contrast, a subjective account of atonement emphasizes the effect the work of Christ has upon the individual. It depends upon a personal response or experience. This often has to do with some response Christ's work elicits in fallen human beings that makes a significant moral difference to the individual. Now, suppose that instead of leaving you a fortune in her will, your distant relative turns up on your doorstep, becomes your personal mentor and teaches you how to earn your own fortune. This is more like a subjective account of the atonement.

Although this distinction between objective and subjective views of the atonement is still in frequent use, I do not find it particularly helpful, and it will not be part of the discussion in subsequent chapters. Often the distinction is used as a heuristic device; that is, a means of trying to teach something about different accounts of atonement.[5] So satisfaction is often said to be a classic example of an objective atonement doctrine because God transacts with Christ to bring about human salvation independent of us, whereas the moral exemplar view is much more subjective because it has to do with our response to Christ's act of self-sacrificial love on the cross. As these examples indicate, the problem is that neither of these views is entirely objective or entirely subjective. They both include elements that are objective and elements that are subjective. Christ satisfies divine justice (objective), but then that is applied to the individual believer (subjective). Christ's work on the cross is an example of self-sacrificial love for us (objective) that we should emulate (subjective). But then it looks like the most this distinction can do is show that some accounts of atonement emphasize one approach to Christ's work over the other, either more objective than subjective, or more subjective than objective. That doesn't seem very illuminating. Nevertheless, in the succeeding chapters we shall see that any adequate account of atonement has both an objective and subjective aspect. God provides for our reconciliation and for the manner in which we may appropriate it through Christ.

THEORIES, MODELS, METAPHORS, AND MOTIFS

Having looked at some important theological distinctions in approaching the doctrine of atonement, let us now consider the important issue of how we should think about the different views of the atonement that the history of Christian thought has generated. This is an important question to ask in

---

[5]See, e.g., Ben Pugh, *Atonement Theories: A Way Through the Maze* (Eugene, OR: Cascade Books, 2014), who uses this distinction to frame his otherwise helpful introduction to the atonement.

approaching the atonement, and has been the subject of some discussion in recent theology.

We begin by thinking about *doctrine*. A doctrine is a comprehensive account of a particular teaching about a given theological topic held by some community of Christians or some particular denomination. So a doctrine of the atonement is a comprehensive account of the atonement that has been taught by a particular group of Christians (such as Baptists, Anglicans, Mennonites, Eastern Orthodox, and so on). Some recent theologians, most notably, the English Reformed theologian Colin Gunton, have taught that the different accounts of the atonement we find in contemporary theology can be boiled down to different metaphors, which have been taken up by theologians for their own purposes. There is the metaphor of the battlefield and of victory over a demonic enemy; there is the metaphor of divine justice being meted out to sinners or to Christ; and there is the metaphor of sacrifice, with its cultic overtones. "The common feature that makes a metaphor a metaphor," observes Gunton, "is that words come to be used in a new and unusual way in human speech."[6] A word used literally in one context can become metaphorical in another. For instance, the sacrificial lamb in the Old Testament (Gen 22:8) becomes the Lamb of God who takes away the sins of the world in the New Testament (Jn 1:29).

Yet it is difficult to see how Christian doctrines can be purely metaphorical all the way down, so to speak. There must be some non-metaphorical work being done in order for us to have a clear conceptual content to particular doctrines. For one of the things that is true of metaphors, and is not true of doctrines as such, is that metaphors have a surplus of meaning. That is, they mean more than one thing at-one-and-the-same-time. In one respect, that is the whole point of a metaphor. We use them to help fill in conceptual gaps, or to make a certain sort of connection that would otherwise be difficult to do without metaphors. So "the Lamb of God" connotes several different things: that Christ is innocent, that he is spotless, that he is pure, that he is sacrificed for human sin, that his death may bring about atonement, that his own atoning act is deeply connected to the Passover feast, and so on. But a doctrine of atonement, such as the satisfaction view, is more than just a metaphor, although

---

[6]Colin E. Gunton, *The Actuality of Atonement: A Study of Metaphor, Rationality and the Christian Tradition* (London: T&T Clark, 1988), 29.

metaphor may play an important role in it. It is a particular conception of the nature of Christ's saving work that provides an account of the mechanism by means of which his work reconciles us to Godself: Christ's death satisfies divine honor. In a similar manner, in contemporary scientific optics a model of light as a wave is more than a metaphor, though metaphor plays a crucial role in helping to convey something of the behavior of the packets of photons that make up visible light under certain conditions.

So, doctrines of atonement are particular conceptions of the nature of Christ's saving work that provide an account of the mechanism by means of which his work reconciles us to Godself. These include metaphors, but are not reducible to metaphors. They may also reflect certain motifs found in Scripture, of ransom, or sacrifice, or whatever, though they are not reducible to these motifs.

Often in contemporary accounts of atonement, though much less frequently in historic accounts, one finds talk about theories of atonement. This talk about theories may be a little overblown. A theory is some overarching conceptual framework or system of ideas based upon general principles independent of those that require explanation, such as a "theory of education," or the "theory of evolution." Accounts of the atonement are not really theories in that sense.

If we have to use language other than doctrines of atonement, it might be more appropriate to speak about *models* of atonement instead. In the contemporary natural sciences, a model is a simplified account of complex data that is not the sober truth of the matter, but which is an approximation to the truth, such as the model of light functioning as waves, or the familiar pictorial model of an atom one finds in high school physics textbooks. Atonement doctrines may be thought of as models in this sense. They are approximations to the truth of the matter, attempts to represent in a simplified form something of the complexity of the saving work of Christ, which is beyond the complete explanation of any one account of the atonement.

There are several reasons for thinking that language about models of atonement may be theologically appropriate. First, in recent times many theologians working on the atonement have become skeptical of the idea that one and only one account of the atonement is the right way to think of the matter. There are a number of different reasons for this. One concern is that there are multiple metaphors of atonement in Scripture, so that any attempt to provide a doctrine of the reconciling work of Christ must be able to take account of these different pictures. Christ's work is a ransom (1 Tim 2:6), a sacrifice (Heb 10:1-10), a substitution (1 Pet 2:24), an example (Phil 2:5), and much more. Our theologizing needs to reflect this. A doctrine of atonement that excludes or overlooks one of these metaphors fails to give an adequate account of Scripture's witness to this saving act. But a model of atonement that does not presume to give the whole truth of the matter is able to account for this—or at least, make room for it.

Second, the atonement, like the incarnation, or the Trinity, is in some important respects a mystery. It is beyond our comprehension. Just as we cannot fully grasp what it means to say God is triune, or Jesus is God incarnate, so we cannot fully grasp what it means to say Christ atones for our sin. Any approach to the atonement that attempts to offer a complete explanation of it is almost certainly overreaching what it is possible for mere humans to say this side of the grave. This doesn't mean we should avoid any attempt at understanding the saving work of Christ. It just means we should approach the doctrine with a healthy dose of intellectual humility in the face of God's saving design. Such intellectual humility is a virtue rather than a vice, something that we prize in other areas of human endeavor especially in the most talented and capable individuals. So it is not surprising that in matters of a theological nature, where we are dealing with God, whose essence is deeply mysterious, that we should cultivate a similarly virtuous approach to understanding the faith we possess. Models of atonement are also able to accommodate this sort of worry about the limits on what we can know of the nature and purposes of redemption. For a model is by definition an approximation to the truth of something much more complex.

TYPOLOGIES OF ATONEMENT

A final issue that an approach to the atonement needs to tackle is typologies. Although he was not the first theologian to distinguish different accounts of atonement, the Swedish theologian Gustaf Aulén did make popular the idea that there are different types or families of doctrine into which particular accounts of the atonement can be grouped.[7] Aulén wrote about the "classic"

---

[7]In Gustaf Aulén, *Christus Victor: An Historical Study of the Three Main Types of the Idea of Atonement* (London: SPCK, 1931).

account of the atonement, which, as we shall see in chapter three, was a version of the ransom view. He maintained that this doctrine was the view of the primitive church, which had been displaced by the variations on vicarious atonement such as satisfaction in the medieval and Reformation periods. This, in turn, had been replaced by moral exemplar views of Christ's work in modern theology since the Enlightenment. Although his typology continues to be influential in a number of recent works on atonement, the particular "decline and fall" narrative that accompanied it has fared less well.

There certainly are families of atonement doctrine, where different views share in common certain ideas that inform the particular view of Christ's saving work, even though these different views offer distinct accounts of the mechanism of atonement. Thus the satisfaction doctrine (chapter four) and penal substitution (chapter six), as well as the governmental view and vicarious penitence view (chapter seven), all share in common certain ideas about the divine nature in general, and divine justice in particular, which they conceive of as being retributive in nature so that the punishment for sin is backwards looking, and must fit the crime. They also all have a strong view about the effects of sin in fallen human beings that requires atonement in order to bring about reconciliation with God. Although they give different accounts of how Christ's work is an atonement, they all think of it as a matter of reparation for sin being met by the sinner in hell or by Christ on the cross. By contrast, the family of views that maintains Christ's work is a demonstration of divine love, or a moral example for us to follow, do not have the same notions of divine justice and the need for atonement from sin in view.

That said, it is not clear to me that there are only three types of atonement doctrine, or three families of views. As we shall see, matters are more complicated than this, and often it is difficult to know how to categorize a given account of atonement. In some cases, we shall see that this is because the view is not actually an account of atonement as such (e.g., some versions of moral exemplarism). In other cases, it is because the view is not so much a model of atonement as a theory about how to think about different models of atonement (e.g., kaleidoscopic accounts).

I mentioned earlier that the idea of a classic view from which later theology sadly departed in a slow decline has been called into question since Aulén wrote his book. Nevertheless, there has also been a desire in recent theology to return to some of the patristic accounts as important and neglected sources for atonement doctrine. I am very sympathetic to that concern. However, two other factors are also relevant in this connection. The first is recent Pauline scholarship that has focused on the notion of union with Christ and our identification with Christ's saving work as fundamental themes in the Apostle's account of salvation in his letters.[8] The second is recent historical-theological scholarship, which has shown how the idea of divinization or theosis is an important constituent of much historic Western Christian theology, not just Eastern theology, as was previously thought. For present purposes, theosis or divinization is the idea that we are united to God in Christ by the power of the Spirit, and that the Christian life is principally about becoming ever more "partakers of the divine nature" (2 Pet 1:4). Not that we lose ourselves in God as a drop in the ocean is lost, but that we are forever on a trajectory into more intimate communion with God. This notion, which has long been a fundamental component of Eastern Orthodox accounts of salvation, is now recognized as an important and neglected theme in Roman Catholic and Protestant thought too. These important developments in scholarship need to be reflected in our thinking about the atonement.

Some recent theology has attempted to disrupt the typological approach to the atonement by arguing that adequate accounts of the saving work of Christ should be more of a mashup of different types of doctrine. Consequently, there have been a spate of works that put forward atonement doctrines that include something of, say, a vicarious component, alongside a ransom component, borrowing from different theological sources to form a new composite doctrine.[9] There is real promise to such an approach, which better tracks with the ways in which different atonement themes are reflected in the New Testament and earliest Christian accounts of Christ's redemptive work.

Having furnished ourselves with some important conceptual tools for approaching the doctrine of atonement, we should now be in a position to consider some of the most influential historic and contemporary doctrines

---

[8]Here I have in mind the recent work of scholars like Douglas Campbell, Michael Gorman, Morna Hooker, Grant Macaskill, and N. T. Wright, amongst others.

[9]See, for example, Hans Boersma, *Violence, Hospitality, and the Cross: Reappropriating the Atonement Tradition* (Grand Rapids: Baker Academic, 2004). We will return to the discussion of his work in Chapter 9.

of atonement. We begin with several patristic accounts of Christ's saving work in the next chapter.

FURTHER READING

Aulén, Gustaf. *Christus Victor: An Historical Study of the Three Main Types of the Idea of Atonement.* London: SPCK, 1931.

Boersma, Hans. *Violence, Hospitality, and the Cross: Reappropriating the Atonement Tradition.* Grand Rapids: Baker Academic, 2004.

Crisp, Oliver D. "Methodological Issues in Approaching the Atonement." In *T&T Clark Companion to Atonement,* edited by Adam J. Johnson, ch. 17. London: Bloomsbury T&T Clark, 2017.

——. *Saving Calvinism: Expanding the Reformed Tradition.* Downers Grove, IL: IVP Academic, 2016.

——. *The Word Enfleshed: Exploring the Person and Work of Christ.* Grand Rapids: Baker Academic, 2016.

Forsyth, P. T. *The Cruciality of the Cross.* London: Hodder and Stoughton, 1910.

Gunton, Colin E. *The Actuality of Atonement: A Study of Metaphor, Rationality and the Christian Tradition.* London: T&T Clark, 1988.

Johnson, Adam. *Atonement: A Guide for the Perplexed.* London: T&T Clark, 2015.

Stump, Eleonore. *Atonement.* Oxford Studies in Analytic Theology. Oxford: Oxford University Press, 2018.

Swinburne, Richard. *Responsibility and Atonement.* Oxford: Oxford University Press, 1989.

Tanner, Kathryn. *Jesus, Humanity and the Trinity: A Brief Systematic Theology.* Minneapolis: Fortress Press, 2001.

SEVERAL PATRISTIC
ACCOUNTS OF ATONEMENT

There is widespread popular misunderstanding about the doctrines of atonement that can be found in the works of the early church fathers. These leaders of the early church sought to pass on the apostolic witness and to safeguard it against various inroads being made into the churches by ideas that were destructive to the Christian faith. Their writings reflect the fact that they were church leaders combating significant challenges to the faith, not tenured professors on research leave constructing academic monographs in the seclusion of university libraries. Their works are often characterized by the bold use of rhetorical flourishes, narrative, metaphor, and exhortation—just as one might expect from pastors used to dealing with the practical needs of their congregations. Nevertheless, the fluidity of their thinking means that it is sometimes difficult to pin down exactly what they are after, and this can easily lead to misunderstanding or misinterpretation.

For instance, in the recent literature, Athanasius, the fourth century bishop of Alexandria, has been appealed to as a thinker whose work supposedly incorporates an embryonic version of penal substitution. In their book *Pierced for Our Transgressions,* authors Steve Jeffery, Michael Ovey, and Andrew Sach maintain that "Athanasius not only affirmed the doctrine of penal substitution, but also placed it squarely at the centre of his theology as integral to the purpose of the incarnation, the restoration of human society and the renewal of creation."[1] They have in mind passages in Athanasius's works like this one:

---

[1]Steve Jeffery, Michael Ovey, and Andrew Sach, *Pierced for Our Transgressions: Rediscovering the Glory of Penal Substitution* (Wheaton, IL: Crossway, 2007), 173.

It was by surrendering to death the body which he had taken, as an offering and sacrifice free from every stain, that He forthwith abolished death for His human brethren by the offering of the equivalent. For naturally, since the Word of God was above all, when He offered His own temple and bodily instrument as a substitute for the life of all, He fulfilled in death all that was required.[2]

There is certainly what we might call a vicarious component to Athanasius's view in this passage. By a "vicarious component," I mean an element of Athanasius's position that presumes Christ stands in our place, acting on our behalf in his act of reconciliation. But, as we shall see later in this chapter, the presence of substitutionary language does not necessarily mean that he holds to an early version of *penal* substitution any more than a substitute player in a soccer match is a *penal* substitute for the player that leaves the field—he is a substitute of a different sort. Clearly, care must be taken when treating ancient authors lest we fall into anachronism and read back into their works later views that postdate them.

The Scandinavian theologian Gustaf Aulén represents a different sort of mistaken account of patristic authors like Athanasius. He famously wrote of the "classic" or "dramatic" view of the atonement, identifying this with the early church fathers as if there were a single doctrine of atonement, or family of views about the atonement, that they all agreed upon. This he identifies as the *Christus Victor* ("Christ the Victor") view. There are several levels of confusion here that need to be teased out.

First of all, there is no single doctrine or family of doctrines that the early church fathers agreed upon and that constitute a "classic view" of atonement that was displaced by later theology. As in any period of church history, things are much more complicated than that, with different views being held by different thinkers. Moreover, the fact that a particular account of a given doctrine is the oldest view on that topic does not necessarily confer upon it a special status. A doctrine can be old and mistaken, after all. If that were not so, we would all still believe the classical Ptolemaic view of the cosmos, in which all the other heavenly bodies, including the sun, rotate around the earth. That is an older view than the Copernican one, according to which the earth and a number of other heavenly bodies rotate around the sun. Yet today

---

[2]Athanasius, *On the Incarnation*, trans. John Behr (Crestwood, NY: St. Vladimir's Seminary Press, 2006), §9.

we know that the Ptolemaic view is false because we have a better grasp of cosmology than the ancients did. So the age of a view does not in and of itself guarantee closer proximity to the truth of the matter. Other factors need to be taken into account as well. In the case of the atonement, this includes the witness of divine revelation in Scripture, against which all atonement doctrines must be measured. The early fathers of the church are important figures whose work is well worth studying and (I think) very close to the truth of the matter when it comes to the atonement. But that isn't just because they are the oldest witnesses to the apostolic teaching. It is because their teaching reflects the content of the message the apostles sought to convey, which we now have preserved for us in Scripture.

Another sort of confusion Aulén made popular was the idea that the "classic" view of the atonement is a version of *Christus Victor*/ransom doctrine. In other words, and in large measure because of the influence of Aulén's work, it has become popular to think that the early fathers of the church, particularly those in the Greek-speaking East, were advocates of a ransom view of atonement. This is a more difficult mistake to displace largely because it is based on a partial truth. There are early church fathers whose view is a ransom account of atonement—or at least, who include ransom metaphors and motifs in what they say about the atonement. The most famous of these is Gregory of Nyssa with his analogy of the bait and hook. He writes,

> In order to secure . . . the ransom . . . the Deity was hidden under the veil of our nature, that so, as with ravenous fish, the hook of the Deity might be gulped down along with the bait of flesh, and thus, life being introduced into the house of death, and light shining in darkness, that which is diametrically opposed to light and life might vanish.[3]

Now, although this passage does seem to include a ransom motif, this fact on its own cannot be used to show that all the church fathers taught the same view of atonement. One cannot extrapolate from a sample of one or two theologians the conclusion that all or almost all theologians working at that time held the same view. That is just fallacious reasoning. At best, it shows that an influential father of the Eastern Church articulated a view of the atonement that includes a ransom motif, which is a much more modest

---

[3]Gregory of Nyssa, *The Great Catechism*, ch. 24, *NPNF*[2], vol. 5 (Edinburgh: T&T Clark, 1892).

outcome than is sufficient for Aulén's view to be sustained. For, as we noted in the first chapter, a motif or metaphor is not sufficient to generate a doctrine of atonement. We shall see that Athanasius also uses the language of "ransom" to describe Christ's work.[4] But this is not the mechanism of atonement; it is not the complete doctrine of atonement he wishes to pass on to his readers. It is more like a motif that features in passing as part of a larger, richer account of Christ's reconciling work, which has a rather different understanding of the means by which atonement is brought about.

A third sort of confusion that Aulén made popular was the idea that the *Christus Victor* view is a version of the ransom doctrine of atonement. In more recent theology these two things have been prized apart so that now there are examples of *Christus Victor* views that are not clearly ransom doctrines as well. This is surprising to many unfamiliar with the relevant literature on the topic, and it is a matter that we shall return to in the next chapter when we tackle the ransom doctrine in more detail. For now it will suffice to say that the claim that Christ is victorious over the powers of evil, which is a central plank of the *Christus Victor* view of Christ's saving work, is not necessarily the same as the claim that Christ's atonement ransoms us from the powers of sin, death, and the devil. Triumphing over the powers of evil could depend on a very different narrative of atonement than that provided by the notion of paying a ransom.

TWO PATRISTIC CASE STUDIES

Well, then, what did the early fathers of the church teach about the atonement? It is not possible to provide a close study of all the great theologians of this period within the covers of a short work like this one. After all, this includes some of the most formative Christian writers in church history! Rather than attempting to give short cameos of a range of different authors, or providing a synthesis of a large number of Fathers, it might be better to begin by looking at two important voices in the early church whose work is often cited in discussion concerning what the Fathers taught about the reconciling work of Christ. Although this will not give us a complete account of all the church fathers, it will help to show how these two particular authors approach the

---

[4]The Greek word is *lytron*, which he uses to good effect at the end of in §21 in *On the Incarnation*.

atonement, and give us some insight into the key issues that make up their respective views on the subject. It will also furnish us with a point of comparison, so that we can see whether two representative early Christian authors on this topic really do say different things about the saving work of Christ.

The two theologians we shall consider are Irenaeus and Athanasius. According to tradition, Irenaeus was a disciple of Polycarp, bishop of Smyrna and Christian martyr, who was himself reportedly a disciple of the Apostle John in his old age. Thus, Irenaeus can trace his theological lineage through his own teacher directly to the apostles, which is an important consideration when reading what he says on the atonement. For one thing, we normally trust the testimony of someone whose information is better sourced, especially if they have access to eyewitness reports of the events in question. If the traditional attribution is right, Irenaeus is just such a theologian. Eventually, Irenaeus became a bishop as well, serving in the city of Lyons (i.e., the Roman city of Lugdunum) in France. Little is known of his life, though he flourished around the second half of the second century AD. More is known about Athanasius. He was born at the end of the third century, and played a decisive role in the defense of orthodoxy against the Arians at the time of the ecumenical council of Nicaea in AD 325. He died in AD 373. Each of these two early church theologians wrote classic works dealing with Christ's reconciliation. Athanasius's treatment is titled *On the Incarnation*. It is the second part of a two-volume work, the first of which was called *Against the Gentiles* (*contra gentes*). Whereas the first work set out to give an account of God and creation, *On the Incarnation* turns to the work of Christ from his incarnation to resurrection. Two of Irenaeus's works survive, and they both tackle the atonement as part of the work of Christ. The first is his monumental and difficult work, *Against Heresies*. The second is his brief study, *On the Apostolic Preaching*, which was rediscovered in an Armenian translation at the beginning of the twentieth century. It is this shorter and more accessible work that is the focus of our attention here.

IRENAEUS: *ON THE APOSTOLIC PREACHING*

Irenaeus's view can be summed up in his famous remark in the preface to book five of *Against Heresies*, where he tackles Christ's saving work in earnest. There he writes, "The Word of God, our Lord Jesus Christ . . . did, through

His transcendent love, become what we are, that He might bring us to be even what He is Himself."[5] In other words, he stooped down to become human that he might scoop up our humanity, so to speak, uniting it to himself, in order that we too might be united with him and participate in his divine life. Or as he puts is in *On the Apostolic Preaching*, Christ's saving work calls "man back again to communion with God, that by this communion with Him we may receive participation in incorruptibility."[6]

Such strong participatory language is rooted in Scripture, in the Pauline epistles, as well as in passages like 2 Peter 1:4, "Through these he has given us his very great and precious promises, so that through them *you may participate in the divine nature*, having escaped the corruption in the world caused by evil desires." Yet how we participate in the divine life through union with Christ is a matter that has generated considerable theological debate. For our present purposes, we need to see that this language of participation in the divine life does not mean we lose ourselves in the divine, or even that we eventually become the same as God—having all the same powers and nature. That is impossible. Rather, the claim is that we are forever on a trajectory "into" God, so to speak, and will enjoy ever greater communion with God as we become ever more like him through ever closer intimacy by means of union with Christ. Think of it like a mathematical asymptote. In an asymptote the curve of a graph approaches a line on a trajectory without ever touching it. It gets ever closer to the line, but the two never meet. In a similar manner, the idea here is that union with God in Christ begins a process of drawing ever closer to God in intimate communion, yet without ever becoming God. Irenaeus, like many early theologians, thinks of the saving work of Christ in part as his becoming human in order that we might be able to participate in the divine life in a way that later theologians developed into the doctrine of theosis or divinization. This is the idea that Christ literally lifts our human natures up out of the mire of sin in order that we can be united with God, participating in intimate union with the divine nature forevermore.

Irenaeus is also well-known for his doctrine of recapitulation, which he sets forth at length in *Against Heresies*. He also makes mention of it in *On*

---

[5]Irenaeus, *Against Heresies* 5, *ANF*, vol. 1 (Edinburgh: T&T Clark, 1885).
[6]Irenaeus, *On the Apostolic Preaching*, trans. John Behr (Crestwood, NY: St. Vladimir's Seminary Press), §40.

the Apostolic Preaching. There he lays out the three key claims of the Christian faith regarding God's nature as Father, Son, and Holy Spirit. In explaining what he affirms regarding Christ, the Son incarnate, he says he came "to recapitulate all things" becoming "a man amongst men, visible and palpable, in order to abolish death, to demonstrate life, and to effect communion between God and man."[7] He repeats the same phrase later in the work, where, having set out the preparation for salvation God wrought through key events in the Old Testament, he speaks of Christ "'recapitulating all things in Himself,' the Word of God, 'things in heaven and things on earth.'"[8] Later still, he explains that Christ's work must recapitulate Adam's mistake so that "mortality might be swallowed up in immortality," a reference to 2 Corinthians 5:4.[9] As he explains in *Against Heresies*, Christ recapitulates in himself each stage of humanity, yet without sin, in order that he might be able to present a perfect life of obedience fulfilling what we are incapable of doing.

These two notions, of participation in the divine life through union with Christ, and of Christ's recapitulating the stages of human existence in his own life in order to heal humanity from the inside-out, as it were, come together in the following passage in *On the Apostolic Preaching*. In it, he underlines the fact that our participation in the incorruptibility of God is entirely contingent upon the incarnation and death of Christ, the incorruptible and invisible God who assumes corruptible, visible flesh in order to make possible our participation in the divine life through his conquest of death:

> So He united man with God and wrought a communion of God and man, we being unable to have any participation in incorruptibility if it were not for his coming to us, for incorruptibility, whilst being invisible, benefitted us nothing; so He became visible, that we might, in all ways, obtain a participation in incorruptibility. And because all are implicated in the first formation of Adam, we were bound to death through the disobedience, for it was fitting [therefore], by means of the obedience of the One, who on our account became man, to be loosed from death. Since death reigned over the flesh, it was necessary that, abolished through flesh, it release man from its oppression.[10]

---

[7]Irenaeus, *On the Apostolic Preaching* §6.
[8]Irenaeus, *On the Apostolic Preaching* §30.
[9]Irenaeus, *On the Apostolic Preaching* §33.
[10]Irenaeus, *On the Apostolic Preaching* §31.

Like the apostle Paul, Irenaeus is concerned to emphasize Christ as the second Adam who does what Adam failed to do, down to "the transgression which occurred through the tree" of the knowledge of good and evil in Eden, which was "undone by the obedience of the tree"—that is, the obedience of Christ to God's will in being crucified.[11]

These are powerful images of salvation in Christ. Nevertheless, Irenaeus has come in for his fair share of criticism in subsequent theology. Here are two of the most important critiques. First, he has been accused of having a *physical doctrine of atonement*. This is the idea that the very action of assuming a human nature in the incarnation is what brings about human reconciliation, nothing more. This objection goes back to the great early twentieth century German liberal historian of doctrine, Adolf von Harnack. It is easy to see how one might think this of Irenaeus, and, to some extent, of other early patristic writers like Athanasius as well, given his emphasis upon the incarnation.

A second sort of objection to Irenaeus's understanding of the atonement is that he doesn't provide his readers with a single account of the work of Christ, and certainly no mechanism of atonement. Instead, he gives us a cluster of different motifs and metaphors strung together like pearls on a necklace. They amount to different images of Christ's reconciling work, like each distinct pearl in the necklace, and do not amount to one coherent whole. Instead, they are various parts thrown together, or various pearls placed beside one another in a necklace. These parts are taken up in subsequent theology and developed into separate, and sometimes incommensurate, atonement doctrines. So, according to this objection, Irenaeus presents us with embryonic versions of a vicarious act of substitution, of Christ paying a debt, of Christ being a moral example, and so on, but nothing more. He does not give us a doctrine of atonement as such, which, as we saw in the previous chapter, is a comprehensive account of a particular teaching about a given theological topic held by some community of Christians or some particular denomination.

Both of these objections seem wide of the mark. As to the first, although Irenaeus does regard the incarnation as a constituent of the atoning work of Christ rather than as merely a prerequisite necessary to bring about the atonement, he also has much to say about the cross of Christ as integral to

---

[11]Irenaeus, *On the Apostolic Preaching* §33.

this work as well. It would be unfair to say he has a diminished role for the death of Christ, or that it is superfluous to his account of the atonement; far from it. He is clear that "by means of the obedience by which He obeyed unto death, hanging upon the tree [that is, the cross], he undid the old disobedience occasioned by the tree [of the knowledge of good and evil in the Garden of Eden]."[12]

The second objection is harder to rebut because a cursory reading of Irenaeus's work is likely to raise this problem in the mind of even the most sympathetic reader. Nevertheless, although he does use different motifs in order to explain various aspects of the work of Christ to his readers, there do seem to be several overarching themes in his work. Although these may not amount to a clear, well-reasoned, or complete account of the means by which Christ's work reconciles us to God, he certainly seems to think in terms of what we might call a conceptual framework for thinking about the atonement. This framework has to do in important respects with the two fundamental notions in his doctrine of atonement with which we began. These were the idea of participation in the divine through Christ's action of becoming incarnate, and Christ uniting himself to our humanity in order to recapitulate in his human nature each age and stage of human life so as to heal it, and thereby (somehow) unite us to God.

Of course, this does not really offer any explanation of how it is that this recapitulating work, including his work on the cross, actually brings about this union, or how it is that Christ is able to represent all of humanity in his vicarious work of atonement. In the background seems to be a way of thinking about Christ that presumes his particular actions can in some manner stand in for our own fallen actions, but not just by his representing us as an ambassador represents a head of state. Rather, Christ represents us in such a way that his action *really is* an action that affects us and our humanity. This seems rather obscure. How can we make sense of it? Perhaps an analogy might help to illuminate the point being made here.

Suppose that we have an acorn, which we infect with some chronic contagion. After the acorn is planted, this contagion affects the way in which the tree grows, at each stage of its existence. The sapling, the young tree, and the mature oak all share in this contagion passed on by earlier stages of the life

---

[12]Irenaeus, *On the Apostolic Preaching* §34.

of the oak. Each stage is contaminated because of the acorn. Similarly, we, as stages of humanity that come after the first humans, are infected with the contagion of sin that was introduced to the human race through their fault. However, at a certain stage in its life, a new oak-branch is grafted into the existing oak, fusing with the parent tree. This graft has been imbued with an antidote to the contagion. As the graft is united with the existing tree, so the antidote is gradually transferred to the other parts of the oak, healing the whole organism. Christ is like this oak-graft, and his atonement is like the antidote that heals the tree of its contagion.

Now, this analogy is different from Irenaeus's views in some respects. Yet it does provide a way of making sense of his idea of participation with Christ, which presumes some sort of real organic union between Christ and fallen humanity that brings about the healing or restoration of the whole. Of course, like any analogy, the one offered here is limited. For instance, it doesn't really illuminate how Christ recapitulates our humanity in his own human nature. But the purpose of the analogy was to make clearer how the action of one entity (the branch/Christ) can somehow affect the rest of an entity (the oak/humanity) with which it has been "fused" or united. This seems to be a very illuminating aspect of Irenaeus's doctrine, and one that could be taken in a direction that yields a doctrine of atonement that makes a lot of sense of the biblical imagery of union with Christ and of Christ's vicarious action in atonement. This is a project we shall return to in the final chapter of the book.

SUMMARY OF IRENAEUS'S DOCTRINE

Let us summarize some of the key aspects of Irenaeus's doctrine. In order to see the overall shape of his position as clearly as possible, it will help if we set it out in numbered statements, with references to relevant sections in Irenaeus's *On the Apostolic Preaching* where these ideas can be found.

1. God is incorruptible in his very nature (§31).

2. Human beings have alienated themselves from God through sin (§15-16).

3. The penalty of sin is death (§15-16).

4. Fallen humanity cannot participate in God's life because they are corrupted (§31).

5. The Word of God unites himself to human nature in order to heal humanity and enable them to participate in the divine life (§31, 40).

6. Christ vicariously recapitulates in himself each stage and age of human existence as a second Adam (§6, 30, 33).[13]

7. Christ dies on the cross to release fallen human beings from the power of death. By dying in our stead, he releases us from the reign of death (§33-34, 38, 68-69).

8. His resurrection destroys the power of death, demonstrating his preeminence over all things, and reconciling us to God (§39-40).

9. This reconciliation obtains for all those who believe in his name (§52).

ATHANASIUS: *ON THE INCARNATION*

Let us turn to our second patristic author, Athanasius. Like Irenaeus, the structure of Athanasius's work follows the creation-fall-redemption narrative of the Christian gospel. He begins with an account of the creation and fall of human beings. The entrance of sin into the created order generates a significant moral dissonance in the creation that God had to address. It would have been unthinkable for God to rescind the curse following the sin of the first humans that brought about death, reasons Athanasius, and unfitting for human beings to be destroyed as a result of their sin. Consequently, God provided a means of expiating sin in order to restore human beings to their place in communion with Godself, namely, the Word of God incarnate. The Word, being divine, is everywhere present, is without a body, and is incorruptible, being in his nature immutable or incapable of change. Nevertheless, he became incarnate and underwent bodily corruption in order to abolish death. "This he did out of sheer love for us," says Athanasius, "so that in his death all might die, and the law of death thereby be abolished because, when he had fulfilled in his body that for which it was appointed, it was thereafter voided of its power for men."[14]

A central motif in Athanasius's treatment of the atonement is that of sacrifice: "It was by surrendering to death the body which he had taken, *as an*

---

[13]This can also be seen in the famous passage of *Against Heresies*, book 2, ch. 22, §4, in which he claims that Christ recapitulates every age of humanity, including old age, because Christ died when he was an old man!

[14]Athanasius, *On the Incarnation* §8.

offering and sacrifice free from every stain, that He forthwith abolished death for His human brethren by the offering of an equivalent."[15] And, as we noted earlier in the chapter in dealing with mistaken interpretations of Athanasius, there is an important substitutionary element to his thinking as well. Christ offers up an equivalent to his human brethren, namely his own human body, in order to vanquish death.

But importantly, Christ's death is not regarded by Athanasius as a punishment as would be the case if this vicarious action were a version of penal substitution. Nor is Christ's death regarded as a sort of merit to be offered as a satisfaction of divine honor or some moral debt to God, as is true with the Anselmian picture of atonement. There is a debt that must be paid by Christ's death, that much Athanasius affirms. But the debt is not owed to God. It is owed to death itself, which is personified in Athanasius's thinking as a sort of shadowy power that holds sway over fallen humanity. We have become subject to the "law of death," the power of which Christ's saving work destroys.[16] In fact, as one recent commentator has pointed out, in Athanasius's thinking Christ's sacrifice is offered to death, not to God.[17] This is particularly clear in the following passage:

> There was a debt owing which must needs be paid; for, as I said before, all men were due to die. Here, then, is the second reason why the Word dwelt among us, namely that having proved His Godhead by His works, He might offer the sacrifice on behalf of all, surrendering His own temple to death in place of all, *to settle man's account with death*, and free him from the primal transgression. In the same act He also showed Himself *mightier than death*, displaying His own body incorruptible as the first-fruits of the resurrection.[18]

Rather like Aslan in *The Lion, The Witch, and the Wardrobe*, who offers himself as a sacrifice to the White Witch in place of the human child, Edmund, so, according to Athanasius, Christ offers himself as a ransom paid to death in the place of all fallen humans.[19] Suppose with Athanasius we allow that

---

[15] Athanasius, *On the Incarnation* §9, emphasis added.

[16] Athanasius, *On the Incarnation* §8.

[17] Benjamin Myers, "The Patristic Doctrine of Atonement," in *Locating Atonement: Explorations in Constructive Dogmatics*, ed. Oliver D. Crisp and Fred Sanders (Grand Rapids: Zondervan Academic, 2015), 85.

[18] Athanasius, *On the Incarnation* §20, emphasis added.

[19] Athanasius, *On the Incarnation* §21.

Christ's reconciling work does indeed have to do with offering a sacrifice that does away with the law of death by offering his own body on our behalf to death.[20] This raises a question about how the death of this one human being can bring about release from the law of death for all of fallen humanity.

Athanasius thinks that Christ is the image of God, in whose image we are fashioned (2 Cor 4:4-6; Col 1:15). When sin defaces that image in us, Christ comes to renew it through his work of reconciliation. He is like the prototype model of humanity, and we are like the production-line versions of humanity made in conformity to the blueprint of the prototype. On Athanasius's way of thinking, this prototypical human being can act on behalf of the rest of humankind so that he alters our condition as a consequence. On the face of it, this is a rather puzzling notion. Athanasius seems to think that Christ's vicarious sacrifice not only purchases us back from the power of death, but also affects our human natures through some sort of union with Christ in language that echoes something of the ideas we found in Irenaeus. How are we to understand this?

Some modern theological interpreters of Athanasius have argued that Christ's humanity is a *vicarious humanity*: his action as one human being not only stands in the place of all other human beings, representing us, but also brings about a moral change on behalf of all other human beings that transforms them as well. Similar ideas can be found in New Testament passages like Ephesians 5:29-32, where the union between Christ and the church is said to be more intimate than the "one flesh" principle of human marriage. That is helpful as far as it goes, but it doesn't really help explain *how* Christ's human nature somehow affects all other human natures.

Perhaps another organic analogy will help illuminate the point Athanasius is making. Consider the case of a human body. Suppose, as the New Testament writers tell us, humanity is like a body, with Christ as its head (see 1 Cor 12; Eph 3:6, 5:23; Col 1:18). In a real human body when we consume food it is distributed throughout the parts of the body, nourishing the whole. The food is taken in through the head, so to speak, but it affects all the parts of the body, not just the head, so that the action of one part of the body brings about a change to the whole. In a similar fashion, Athanasius seems to think that Christ's work of reconciliation involves the sacrifice of his body to death in order that through this action all the other "parts" of the human race are

---

[20]Athanasius, *On the Incarnation* §10.

affected, like the parts of a normal human body nourished through the consumption of food. In this way, one "part" of a whole (the head; Christ) can affect all the other "parts" of a whole (the body; humanity) through an act that distributes benefits to the entire organism. Although Athanasius doesn't use this sort of analogy, there is much in what he does say that resonates with this sort of idea, with its roots in the teaching of the New Testament.

A final component of Athanasius's view is the resurrection. Towards the end of *On the Incarnation* he writes this regarding the human body of Christ:

> Mortal and offered to death on behalf of us all as it was, it could not but die; indeed, it was for that very purpose that the Savior had prepared it for Himself. But on the other hand it could not remain dead, because it had become the very temple of Life. It therefore died, as mortal, but lived again because of the Life within it; and its resurrection is made known through its works.[21]

Athanasius regards the resurrection as the act that confirms the destruction of death. Because Christ's corruptible human body is joined to the incorruptible Son of God, it contains divine life and cannot be destroyed by death. Instead, it destroys death from the inside out, as it were. The image here is rather like the conclusion to the fairytale *Red Riding Hood*. At the end of the original version of that story, the wolf eats Red Riding Hood whole, apparently consuming and destroying the poor child. However, she is cut out of the stomach of the wolf alive and well, and in the process the wolf itself dies. In a similar manner, Athanasius envisages the human Christ being "swallowed whole" by death, and then destroying death from the inside-out in his resurrection. His return to life literally spells the end of death.

Like Irenaeus, Athanasius believes that Christ's work is fundamentally about enabling human beings to participate in the divine life. He writes,

> He, indeed, assumed humanity that we might become God. He manifested Himself by means of a body in order that we might perceive the Mind of the unseen Father. He endured shame from men that we might inherit immortality. He Himself was unhurt by this, for He is impassible and incorruptible; but by His own impassability He kept and healed the suffering men on whose account He thus endured.[22]

---

[21] Athanasius, *On the Incarnation* §31.
[22] Athanasius, *On the Incarnation* §54.

Participation is the goal, but the means to that goal is atonement, and that is brought about through the destruction of death by the life-giving power of the Savior.

SUMMARY OF ATHANASIUS'S DOCTRINE

Let us take stock. As before, when we considered Irenaeus's doctrine, we shall summarize the main points in numbered sentences making reference to the passages in *On the Incarnation* from which they are drawn.

1. God is incorruptible in his very nature (§8–9).

2. Human beings are God's creation, being made in the image of Christ, who is the image of God (§11–13).

3. Human beings are not merely corruptible in principle, but actually corrupt because of the sin of our first parents (§3–5).

4. The consequence of the fall is the curse, and its penalty, death (§3–5).

5. The penalty of death must be met either in the person of the sinner, or in the person of some suitable substitute (this is not stated as a principle by Athanasius, but seems to be an implication of the whole work).

6. God will not permit human beings to be left to suffer the penalty of death; he will renew the divine image in us through an act of recreation (§6, 13).

7. This recreative act is brought about by the reconciling work of Christ, who is the incorruptible Word of God joined with corruptible humanity (§9).

8. Christ's recreative act is also an act of reconciliation (§10, 13).

9. Christ reconciles fallen human beings to God through his act of sacrifice on the cross (§10).

10. This he does by giving up his human body to death, in order to pay the penalty of the curse (§8, 10, 16, 20, 25).

11. Death is unable to "contain" Christ, whose human nature is imbued with Life in virtue of being united to the incorruptible divine nature of God the Son. Instead, Death is destroyed by Christ from the inside-out, so to speak (§31).

12. Christ's resurrection confirms his substitutionary work on our behalf, showing in a visible manner that he has conquered death, thereby restoring the divine image in human beings, and reconciling us with God by union with himself (§21, 26-27).

13. By means of Christ's saving work we are enabled to participate in the divine life (§54).

CONCLUSION

In this chapter we have seen that two important early works on the atonement by Irenaeus and Athanasius give us distinct views of the atonement that share in common a number of overlapping themes and ideas. Nevertheless, these ideas do not amount to some later doctrine of atonement such as penal substitution, or satisfaction—though they contain vicarious elements or components. Nor are they merely physical doctrines of atonement, or even different versions of a *Christus Victor* or ransom account of the atonement, as has sometimes been alleged. Instead, they represent two variations on the atonement, rather like two variations on a musical theme, both of which emphasize his vicarious act of atonement in Christ's incarnation, life, death, and resurrection. This one atoning act abolishes the curse of the fall, destroying death. It also secures our participation in the life of God through our union with Christ, the incorruptible God who takes on corruptible human flesh in order to assure our salvation.

FURTHER READING

Athanasius. *On the Incarnation*. Translated by John Behr. Crestwood, NY: St. Vladimir's Seminary Press, 2006.

Aulén, Gustaf. *Christus Victor: An Historical Study of the Three Main Types of the Idea of Atonement*. London: SPCK, 1931.

Boersma, Hans. *Violence, Hospitality, and the Cross: Reappropriating the Atonement Tradition*. Grand Rapids: Baker Academic, 2004.

Irenaeus. *Against Heresies*. In vol. 1 of *The Ante-Nicene Fathers*. Series 1. Edited by Philip Schaff and Henry Wace. Edinburgh: T&T Clark, 1885.

——— *On the Apostolic Preaching*. Translated by John Behr. Crestwood, NY: St. Vladimir's Seminary Press, 1997.

Jeffery, Steve, Michael Ovey, and Andrew Sach. *Pierced for Our Transgressions: Rediscovering the Glory of Penal Substitution*. Wheaton, IL: Crossway, 2007.

Johnson, Adam. *Atonement: A Guide for the Perplexed*. London: T&T Clark, 2015.

Myers, Benjamin. "The Patristic Doctrine of Atonement." In *Locating Atonement: Explorations in Constructive Dogmatics*, edited by Oliver D. Crisp and Fred Sanders, 71-88. Grand Rapids: Zondervan Academic, 2015.

Gregory of Nyssa. *The Great Catechism*. In vol. 5 of *The Nicene and Post-Nicene Fathers*. Series 2. Edited by Philip Schaff and Henry Wace. Edinburgh: T&T Clark, 1892.

THE RANSOM ACCOUNT
OF ATONEMENT

In the previous chapter we looked at Athanasius and Irenaeus and considered what they had to say about the doctrine of atonement in two of their works. We saw that their views on the atonement were similar, though distinct accounts of the work of Christ that can be summed up in the adage *Christ became human that we might become divine*. This is at the heart of the doctrine of theosis, an important constituent of the doctrine of salvation in Eastern Orthodox theology, but also in much Western theology as well, from Thomas Aquinas to Jonathan Edwards.

In this chapter, we turn our attention to a closely related doctrine of atonement, that is, the ransom account. The motif of Christ's work as a ransom paid to atone for human sin can be found in the New Testament in several places, though it is not developed in detail. For instance, in Mark 10:45 (with a parallel passage in Mt 20:28) we read, "For even the Son of Man did not come to be served, but to serve, and to give his life a ransom for many." The word for ransom used here is *lytron*, and has the connotation of buying something back at a price. This notion is repeated elsewhere in the New Testament. For instance, 1 Timothy 2:5-6 states "For there is one God and one mediator between God and mankind, the man Christ Jesus, who gave himself as a ransom for all people. This has now been witnessed to at the proper time." (Compare Titus 2:14 for similar sentiments.) Also present in the New Testament is the notion of Christ's victory over sin, death, and the devil, which is a cluster of concepts often closely associated with the ransom motif in atonement theology. For instance, in Hebrews 2:14-15 we read, "Since the children have flesh and blood, he too shared in their humanity so that by his death he might break the power of him who holds the power of death—that is, the devil—and free those who all their lives were held in slavery by their fear of death." Earlier in the New Testament in the letter to the Colossians we read of how God has "canceled the charge of our legal indebtedness, which stood against us and condemned us; he has taken it away, nailing it to the cross. And having disarmed the powers and authorities, he made a public spectacle of them, triumphing over them by the cross" (Col 2:14-15). Christ triumphs over the power of death, the devil, and the powers and authorities in his death on the cross. He also sets us free from the law of sin and death in his atonement (Rom 8:2). So Christ's work is both a ransom, and also a victory over sin, death, and the devil. As we saw in the previous chapter these are ideas that are also prevalent in patristic thought, which takes up these different threads of the apostolic witness.

That said, there is a difference between utilizing a particular image, metaphor, or concept, and making a given image, metaphor, or concept one of the main structures that hold together the different parts of one's understanding of Christ's reconciling work like glue that holds together the parts of a model airplane. This is an important consideration to bear in mind when thinking about the ransom account of atonement because it is often conflated with the patristic authors, as if it were the central view common to all, or almost all, theologians in the first thousand years of the life of the church until Anselm of Canterbury. Our investigation in the last chapter demonstrates that this is not a sustainable position. Nevertheless, the ransom view is present in these authors as an aspect of their understanding of atonement. There it functions as a sort of motif in a larger composite whole. In the contemporary theological literature, ransom has once again become popular as an account of the atonement, with a number of prominent theologians claiming that it is arguably the best or most comprehensive way of thinking about Christ's reconciling work.[1] Others have claimed that it is an important aspect of atonement that needs to be present in an adequate understanding of Christ's reconciling work. As we consider the ransom account we will have to assess these claims.

In this chapter we will argue for two conclusions that are theologically significant, and then attempt some theological construction. The first of these

---

[1]Examples include the work of the Mennonite theologian J. Denny Weaver, and, with some careful nuance, the Anglican theologian N.T. Wright.

is that the ransom motif (the notion that Christ buys fallen humanity back at the cost of his life) is not the same as *Christus Victor* (the notion that Christ is victorious over sin, death, and the devil), though these two terms are often used as synonyms in the atonement literature. The second conclusion is that both the *Christus Victor* and ransom views do not yield a complete model of the atonement taken separately or together because neither view can provide a clear mechanism for atonement. As we noted in the first chapter, a mechanism is needed in order for an account of the reconciling work of Christ to be considered a doctrine of atonement. However, it may be that we can repair this gap in the ransom/*Christus Victor* views by providing a treatment of the atonement that brings together both of these motifs into a composite whole, and supplies the missing mechanism of atonement in the process. This is the constructive third element of the chapter. If it is possible to supply the missing mechanism, then a repaired or refurbished version of the ransom account may constitute a model of atonement after all.

THE *CHRISTUS VICTOR*/RANSOM MOTIF

Let us begin our assessment with the work of Gustaf Aulén, whom we first encountered when discussing Irenaeus and Athanasius in the previous chapter. He is widely regarded as having put the ransom doctrine of atonement back on the theological map with his study entitled *Christus Victor*, which was first published in 1931. He claimed that the "classic" view of the atonement, which, he maintained, was the position of the early church, had become obscured by later layers of theological reflection that need to be removed in order to reclaim the classic view for contemporary theology. Aulén writes,

> I have tried to be consistent in speaking of the classic idea of the Atonement, never of the, or a, classic theory; I have reserved the word theory, and usually the word doctrine, for the Latin and "subjective" types [of doctrines of atonement]. For the classic idea of the Atonement has never been put forward, like the other two, as a rounded and finished theological doctrine; it has always been an idea, a motif, a theme, expressed in many different variations. It is not, indeed, that it has lacked clearness of outline; on the contrary, it has been fully definite and unambiguous. But it has never been shaped into a rational theory.[2]

---

[2]Gustaf Aulén, *Christus Victor: An Historical Study of the Three Main Types of the Idea of Atonement* (London: SPCK, 1931), 174-75.

This classic "motif" or "theme" (or the "dramatic view" as he sometimes calls it) is the *Christus Victor* view. On his way of thinking, *Christus Victor* is a way of speaking about the manner in which Christ is victorious over sin, death, and the devil. Moreover, Christ buys back human beings from the powers of sin, death, and the devil. His work is a ransom price that is paid to these powers in order that some number of fallen humanity may be redeemed from destruction, and brought to salvation. This twofold central claim of the view that Christ is victorious over sin, death, and the devil, *and* that his atonement buys back fallen humanity from destruction—which, we have seen are motifs that can be discerned in the New Testament—are often embedded in a larger story about salvation. Perhaps the most famous example of this is in Gregory of Nyssa's *Great Catechism*. There he says this:

> For since, as has been said before, it was not in the nature of the opposing power to come in contact with the undiluted presence of God, and to undergo His unclouded manifestation, therefore, in order to secure that the ransom on our behalf might be easily accepted by him who required it, the Deity was hidden under the veil of our nature, that so, as with ravenous fish, the hook of the Deity might be gulped down along with the bait of flesh, and thus, life being intro- duced into the house of death, and light shining in darkness, that which is diametrically opposed to light and life might vanish.[3]

This story, or some variation on it, appears in the writings of a number of patristic authors including Irenaeus, Origen, John Chrysostom, Augustine (who uses the example of a mousetrap[4]), and John of Damascus (who uses the same picture as Gregory of Nyssa[5]). Although the core claims of the view are independent of the narrative into which Gregory and these other great theologians set them, the narrative does a lot of work in communicating how these different elements might fit together into one whole explanation of salvation. Often this bait-and-hook analogy has been taken to be

---

[3] Gregory of Nyssa, *The Great Catechism*, ch. 24, *NPNF*², vol. 5 (Edinburgh: T&T Clark, 1892). Chapter 26 of the *Great Catechism* makes it clear that Gregory thinks God deceives the devil in proceeding as he does.

[4] The so-called *muscipula diaboli*, as it was known in Latin. A good example of this can be found in Augustine's Sermon 263, "On the Ascension," in Augustine, *Sermons on the Liturgical Seasons*, Fathers of the Church Patristic Series, trans. Mary Sarah Muldowney (Washington, DC: The Catholic University of America Press, 1984).

[5] John of Damascus, *On The Orthodox Faith*, bk. III, ch. XXVII, *NPNF*², vol. 9. (Edinburgh: T&T Clark, 1892).

problematic because it implies God deceives the devil (the fish), tricking him into attempting to destroy the human nature of Christ by swallowing it so as to destroy it in death. However, we shall see in the third section of this chapter that this need not be the case. The story of redemption told by the defender of a ransom account of atonement need not have this problematic moral consequence.

DISTINGUISHING *CHRISTUS VICTOR* FROM RANSOM

Before elaborating upon the constructive theological section of the chapter, we need to think a little more carefully about the relationship between the notion of ransom and the notion of Christ as victor over sin, death, and the devil. As we noted in the introduction to this chapter, the *Christus Victor* view has come back into vogue. One interesting feature of this recent return to the limelight is that there has been a bifurcation of the *Christus Victor* and ransom accounts of atonement in some of the retrievals of this atonement motif. A clear example of this is the work of the anabaptist theologian J. Denny Weaver. Amongst other things he holds that *Christus Victor* is not about the death of Christ at all, but about the reign of God. This is seen in Christ's life, death, and resurrection. But it is not synonymous with these things. Weaver says, "Since Jesus' mission was not to die but to make visible the reign of God, it is quite explicit that neither God nor the reign of God *needs* Jesus' death in the way that his death is irreducibly *needed* in satisfaction theory." This, he says, represents, "one of the most profound differences between narrative *Christus Victor* and satisfaction atonement."[6] It seems that for Weaver, Christ's victory over the powers of sin, death, and the devil is independent of him buying back fallen human beings at the price of his own life. Christ's death is not so much a ransom, on Weaver's account, as it is a consequence of his dedication to living out the reign of God.

Other contemporary theologians seek to privilege a ransom account of atonement over other "motifs" or "metaphors" that can be found in the biblical material. A good example of this sort of interpretive strategy can be found in the work of the New Testament scholar and theologian N. T. Wright. He says,

---

[6]J. Denny Weaver, *The Nonviolent Atonement*, 2nd ed. (Grand Rapids: Eerdmans, 2011), 89. Emphasis in the original.

The cross is for Paul the symbol, as it was the means, of the liberating victory
of the one true God . . . over all the enslaving powers that have usurped his
authority. . . . For this reason I suggest that we give priority—a priority among
equals, perhaps, but still a priority—to those Pauline expressions of the crucifixion of Jesus which describe it as the decisive victory over the "principalities
and powers." Nothing in the many other expressions of the meaning of the
cross is lost if we put this in the centre.[7]

The Dutch-Canadian Reformed theologian Hans Boersma is another contemporary scholar who thinks highly of the *Christus Victor* account, although
he admits that it does not provide a clear explanation of how Christ gains the
victory over sin, death, and the devil. He makes clear what Wright hints at,
namely, that this victory motif should be used as one metaphor amongst
several others, which may be "mashed up" together into a new account of
atonement (a matter to which we shall return in chapter nine). His chosen
complement to the *Christus Victor* account is the recapitulation motif we noted
in Irenaeus's work in chapter two. "Christ's victory over the powers of darkness
is the telos and climax of his work of recapitulation," says Boersma. "In other
words, the victory is the *result* of the entire process of recapitulation."[8] Here,
the *Christus Victor* motif is not so much one privileged motif amongst several
to be found in Pauline theology, as with Wright, but more like the upshot of
Christ's reconciling work, understood as his recapitulating each stage of fallen
humanity in his own life (as per Irenaeus's account of the atonement). Each of
these three contemporary theologians adopts a slightly different interpretive
strategy with respect to the *Christus Victor*/ransom motif in their work on
atonement. But notice how both Wright and Boersma, like Weaver, think of
the main claim of *Christus Victor* as Christ's victory over the "powers" of sin,
death, and the devil. In each of these three instances the notion of ransom
plays a much less significant role in the discussion. In the case of Weaver in
particular it appears to have largely dropped out of the discussion altogether.

Let us take stock. As even this cursory sketch of several recent treatments
of the topic suggest, there appear to be what I have been calling different

---

[7]N. T. Wright, *What St. Paul Really Said: Was Paul of Tarsus the Real Founder of Christianity?* (Grand
Rapids: Eerdmans, 1997), 47.
[8]Hans Boersma, *Violence, Hospitality, and the Cross: Reappropriating the Atonement Tradition* (Grand
Rapids: Baker Academic, 2004), 181.

interpretive strategies being deployed by these different theologians in order to make sense of the *Christus Victor*/ransom account of atonement. Whereas Aulén thought of them as two aspects of one whole account of atonement, an account he thought common in primitive Christianity, recent work on the atonement has tended to separate these two things out at different and apparently distinct motifs. The ransom material has largely been eclipsed in some of this recent work by the *Christus Victor* theme. Christ's triumph over the powers—especially the powers of sin, death, and the devil—has taken center stage in several important pieces of recent atonement theology, either as the substantive claim being made about Christ's work (as with Weaver), or as an important and potentially fundamental motif in considering New Testament notions of atonement (as with Wright), or even as a motif that can be mashed up with other, patristic themes, like recapitulation, to produce a new way of thinking about Christ's atonement (as with Boersma).

IN SEARCH OF A MECHANISM OF ATONEMENT

From the foregoing it should be clear that there are different interpretive strategies used in the contemporary theological literature in deploying the *Christus Victor* and ransom motifs. But are these two concepts merely motifs or metaphors for the atonement or are they more than that? Do the twin notions of ransom and Christ as victor constitute a doctrine or doctrines of atonement—a complete model or models for understanding the reconciling work of Christ? As it stands, I think ransom and *Christus Victor* are not more than atonement motifs (as Aulén himself admits), though there may be a way of adding to them a mechanism of atonement in order to generate a doctrine of Christ's reconciling work. Before coming to that more constructive component, let us consider why these motifs do not yield a doctrine of atonement.

To assist us in our deliberations, it will be helpful to have a clear idea of the conceptual content of ransom and *Christus Victor*. Earlier I said that ransom is the notion that Christ buys fallen humanity back at the cost of his life. But how should we think of this claim? Some Christian theologians seem to think Christ's reconciling work is literally a ransom; it literally buys back fallen human beings at the cost of his life. But then, to whom is the ransom paid? To whom is Christ's life owed? Not to God, for Christ is God incarnate, and he can hardly be said to owe himself his own (human) life. Well then, perhaps the idea is that Christ pays the ransom price of his life to sin, death, and the devil, or to some combination of these three entities. Certainly they are all treated in quasi-personal ways by some patristic theologians, as "powers" to which we are somehow beholden. But without much more explanation of this, it is difficult to see how Christ's work can be a ransom paid to such entities. Death is not a thing, but (according to much historic theology, at least) a *privation* of something—the privation of life. Sin is not a thing but (again, according to much historic theology) the *privation* of something, that is, the privation of a good thing that should have been present.[9] Compare the idea of a hole in a garment. We do not normally think that a hole is a thing added to the garment when it first appears. It is not as if there is the garment, and then later there is the garment plus this thing called a "hole" that has been added to it. Rather, we think that the hole is a "lack" or a "privation" of the cloth that has torn or been eaten by moths. In a similar manner, much historic theology has treated both death and sin as essentially privative, that is, the lack of a thing rather than something substantive.

The devil is rather different in this regard. Plausibly (according to much historic theology) the devil *is* a thing. In fact, he is a creature, a fallen angel. But how could a ransom be paid by God to the devil? Why would we think God "owed" the devil the price of the lives of all of fallen humanity? That seems a very strange view. If the response is that in sinning human beings sold themselves into slavery, with the devil as their master, this seems to be a distorted picture of the role played by the devil in traditional theology. He is not lord over humanity, but a fallen creature seeking to create mischief. Yet, because he is a creature, his actions are circumscribed by God's power and design. It is not as if the devil acts as a kind of anti-god, creating whatever havoc he wills. No, rather he is a creature whose actions are hemmed in by God and permitted in the knowledge that God has complete control of the outcome, as well as the process that yields the particular outcome.

So perhaps we should think of the ransom motif like this: *the picture of Christ's work of reconciliation by means of which he buys back the lives of fallen human beings subject to sin, and death, and afflicted by the devil—in a way similar to a ransom price that is paid out in order that some number of fallen*

---

[9]The notion that sin is a privation is particularly associated with the work of Augustine. See, for example, Augustine, *Confessions,* trans. Thomas Williams (Indianapolis: Hackett, 2019), Bk. 3, 7.12, p. 36.

humanity may be redeemed from destruction, and brought to salvation. But of course, as soon as we put it in these terms, it should be clear that what is envisaged here in the use of the term "ransom" is a figure of speech, a motif of a sort, but not a complete doctrine of atonement. For it is still not clear on this way of thinking how ransom is doing any work in providing a mechanism for atonement. And I suggest that this is true of much of the theological literature that appropriates this ransom language as well.

Let us turn to the triumphal motif of *Christus Victor.* Does this fare any better? Recall that this is the notion that Christ is victorious over sin, death, and the devil. What does this victory entail? At least some contemporary theologians, like Weaver, think of this as a consequence of a life lived in dedication to God. It is the manifestation of the reign of God, but it has no intrinsic connection to the death of Christ or even, perhaps, to the notion of atonement. Suppose we follow Weaver in this regard. Then, the victory of Christ over the "powers" of sin, death, and the devil are about the manifestation of God's reign in the life and ministry of Christ, as well as (perhaps) in his death and resurrection. But this leaves entirely unexplained how it is that Christ's life, ministry, death, or resurrection are an atonement for human sin, or how they are supposed to be acts that reconcile humans with Godself.

Well, perhaps if we combine the ransom and *Christus Victor* motifs we may yet generate an atonement doctrine. Here is one way that goal might be achieved. Think of Christ's reconciling work as the action by means of which he buys back the lives of fallen human beings subject to sin, death, and afflicted by the devil. It is like a ransom price that is paid out in order that some number of fallen humanity may be redeemed from destruction, and brought to salvation. As a consequence of this ransom-like act, Christ triumphs over sin, death, and the devil in his resurrection from the grave, manifesting the reign of God in the world, and his power to reconcile humanity to Godself.

This is an improvement on the foregoing, but it is still not clear how this ransom-like action, and the resulting triumph over sin, death, and the devil, are supposed to bring about reconciliation with God. Suppose Smith has never seen a smartphone. Upon being shown one, he asks how it works. What is the mechanism by means of which he is able to talk to someone far away, to access the internet wirelessly, and to do a host of other things including listening to music and getting weather reports on the digital display? If the response given was obfuscating, or lacking in real explanatory power, Smith would quickly become frustrated. "You speak in here and it is received elsewhere. There is a flow of power from one smartphone to the other and it communicates the voice in the process," comes the reply. "Yes, but how does that occur?" asks Smith. "Well, it flows into one phone and out of the other," his interlocutor tells him. "Yes, I understand that part. What I want to know is, *how* does that happen? By what means does this 'flow' of information take place?" And so on. This is akin to the worry about ransom/*Christus Victor* views in view here. From what we have seen thus far, it is not clear how they are able to give an account of the means by which the atonement reconciles fallen human beings to Godself.

So, in short, it looks like taken separately the ransom motif and the *Christus Victor* motif do not yield mechanisms of atonement, and so do not qualify as models or doctrines of atonement. The same is true if one combines the two notions. Taken together they still do not provide a clear understanding of how it is that Christ's work reconciles human beings to God.

AN ALTERNATIVE WAY OF THINKING ABOUT THE RANSOM ACCOUNT

However, perhaps we can do something to supply the missing component to the ransom/*Christus Victor* approach to the atonement in order to generate a doctrine or model. Earlier, we mentioned the bait-and-hook story of ransom that a number of patristic theologians use to make sense of the central claims of the ransom and *Christus Victor* motifs. We also noted that the way in which this is often understood—as a problematic story that involves God trying to deceive the devil in order to ransom fallen humanity—may be mistaken in important respects. Having seen that the ransom and *Christus Victor* motifs have come apart in recent theology, and that they can be used separately or recombined as aspects of new composite accounts of atonement, we are now in a position to return to the ransom story with which we began to see whether we can repair it for constructive theological use today.

The Australian theologian Benjamin Myers has recently offered a rather different way of thinking about the bait-and-hook story that is illuminating. Although Gregory of Nyssa does indeed invoke the devil as an actor in his version of the bait-and-hook story, a careful analysis of what he actually says makes it clear that the root problem is not the devil, but death itself. It is death, as the privation of life, that Christ comes to conquer. Death here is privative in the sense that darkness is a privation of light. Once the light is switched on, or the lamp brought into the room, the darkness vanishes. In a similar manner, Gregory is saying that Christ enters the state of death in order to destroy it, so that fallen human beings may be reconciled to Godself. As Myers summarizes it, "When Christ's human nature succumbs to death, the fullness of the divine life enters the privative state of death. As a result, the privation is filled, i.e. cancelled out. In the death of Christ, death dies."[10] This is what he thinks of as the mechanism of reconciliation according to this way of thinking about what he calls the patristic view of atonement.

But we could adapt this insight that Myers applies to the patristic view of atonement to refurbish the ransom/*Christus Victor* view instead, taking the "ransom" and "*Christus Victor*" motifs together as two aspects of one larger composite understanding of Christ's saving work. In order to make this as clear as possible, let us attempt to retell the ransom narrative borrowing freely from Gregory's original bait and hook tale, amending the story where necessary in order to finesse his account and furnish the missing mechanism of atonement. It goes like this:

> Through rebelling against God human beings have fallen into a state of sin that leads to death. Death, the privation of human life, is an evil that has a kind of "power" or hold over fallen human beings as the inevitable result of rebellion against God. What is more, God permits the devil a certain sort of influence over sinful humanity, as he allows Satan in the biblical story of Job to afflict Job in all sorts of ways. How are we to be released from this dreadful state? By the reconciling work of Christ. His work achieves two interrelated, though distinct, ends. First, by his death, he pays the ransom price for human sin. This price is death itself, the privation of life that is "owed" because of human sin. It is a penalty that must be paid either by fallen human beings in succumbing to death, or by Christ as a substitute who can pay the price instead of the sinner, in order to "buy back" the sinner from the clutches of death. By paying this price he releases fallen humanity from the thrall of death, and the sway of the devil by entering this state

---

[10]Benjamin Myers, "The Patristic Doctrine of Atonement," in *Locating Atonement: Explorations in Constructive Dogmatics*, ed. Oliver D. Crisp and Fred Sanders (Grand Rapids: Zondervan Academic, 2015), 73.

of privation and destroying death from the inside out. This redemptive action brings the light of life (that is, Christ) into the darkness of death (that is, the penalty for sin). The second end or goal of Christ's reconciling work is triumph over sin, death, and the devil, brought about by his atoning act of suffering on the cross. This appears to be an act that destroys Christ's human nature. But it is actually the means by which Christ is able to defeat the powers of sin, death, and the devil. His resurrection is a triumph over these powers, a display of his victory against evil, death, and the devil. Because he acts as a substitute for human sinners, paying the ransom price of his life in order to enter and destroy the privative state of death from the inside out in place of fallen human beings, Christ has defeated the penalty of sin. As a result he has destroyed its power over fallen human beings, thereby frustrating the plans of the devil and making reconciliation with God possible for all humanity.

This story shows that defenders of a ransom/*Christus Victor* account of atonement need not include the notion of a divine deception in their account of Christ's reconciling work. It also tracks the New Testament material with which we began, and reflects some of the important claims made by some patristic theologians such as Gregory regarding the atonement as a work that defeats the power of death and thereby overcomes the penalty of sin, frustrating the plans of the devil. However, this story is rather different from the account given of ransom/*Christus Victor* in Aulén's work, or, indeed, the work of Weaver, and to some extent Wright, or Boersma. It is also different from many of the textbook treatments of this topic, which often repeat Aulén's mistaken way of thinking about the matter.

The main difference between this version of the ransom account and the others we have surveyed thus far is that this version provides a clear mechanism of atonement. The mechanism in this story depends on a claim about Christ's work being a vicarious substitution. It is vicarious because he acts on behalf of fallen humanity. It is substitutionary in nature because he takes the place of fallen human beings. The vicarious work he performs involves him taking upon himself the penalty that is due for human sin, namely, death. But death is not understood on this way of thinking as a punishment (as with classic penal substitution doctrines of atonement). Nor is it exactly true to say that he takes upon himself the penal consequences of human sin—that is, the consequences that would be punishment for us, for while they are not punishment for the innocent Christ, he assumes these consequences in our place. Rather, it is that he enters the privative state of death that is the penalty set for human sin, and destroys that state from the inside out. By performing this action, he does several things at once. First, he destroys the power of death and its hold over fallen human beings, for whom death is the "last enemy," the consequence of the curse upon humankind as a consequence of sin. Second, in breaking the power of death, he removes the curse accompanying sin. By undergoing the privative state of death on behalf of fallen human beings, he takes away the penalty of sin thereby freeing human beings from the thrall of sin. And finally, in performing this vicarious substitutionary act of ransom-paying, Christ frustrates the plans of the devil. So he really does triumph over sin, death, and the devil in his resurrection, which really is a victory over these powers that he leads captive in his train (Eph 4:8).

It should be clear from the foregoing that this amended account of ransom is very similar to the views of Irenaeus and Athanasius encountered in the previous chapter. This is not accidental. The reason why this is the case is that the missing element from the ransom/*Christus Victor* accounts of atonement is, in large measure, what is supplied in the writings of Irenaeus and Athanasius. In order to make the ransom/*Christus Victor* motifs more than mere metaphors, they need to have added to them something like the vicarious-substitutionary element found in Irenaeus and Athanasius, as well as making more prominent the way in which Christ's atonement has to do with the defeat of death as the penalty of human sin.

This revised account also provides some explanation of why it is that ransom/*Christus Victor* is so often mistaken as the patristic view of atonement. It is certainly a component part of many patristic views, including those of Irenaeus and Athanasius. But only when it is conjoined with a clearer, more developed account of the vicarious and substitutionary nature of Christ's work, and how Christ's atonement defeats death, thereby dealing with the penalty due for human sin—ransoming fallen humans from death, so to speak—does it compose a complete doctrine or model of Christ's reconciling work. When the ransom/*Christus Victor* motifs are taken out of this richer conceptual context, they do not function as part of the larger theological whole that includes the explanatory element of the mechanism of atonement. Shorn of this mechanism, the motif of ransom makes little sense other than as a metaphor for Christ's redeeming work (which is conceptually fuzzy about the nature of the ransom), the same being true of *Christus Victor*, which becomes simply a way of speaking about the victory of Christ over sin, death, and the devil, or about the reign of God made manifest in Christ's life, ministry, and passion (in the case of Weaver's treatment of the victor theme). But when these elements are combined with the vicarious and substitutionary story that makes clear how Christ pays the penalty of death, the "ransom price" for human sin, destroying death and the consequences of sin in the process (and frustrating the devil), the ransom account does indeed rise to the level of a doctrine of atonement. Such a refurbished and expanded ransom view offers a striking way of thinking about the reconciling work of Christ that reflects patristic teaching and important elements of the New Testament witness.

CONCLUSION

I have provided an argument for two conclusions. The first is that the ransom/ *Christus Victor* motifs are distinct, and have been treated that way in some of the contemporary atonement literature, where they have "come apart" and been used in rather different ways by different scholars. The second conclusion is that neither separately, nor together do these motifs constitute a complete doctrine or model of atonement. Something more is required, specifically, a clear mechanism of atonement consistent with the metaphors of ransom and Christ as the victor over sin, death, and the devil. This missing mechanism we saw could be supplied by borrowing a concept of vicarious substitution from Irenaeus and Athanasius, and by making clearer the manner in which Christ's defeat of death deals with the penalty and consequences of human sin. This reparative action not only provides a ransom doctrine of atonement, it also provides an explanation of why this has so often been misunderstood in the atonement literature.

FURTHER READING

Athanasius. *On the Incarnation*. Translated by John Behr. Crestwood, NY: St. Vladimir's Seminary Press, 2006.

Aulén, Gustaf. *Christus Victor. An Historical Study of the Three Main Types of the Idea of Atonement*. London: SPCK, 1931.

Boersma, Hans. *Violence, Hospitality, and the Cross: Reappropriating the Atonement Tradition*. Grand Rapids: Baker Academic, 2004.

Irenaeus. *Against Heresies*. In vol. 1 of *The Ante-Nicene Fathers*. Series 1. Edited by Philip Schaff and Henry Wace. Edinburgh: T&T Clark, 1885.

———. *On the Apostolic Preaching*. Translated by John Behr. Crestwood, NY: St. Vladimir's Seminary Press, 1997.

Jeffery, Steve, Michael Ovey, and Andrew Sach, *Pierced for Our Transgressions: Rediscovering the Glory of Penal Substitution*. Wheaton, IL: Crossway, 2007.

Myers, Benjamin. "The Patristic Doctrine of Atonement." In *Locating Atonement: Explorations in Constructive Dogmatics*, edited by Oliver D. Crisp and Fred Sanders, 71-88. Grand Rapids: Zondervan Academic, 2015.

Gregory of Nyssa. *The Great Catechism*. In vol. 5 of *The Nicene and Post-Nicene Fathers*. Series 2. Edited by Philip Schaff and Henry Wace. Edinburgh: T&T Clark, 1892.

Ray, Darby Kathleen. *Deceiving the Devil: Atonement, Abuse, and Ransom*. Cleveland, OH: Pilgrim Press, 1988.

THE SATISFACTION
DOCTRINE OF ATONEMENT

One of the greatest Christian thinkers of all time and a Doctor of the Church (*Doctor Magnificus*), Anselm was born in AD 1033 to a family of minor nobility in Aosta, Italy. As a young man, he left home and wandered Europe in search of his destiny, eventually settling to the religious life at the monastery of Bec in Normandy, France. Scholarship and an ecclesiastical vocation beckoned, and he was ordained a monk of the Benedictine order there. He served as prior and abbot of Bec and then succeeded his teacher Lanfranc as Archbishop of Canterbury in England, where he had a stormy relationship with successive monarchs and spent several periods in exile in Europe as a consequence. He died in April of AD 1109, surrounded by his monks at Canterbury, and he was buried in the cathedral church.

Anselm was a remarkable figure by the standards of any age. More remarkable, perhaps, is the body of work, mainly of a theological nature, that he left behind. Composed in a relatively short period, and begun in mid-life, his major dogmatic outputs show a marked consistency of thought. He often refers readers in one work back to others he has written in a kind of informal, internal cross-referencing system. This is one indication of the fact that he was a thinker who had worked out his views in a systematic manner by the time he came to writing. There are really no significant retractions or revisions to his thought in the different treatises, meditations, and prayers he produced.

Not only is his body of work relatively stable and coherent, it is also written in some of the clearest and most direct prose of any religious thinker. This makes him one of the easiest theologians for the beginning student to read, and one of the most rewarding to study. It is particularly true of one of his most famous works that is known by its Latin title, *Cur deus homo* (*Why The God-Man*).[1] It is arguably one of the greatest accounts of the atonement ever produced. In fact, in terms of its influence on later theology, it may rank as the single most influential historic doctrine of atonement. For Anselm's position was taken up and modified by later medieval theologians such as Thomas Aquinas and was a major influence upon magisterial reformers such as Martin Luther and John Calvin, and subsequent post-Reformation theology. It is, in fact, the first truly systematic account of the atonement in Western theology.

For these reasons, it is worth studying Anselm's doctrine of atonement with some care. That is the principle task of this chapter. To begin with, we will set out the shape of his position. Having done that, we will be in a position to consider some objections to it. Some traditional textbook objections to Anselm's work are wide of the mark, though they are often repeated. However, there are some conceptual worries that his account raises, some of which we shall return to when considering the "successor" to Anselm's doctrine, that is, penal substitution.

THE SHAPE OF ANSELM'S DOCTRINE OF SATISFACTION IN *CUR DEUS HOMO*

The argument of *Cur deus homo* (hereafter *CDH*) is divided into two parts. In the first part, Anselm explores why atonement is necessary for salvation (if, indeed, it is necessary). In the second section, he explains why satisfaction must be brought about by one who is at-one-and-the-same-time fully God and fully human (i.e. a God-man). It is cast in the form of a dialectic, or discussion between Anselm and one of his monks, Boso. The student asks questions, and the teacher (in this case Anselm's literary self) provides answers. This artifice provides a way of framing the discussion that gets to the main issues quickly and effectively.

At the outset, it is important to grasp two theological assumptions that underpin the work as a whole. The first is Anselm's commitment to a faith seeking understanding approach to theology. This is the notion that one begins from a position of faith and works from there to a place of understanding, by

---

[1] All references in this chapter are to Thomas Williams's translation of *Cur deus homo* in *Anselm, The Basic Works* (Indianapolis: Hackett, 2007), 237-326.

reasoning through the conceptual commitments of that faith. Thus, in the Commendation of *CDH* to Pope Urban II with which the work is prefaced, Anselm writes, "I will endeavor to raise myself up just a little to gaze upon the reason of the things we believe, as far as heavenly grace sees fit to grant it to me." Beginning from faith, he seeks to reflect upon what he believes.

Anselm also explains in the preface to *CDH* how he intends to set out his argument *"remoto Christo"*—that is, bracketing out what he knows of salvation from divine revelation and proceeding on the basis of more general theological and metaphysical principles to ascertain whether the incarnation and atonement were required for salvation. He seeks to prove "by necessary reasons—leaving Christ out of the picture, as if nothing concerning him had ever taken place—that it is impossible for any human being to be saved apart from Christ." We shall see that this rather unusual manner of proceeding has been the occasion of some of the criticisms that have been raised against his view being too speculative and not appropriately biblical in its orientation.

The core idea of *CDH* can be stated fairly easily. It is this: *God's honor is taken away by human sin. This is intolerable. So his honor must be satisfied by some act of atonement for sin, or by the punishment of sin.* He writes, "Necessarily, then, when God's honor is taken away, either it is paid back or else punishment follows. Otherwise, either God would not be just toward himself, or he would lack the power to enforce either repayment, or punishment. And it is impious to think such a thing."[2]

Behind his notion of divine honor is divine justice, which, on Anselm's way of thinking, is identical with God's nature. Anselm presumes that divine justice is essentially retributive in nature, so that the punishment must fit the crime. God may not set aside his justice in order to forgive sin, for, thinks Anselm, God cannot fail to be just to himself. That is, to fail in respect to the exercise of his justice in pursuit of his own honor would be to fail to act according to his own nature—in effect, to deny himself—which is impossible. "Forgiving sin in this way is the same as not punishing it," says Anselm. "But to order [that is, to organize, or regulate] sin in the right way when no recompense is made *just is* to punish sin. So if sin is not punished, it is left unordered. . . . But it is not fitting for God to leave anything unordered in his

---

[2]*CDH* 1.13.

kingdom. . . . So, it is not fitting for God to leave sin unpunished in this way."[3] The idea seems to be that God is bound to punish sin because he is incapable of leaving anything "disordered" in his creation. We might say that his nature is such that all things must be properly "ordered." It would be unfitting for sin to go unpunished, for this would be to allow sin to go "unordered" or "unregulated." Its proper regulation requires punishment. So sin *must* be punished.

Clearly, by Anselm's reckoning, human sin is a very serious matter. In *CDH* 1.13 he reasons that human sin takes away divine honor. But God must ensure that his honor is preserved. It would be unjust for God to permit his honor to be taken away by human sin, and he cannot act in such an unjust manner. So he must ensure one of two outcomes: either human sin is punished, or his honor is restored through some other act of satisfaction. "Necessarily then," Anselm says, "when God's honor is taken away, either it is paid back or else punishment follows."

Later in *CDH* 1.21-24, Anselm offers a second line of argument, this time concerning the seriousness of sin. He reasons that recompense for sin ought to be proportioned to the magnitude of the sin. Even an apparently trivial sin, such as looking away from God when commanded not to, is immensely grave. This is because the seriousness of sin is connected to the status of the person we have offended. Anselm writes, "You do not make recompense unless what you pay back is greater than the thing for the sake of which you ought not to have committed the sin."[4] All human beings owe their very being to God because he creates and sustains us. So, says Anselm, all sin against God is a sin against our creator and sustainer. Since we owe everything to God even without sin, we are incapable of performing any act that atones for our sin. Any putative act of atonement would fail to repay the debt owed. In which case, it looks like our debt to God is so great that we cannot pay it through any act since we owe everything we are to God.

It appears that, for Anselm, the seriousness of sin depends in part on the status of the person against whom we sin. Because we sin against God, to whom we owe everything, our predicament is grave indeed. We can put it in the form of a Status Principle like this: *The guilt accruing to sin leading to punishment is proportional to both (a) the severity of the actual or intended*

---

[3]*CDH* 1.12.
[4]*CDH* 1.21.

harm to the person or object concerned, and (b) the kind of being against whom the wrong is committed.

At first glance there appears to be something intuitive about this. We may well think that sinning against a monarch, say, is more serious than sinning against our neighbor because there is something about the status of the monarch as the head of state that makes sinning against her more heinous. What might this "something" be? Anselm seems to presume that there is a kind of order of being, and that different beings have different status in this order, depending upon where they stand relative to other entities. So a dog has a more important status than an ant, and a human has more status than a dog, and so on. Today, we tend to be much more skeptical of the claim that difference in kind implies a difference in ontological status, as if there is something about being a dog that makes it more important than being an ant. So we might well be skeptical about Anselm's claim that the status of an individual we have offended is important in weighing the seriousness of the crime committed.

Yet, even if we do harbor such skepticism, all Anselm's argument really needs is the claim that there is a significant difference between the dignity and honor that should be ascribed to God as our creator and sustainer and to any creature he fashions and upholds in being. There does indeed seem to be an ontological gulf between God and creation. Perhaps on this basis we might venture with Anselm to say that any sin committed against a fellow creature pales in significance compared to a sin committed against our creator and sustainer, to whom we owe everything.

This brings us to the matter of the mechanism for atonement on Anselm's view. Given the heinousness of human sin and the honor and dignity of the God we have offended, and given that justice must be served, the only suitable alternative to punishment is some act of atonement. It is at this juncture that Anselm's famous argument for the God-man comes into its own. In the second part of *CDH*, chapters 7–9, he reasons as follows: Only someone who is a human being of the race of Adam can save other human beings of the race of Adam. That is, there must be a "connection" between the God-man and Adam's race; it is not sufficient for a new being to be created out of nothing by God because he would not be of the same race as Adam's progeny, and so could not act on their behalf. At the same time, only someone who is without sin can bring about salvation for fallen human beings, since a sinner already owes everything he has and is to God. So, the God-man must be born without sin, but as a member of the race of Adam. However, it is not sufficient for a sinless human being to bring about salvation, since no human act can generate a merit sufficient to atone for all human sin. Therefore, in addition to being a sinless human of Adam's race, the savior must also be a divine person, since only a divine person is able to unite himself with human nature and satisfy divine justice by performing some atoning act that is sufficiently meritorious that it may atone for human sin. Hence, the savior must be a God-man. As Anselm puts it, "It is necessary that the one who is going to make this recompense be both perfect God and perfect man, since only one who is truly God can make it, but only one who is truly human owes it."[5]

An important consideration here is that it is possible for the God-man to act on behalf of fallen humanity because he is not already obligated to atone for human sin. He is without sin, so he does not owe God his life to atone for the debt of his own sin. This means that the act of atonement is *supererogatory*. That is, it is an act that is above and beyond the call of duty; it is not required in order to satisfy divine justice. Since the God-man is not duty-bound to save human beings from their sin, and since he does not require the merit his saving act generates in order to save himself, he may "apply" it to our account, offering it up as a suitable satisfaction of the debt human sin has generated, in place of the punishment we would otherwise have to face. So, at the heart of Anselm's account of the atonement is something like a trans-action between the First and Second Persons of the Godhead, which satisfies divine justice and deals with human sin. For this reason, in some older text-books of Christian theology Anselm's view is referred to as the commercial doctrine of atonement because there is this transaction or "commerce" between the Father and the Son at the heart of his account.

SUMMARY OF ANSELM'S DOCTRINE

There is much more to Anselm's doctrine of atonement than we have been able to recapitulate here. It is a subtle and carefully reasoned account of the saving work of Christ. However, for our purposes, it may be helpful to have

---

[5]*CDH* 2.7.

a summary statement of what we have seen of his doctrine. Although this doesn't follow every step in Anselm's reasoning, it gives a sense of the central argument for human reconciliation that he sets out in *CDH*:

1. Human sin is heinous because it is committed against a being to whom we owe everything.

2. God's honor is taken away by human sin. This is intolerable.

3. His honor must be satisfied by some act of atonement for sin, or by the punishment of sin.

4. God the Son consents to act as the mediator of salvation.

5. To do this, he assumes human nature in the incarnation (that is, he becomes the God-man).

6. The God-man is sinless; he does not owe his life to God on account of sin.

7. The life and work (including the death) of the God-man is an act of supererogation.

8. Since it is an act of supererogation, the merit it generates is not owed.

9. Since it is an act of supererogation committed by a sinless entity, the God-man does not require the merit it generates.

10. So, the God-man is free to "give" the merit accruing to his act to another.

11. The merit generated by the atoning act of the God-man is more than sufficient to atone for human sin (because it is the action of the Second Person of the Trinity incarnate).

12. There is nothing to prevent the God-man from offering the merit generated by this work as payment for the demerit generated by human sin.

13. The God-man offers this work as a satisfaction to the Father, thereby providing a means by which human beings may be reconciled with God.

IS SATISFACTION THE SAME AS PENAL SUBSTITUTION?

Having set out Anselm's view, we can now turn to some problems it raises. First, though, we should clear up a common misunderstanding. Sometimes satisfaction is confused with penal substitution. The two doctrines do share a family resemblance, and that is no accident. The magisterial Reformers who developed the doctrine of penal substitution did so against the backdrop of the Anselmian doctrine of satisfaction. They share a number of assumptions about the divine nature, about divine justice, about the need for sin to be punished, and about the role Christ plays as the God-man. However, satisfaction and penal substitution are not the same doctrine. The reason is simple: they have different accounts of what the atonement is, including different views of the mechanism by means of which Christ's work reconciles human beings with God.

We have seen that at the heart of the satisfaction doctrine is the idea that the God-man is not indebted to God because of sin, for he is sinless. His life is blameless, which is a prerequisite for atonement, and his death is not a requirement as it is for all other (fallen) humans because he is without fault. For Anselm, Christ's saving work is an act of supererogation. It is for this reason that the merit his work of reconciliation generates can be applied to our account, so to speak. Christ is able to present his meritorious action to God the Father as an act that may satisfy divine honor, so the fallen human beings may be reconciled to God. In effect, their sins are atoned for by this reparative action.

This is rather like a very wealthy friend offering to pay the fee for a parking fine on behalf of the person who has incurred the fine. The friend is not the one fined, does not need to provide the money to pay the fine (that is, is not obligated to do so), and provides it freely. The "merit" in this case is the money needed to pay the fine, and it is credited to the account of the person that has incurred the fine, who is obligated to pay it, and (let us suppose) is in financial difficulties and cannot do so. The action of the friend who steps in to pay the fine is, from one point of view, very like Anselm's notion of satisfaction, for she satisfies the requirements of the law by paying the fine on behalf of her friend. But she is not punished; she does not take upon herself the harsh treatment (in the form of financial cost) that her friend should suffer. Instead, she simply offers up an equivalent amount of money instead of her friend from the wealth she possesses, in order to remit the fine.

By contrast, penal substitution presumes that Christ is *actually punished* in the place of the sinner. His work does indeed generate a merit of sufficient worth to offset our debt of sin. But the mechanism by means of which this is credited to our account is not a free gift of merit that may be applied to us as a satisfaction for our sin. Rather, it is by means of his standing in our place and taking upon himself the punishment that should be ours. Both doctrines of atonement turn upon a vicarious sacrifice made by the God-man in place of the sinner. But unlike the defender of penal substitution, Anselm would never have allowed that Christ is punished in our place.

OBJECTIONS TO SATISFACTION

Having given some account of Anselm's doctrine, we are now able to consider some objections to it. Down through the centuries, the satisfaction doctrine has been subjected to various criticisms. We will consider several of the most pressing of these objections, beginning with the weakest and moving to more serious concerns.

Anselm's doctrine is a product of medieval feudalism. The objection to Anselm's satisfaction doctrine that is most regularly reiterated in the literature on the atonement is that his view is indebted to the medieval feudalism of his social context, where a strict honor-shame code pervaded society and governed much of the social interaction between different classes of people. So, the objection goes, in medieval feudal society those lower in the pecking order (the villeins, and serfs) were indebted to their overlords (the lord of the manor), and owed them a fief, that is, a portion of what they produced. Defaulting on this arrangement had serious consequences, and satisfaction had to be made when this occurred. Anselm's doctrine borrows the idea of satisfaction, and of the context in which this quasilegal concept is situated, in order to construct his particular doctrine of the atonement. Hence, the objector claims, Anselm's work is merely the product of the time and place in which he flourished. Like any particular social context, Anselm's situation limits and constrains what he has to say and makes his doctrine very much a medieval account of the atonement. Since we no longer live in such a society, we no longer feel the constraint Anselm did to think of our relationship to God on analogy with our relationship to other individuals in a society organized along honor-shame lines in a social pyramid with the king at the pinnacle, the masses of indentured agricultural workers at the bottom, and an aristocracy in between the other two social strata.

On the face of it, this objection appears to be a version of the *genetic fallacy*. This is the view that the truth-value of a particular notion or doctrine depends upon its provenance, that is, how or where it originated. For instance, suppose that in medieval feudal societies it was thought that it is a good thing to be kind to small children. The fact that this notion was a common view amongst members of such medieval feudal societies does not mean that it is false. If we apply this reasoning to the objection to Anselm's doctrine based on his medieval feudal context, we find a similar result: the fact that Anselm wrote his doctrine in a particular time and place, with a particular social location may indeed affect the way he frames his doctrine in important respects. It may even be true to say that some concepts he uses are borrowed from the world in which he lived and worked. But that in-and-of-itself has no bearing whatsoever on whether Anselm's doctrine is right about the nature of the atonement. Social location and truth-value must be kept apart, conceptually speaking, so that we are clear in our own minds that the context from which a person writes does not necessarily invalidate the content of what that person says, though it often constrains it in important respects.

But more importantly, it is not clear that Anselm is borrowing the notion of satisfaction from his medieval feudal context. For one thing, it is a concept that can be found in patristic theology. The second century theologian Tertullian compares satisfaction made to God by repentance with someone who turns to offer satisfaction to the devil instead.[6] Later in the same essay he goes on to say, "We confess our sins to the Lord, not indeed as if He were ignorant of them, but inasmuch as by confession satisfaction is settled, of confession repentance is born; by repentance God is appeased."[7]

It is interesting that Anselm takes up this penitential language in his account of satisfaction. Boso's answer to what he will give God in recompense for his sin is "repentance, a contrite and humble heart, acts of self-denial and a great variety of bodily labors, mercy in giving and forgiving, and obedience." (*CDH* 1.20.)[8] It is precisely these acts that Anselm argues are insufficient to satisfy for sin because we owe all we are and all we do to God already. Of course, this brief comparison cannot demonstrate that Anselm discovered

---

[6]See his short work *On Repentance* [*De Poenitentia*], ch. 5. For this English translation, see Tertullian, *On Repentance* (*ANF* 3:657-668). Chapter 5 is on pp. 660-61.

[7]Tertullian, *On Repentance*, chapter 9 (*ANF* 3:664).

[8]I owe this point to Rik Van Neiuwenhove, *An Introduction to Medieval Theology* (Cambridge: Cambridge University Press, 2012), 95, which offers incisive criticism of some of the standard objections to Anselm's doctrine of atonement.

his views in much earlier writings. What it does show, however, is that similar ways of thinking about satisfaction can be found in a theological work composed centuries before feudalism existed.

Anselm's argument is not based on Scripture. We saw at the beginning of our treatment of Anselm's doctrine in the preface to *CDH* that he sets out to provide an account of the atonement, "leaving Christ out of the picture, as if nothing concerning him had ever taken place." For the modern reader, that is a very odd way to go about giving an account of the atonement. It may mislead us into thinking that he is a kind of rationalist, seeking to demonstrate one of the central doctrines of Christianity on the basis of reason alone, and independent of divine revelation in Scripture. However, such worries may be significantly reduced if we pay attention to the assumptions with which we began our summary of Anselm's doctrine. First, we noted that his is a faith-seeking-understanding enterprise. Anselm often writes presuming that his readers share his assumptions about standing within the faith, so to speak, and seeking to understand it better. The Benedictine life was saturated with Scripture, including the singing of all 150 Psalms every week in the daily offices. Although he does not often refer directly to Scripture in the body of the text of *CDH*, this is because his approach is not so much to appeal to prooftexts for views he develops, as it is a reflection upon themes that arise out of the biblical material and from the Christian tradition. These themes have to do with Christ's sacrifice, with God's justice and honor, with the seriousness of human sin, and with the need for some repayment, which must be brought about by a vicarious action on the part of one who is both God and human.

Secondly, it is clear from what he says about his method of proceeding in the preface to *CDH* that he is explicitly not approaching the topic on the basis of biblical arguments. He is approaching it in terms of an elaborate thought experiment. We use thought experiments all the time, often with very helpful results. Take, for instance, the parent who says to her child, "Let us suppose for a moment that you attempted to walk across this freeway. The traffic is traveling so fast, and in such numbers, that the most likely outcome is that you will be hit by a vehicle and be severely injured. So, please don't do that." Anselm is inviting his readers to consider a thought experiment concerning human salvation. He is addressing himself to those already convinced of Christ's saving work in Scripture. But he wants to ask, Why do we need the God-man?

Why did God become human? Is there no other means by which we can be saved? Let us think about this using our sanctified reason to do so. Such an approach will strike many as too speculative to be of much practical theological use. However, for those who see the importance of such thinking for mapping out a kind of conceptual framework for our theologizing, this certainly has a place, and its results have borne much fruit in the history of theology.

Anselm's doctrine valorizes divine violence. One of the most important criticisms of much traditional atonement theology in recent times has come from theologians, especially feminist theologians, who have argued that violence is at the heart of the doctrine of atonement. Such critics of traditional atonement theology believe this raises very serious concerns about the concept of God that stands behind these atonement doctrines. For if God is complicit in acts of violence, what does this say about his character? Is he a violent, angry being? Does he lash out against his creatures? This hardly seems consistent with the deity who is said to be essentially loving, as the apostle John tells us in 1 John 4:8 when he says, "Whoever does not love does not know God, because God is love."

We shall consider this concern more carefully when treating the problem of atoning violence in chapter eight. Nevertheless, it bears directly upon Anselm's doctrine because indisputably Anselm's satisfaction account has at its heart an act of violence, namely, the crucifixion of Christ. However, this does not mean Anselm thinks violence is part of the divine nature. Consider what he says at the close of the second part of *CDH* in chapter twenty:

> As for God's mercy, which seemed to you to vanish when we were considering God's justice and human sin, we have found it to be so great and so consonant with justice that it cannot be thought to be greater or more just. What, indeed, can be understood to be more merciful than for our God and Father to say to a sinner condemned to eternal torments, with no way to redeem himself, "Take my only-begotten Son, and offer him on your behalf," and for the Son himself to say, "Take me and redeem yourself"? . . . . And what is more just than for one who is paid a price greater than every debt to cancel every debt, if the price is paid with the proper affection?

It is *God* who initiates redemption, and *God* who brings it about in the person of the Son incarnate. What is more, as we have been at pains to point out, Anselm does not think that the atonement is an act of punishment, but of satisfaction. God does not require punishment; he requires the repayment of a debt to his honor—a repayment that he brings about on behalf of fallen humanity. This is not inexorable justice pitted against mercy and grace, still less an act of divine violence, but a gracious act of condescension on the part of the Deity that is entirely consonant with justice and with divine love.

The payment of debt. In the opening chapters of the first part of *CDH* (especially chapters six through seven), Anselm does some "ground clearing" before setting out his own positive account of the redeeming work of Christ. There he opposes the idea that the devil has any "rights" over humankind—a matter that was the subject of debate in northern French monastic schools of the time and was a familiar constituent of ransom accounts of the atonement. In *CDH* 1.7 Anselm reasons that humans and devils are subject to God, the devil holds no sway over humanity, and both the devil and fallen humanity are slaves to sin. Anselm's attack on the idea that the devil has "rights" over fallen human beings is much more limited in scope than the ransom account of the atonement. Nevertheless, his remarks do put some distance between his own approach and those earlier accounts of atonement that depend in important respects upon this claim. What is more, they make clear at the outset of *CDH* that the debt paid by Christ is not to the devil or any other creature, but to God himself, the one against whom we have sinned.

With this in mind, we turn to *CDH* 2.6, which is at the heart of the constructive section of Anselm's work. There Anselm reasons, in effect, that if only God can make this satisfaction and only a human ought to make it, it is necessary that a God-man make it. That is, fallen human beings owe God a debt they cannot repay, so that only God can deal with this debt. But only someone who is both divine and human can will to deal with this and therefore atone for the debt. So we need a God-man to do it. But, clearly, the God-man does not owe God in the way that fallen human beings do. So how can the God-man atone for human debt if he does not owe God that debt?

We have already noted that there are situations in which we permit one person to pay the debt of another, though the second person does not owe the debt. One obvious case of this is our earlier example of the parking fine, which is a kind of penalty. What matters is that the fine is paid, not *who* pays it. Perhaps something similar can be said in defense of Anselm's doctrine. The issue is that our debt of sin needs to be remitted. Clearly, the God-man does not owe the debt of sin that mere humans do. However, the logic of Anselm's position is that the God-man can atone for our debt of sin by generating a merit sufficient to meet the deficit. Because he is a human being like us, the merit he generates will be a merit of the right sort, namely, a human merit. Yet because he is divine, it will be a merit that is of infinite worth. So it will be a merit sufficient in principle to meet the debt of all fallen human beings. Of course the God-man does not owe the debt we do, otherwise he would not be able to offer satisfaction because what he has he would already owe to God.

Anselm's argument turns on the claim that the God-man is able to generate a merit that is relevantly similar for the purposes of satisfying divine honor and justice, and that can be offered in place of our debt, to offset our debt. This human sin-debt is treated by Anselm as a kind of penalty. If satisfaction is blind to the question of who pays the debt, as is the case in parking fines, then the fact that he is innocent of the debt does not necessarily preclude him from performing an act that can be counted in place of that debt, as with the paying of the parking fine by the wealthy friend instead of the one guilty of incurring the fine. In which case, the issue of the payment of the debt by a substitute can be resolved.

It might be thought that this worry about debt payment generates a further issue concerning the transfer of merit from one person to another, and, specifically, from one innocent person to another that is guilty. But this is not actually a problem for the advocate of Anselmian satisfaction because Christ does not take upon himself our guilt, and he is not punished in our place. We remain the guilty parties, and Christ remains innocent. He acts on our behalf in generating satisfaction. But this involves no transfer of merit or guilt, although it does involve a substitutionary act of a sort—the sort we encountered in the example of the payment of a fine by an innocent friend. To put it in terms that are often used in contemporary legal theory, Anselm's view seems to be that satisfaction works on the same principles as a penalty (e.g., parking fines), not like a punishment (e.g., a custodial sentence).

A complete account of atonement? A final issue concerns a lacuna or gap in Anselm's doctrine. Is Anselm's doctrine incomplete as it stands? What he provides is a mechanism of atonement situated in a carefully worked out account of our sinful state and the need for satisfaction. But he doesn't really explain how the benefits of Christ's reconciling work are to be accessed by those he came to save, or how they are applied to such persons. It is like saying to a blind person, "Suspended over your head is a small phial containing a liquid that, once swallowed, shall infallibly return to you your powers of sight." Of what use is such a remedy if the blind person is incapable of finding and accessing this cure, on account of his disability? Similarly, Anselm doesn't really give his readers an indication of how may we appropriate Christ's benefits. It would be fairly easy to provide such an account. It is just that Anselm doesn't really do that work for his readers. This is important because there is more than one way of thinking about the reception of Christ's benefits in the Christian tradition. For instance, we might offer up Christ's reparative act of satisfaction through prayer as our own act of penitence, thereby joining our desires with Christ's work in the hope that God will apply the benefits of his satisfaction to us. Or, we might believe that God applies Christ's benefits directly to us in the gift of faith; or something else. These different acts may be complementary, of course. But they could represent distinct ways of appropriating Christ's benefits each of which is consistent with Anselm's doctrine. That alone gives us reason to think that his view is underdeveloped in what it says about the connection between Christ's finished work and our appropriation of it.

CONCLUSION

In this chapter, we have seen that Anselm's influential doctrine of satisfaction represents a powerful understanding of the atonement and one that is still worthy of our serious consideration. Although it is not without shortcomings, and although it does not necessarily provide us with a complete account of Christ's reconciling work, it nevertheless goes a long way towards doing so— much further, in fact, than some of its critics are willing to allow.

FURTHER READING

Anselm of Canterbury. *Cur Deus Homo*. In *Anselm: Basic Writing*, translated by Thomas Williams, 237-326. Indianapolis: Hackett, 2007.

Baker, Mark D., and Joel B. Green. *Recovering the Scandal of the Cross: Atonement in New Testament and Contemporary Contexts*. 2nd edition. Downers Grove, IL: IVP Academic, 2011. Chapter 5, "Models of the Atonement: A History and Assessment (Part One)."

Brown, David. "Anselm on the Atonement." In *The Cambridge Companion to Anselm of Canterbury*, edited by Brian Davies and Brian Leftow, 279-302. Cambridge: Cambridge University Press, 2004.

Evans, G. R. *Anselm*. Outstanding Christian Thinkers. London: Bloomsbury, 2005.

McIntyre, John. *St. Anselm and His Critics: A Re-Interpretation of the Cur Deus Homo*. Edinburgh: Oliver & Boyd, 1954.

Plantinga, Richard J., Thomas R. Thompson, and Matthew D. Lundberg. *An Introduction to Christian Theology*. Cambridge: Cambridge University Press, 2010. Chapter 10, "The Reconciling Work of Jesus Christ."

Sweeney, Eileen C. *Anselm of Canterbury and the Desire for the Word*. Washington, DC: Catholic University of America Press, 2012.

Swinburne, Richard. *Responsibility and Atonement*. Oxford: Oxford University Press, 1989.

Tertullian. *On Repentance*. In vol. 3 of *The Ante-Nicene Fathers*, edited by Alexander Roberts and James Donaldson, 657-668. New York: Charles Scribner's Sons, 1905.

Van Neiuwenhove, Rik. *An Introduction to Medieval Theology*. Cambridge: Cambridge University Press, 2012.

Visser, Sandra, and Thomas Williams. *Anselm*. Great Medieval Thinkers Series. Oxford: Oxford University Press, 2010. See chapter 13.

MORAL EXEMPLARISM
AND ATONEMENT

According to the moral exemplar view, Christ's work is primarily an example that should elicit a particular response in individuals that encounter it, rather like an act of courage that is an inspiration to others in the midst of a pitched battle. By imitating the example of Christ, human beings are saved. Sometimes this view is called the moral influence theory, but this is essentially the same as the moral exemplar view, and I shall refer to the position as the moral exemplar or moral example view in order to make clear the central idea that informs those who take this position. We will see, however, that there are ways of construing the doctrine that include something more than *mere* exemplarism—that is, more than merely the core idea that Christ's work is an example that should motivate us to respond in a particular manner.

Like satisfaction, moral exemplarism is widely misunderstood as a view of the atonement. The main aim of this chapter is twofold: first, to clear up this misunderstanding by giving some historical background to the doctrine; and, second, to provide a clear account of two versions of the doctrine that are seldom clearly distinguished in the theological literature. It is important to make this distinction, however, for only one of these two accounts amounts to a doctrine of atonement. The other offers a way of construing the work, ministry, and death of Christ that does not include commitment to a doctrine of atonement at all. It is not difficult to see that this is a potentially theologically significant conclusion and one that may be an important consideration for those attracted to some version of moral exemplarism.

The chapter proceeds as follows. We begin with a section outlining the history of the doctrine in order to clear up some misunderstandings about its development and shape. This includes discussion of Peter Abelard, Faustus Socinus, and an important recent defender of the view, the British philosophical theologian John Hick. Then, in a second section we will consider two versions of the doctrine. This leads to some remarks about the theological shortcomings of these two different ways of thinking about moral exemplarism in a third section. The chapter wraps up with a short conclusion summarizing our findings.

HISTORICAL BACKGROUND

Let us start by attempting, in a modest way, to help set the historical record straight. It is often claimed in textbooks of Christian theology that the moral exemplar view of the atonement began with the work of the French theologian Peter Abelard (AD 1079–1142). In this connection mention is often made of Abelard's commentary on Romans as the place at which he outlines his "exemplarist" account of atonement, in which God's love takes center-stage. But this is at best a half-truth that denies the redemptive component of Abelard's doctrine of atonement. Although divine love is indeed fundamental to his account of the atonement, it is clear from what Abelard says that he thinks this is bound up with Christ's atonement on the cross as a redemptive action that justifies us before God. In commenting on Romans 3:4-27 he writes,

> Nevertheless it seems to us that in this we are justified in the blood of Christ and reconciled to God, that it was through this matchless grace shown to us that his Son received our nature, and in that nature, teaching us both by word and by example, persevered to the death and bound us to himself even more through love, so that when we have been kindled by so great a benefit of divine grace, true charity might fear to endure nothing for his sake.

He goes on to say, "Therefore, our redemption is that supreme love in us through the Passion of Christ, which not only frees us from slavery to sin, but gains for us the true liberty of the sons of God, so that we may complete all things by his love rather than by fear."[1]

The supreme love of God in Christ, demonstrated in Christ's passion, is indeed the means by which fallen human beings are redeemed. But note

---

[1]Peter Abelard, *Commentary on the Epistle to the Romans,* trans. Steven R. Cartwright (Washington, DC: The Catholic University of America Press, 2011), Book II, 167-68.

that this supreme love in us is *through* the passion of Christ, which frees human beings from slavery to sin so that we may live in love rather than fear. Put differently, divine love is expressed in the passion of Christ, which is redemptive, and which is then communicated to fallen human beings by grace. Salvation is not achieved by the imitation of divine love displayed in Christ's life and work, according to Abelard. Rather, because of God's love demonstrated in Christ's passion, we are redeemed and able to live in love. The passion of Christ does the atoning; the love expressed in this atonement is then communicated to fallen human beings who respond in kind.

From this it should be clear that divine love is certainly the motivating factor for Abelard's account of the atonement. But it would be a travesty of his position to claim that all that occurs in this divine exchange is that Christ demonstrates to us (sinners) God's love for us, which we in turn ought to imitate, or which ought to draw out from us a similarly loving response. This is an element of Abelard's presentation, to be sure. But as even these quotations show, they can hardly be said to be the whole of it. For the expression of divine love in Christ is consequent upon the redemptive work his atonement brings about, echoing the Pauline message upon which he is commenting.[2] So Abelard's work is not an instance of what we might call a *mere* moral exemplar account of Christ's work—that is, an account of Christ's reconciling work that reduces it to his role as a moral example. This is a matter to which we shall return when setting out the two versions of the doctrine later in the chapter.

Something more clearly approximating a full-blown mere moral exemplarist account of Christ's work is argued for by the sixteenth century Socinians, who opposed much of the work of the magisterial Reformers such as Luther, Zwingli, Calvin, and Cranmer. And in modern philosophy and theology notable exponents of the view include Immanuel Kant, Friedrich Schleiermacher, Albrecht Ritschl, Hastings Rashdall, and John Hick. Rather than considering all of these historic figures, let us focus on the most significant historic example, namely, Socinus. This is important because he is the fount of much subsequent moral exemplarism in theology, although his

---

[2]A similar point is made by Richard E. Weingart in *The Logic of Divine Love: A Critical Analysis of the Soteriology of Peter Abailard* (Oxford: Oxford University Press, 1970), 125-26.

views are seldom the subject of sustained discussion today. Then we shall consider a modern heir to Socinus's views in the work of John Hick.[3]

Faustus Socinus on atonement. Faustus Socinus (AD 1539–1604) was descended from minor Italian nobility, the Sozzini, and migrated from his home country via Switzerland to Poland as a consequence of persecution for his eccentric theological views in the later part of the sixteenth century. He is best known for his work on the atonement entitled *De Jesu Christo Servatore* (*On Jesus Christ the Savior*), which is yet to be translated and published in English.[4] The work is remembered mainly for its savage attack upon the whole idea of substitutionary atonement as understood by the Reformers. Indeed, the tenor of his work is largely critical rather than constructive. Nevertheless, it does contain the outline of a positive account of the work of Christ, understood as a moral example of the love of God. It is notable that Socinus argues on the basis of biblical arguments not, as is sometimes claimed, on purely rational grounds. He was not a rationalist. If anything, he is a biblicist, seeking to ground all his arguments in Scripture alone.

Socinus argues that nothing in the character of God constrains him to punish sin; he may simply forgive sin without any satisfaction. He gives the example of Cain in Genesis, whom God forgives freely without requiring punishment of any kind. And from the New Testament, he cites the parable of the unmerciful servant from Matthew 18, where the master cancels the debt of the servant and lets him go, and Christ's audience is told to do likewise, forgiving one another from the heart (Mt 18:35).

Echoing Anselm, Socinus conceives of sin as essentially a debt owed to God. So, like the master in the parable of the unmerciful servant, God may forego all or part of the debt without penalty, because of sheer mercy. If that is right, reasons Socinus, then there is nothing to prevent God from being merciful to all who ask, forgiving them without requiring satisfaction of the

---

[3]There are a number of other places where readers can find treatments of these different historic theologians on this topic. A good place to start is R. S. Franks, *The Work of Christ*, 2nd ed. (London: Thomas Nelson, 1962).

[4]However, Alan W. Gomes translated Section III of the work as part of his PhD dissertation at Fuller Theological Seminary, and has written a very helpful introduction to Socinus' study in his essay, "*De Jesu Christo Servatore*: Faustus Socinus on the Satisfaction of Christ," *Westminster Theological Journal* 55 (1993): 209-31. A Summary of Socinian teaching can be found in *The Racovian Catechism*, trans. Thomas Rees (1605; repr., London: Longman, Hurst, Rees, Orme, and Brown, 1818).

debt owed. In which case, it looks like the very idea of satisfaction of a debt is something God has good reasons not to require. By a similar token, the writer to the Ephesians says, "Be kind and compassionate to one another, forgiving each other, just as in Christ God forgave you" (Eph 4:32), a message echoed elsewhere in Pauline theology (e.g., Col 3:13). But forgiving a person is quite different from requiring some sort of satisfaction—the two notions are incompatible. One cannot forgive by means of satisfaction. For, on the Socinian way of thinking that is like saying to a debtor, "I will forgive you your debt by way of getting someone else to pay your debt." If the debt is paid, either by the debtor, or by someone willing to stand in the place of the debtor taking upon himself the liability for the debt, then it makes no sense to speak of *forgiving* the debt. It has been paid. Socinus pointed out that similar reasoning applies, the relevant changes having been made, to the case of the atonement. If God has forgiven us our sin independent of requiring satisfaction, then there is no need for satisfaction; it is redundant. Saying that our sins are forgiven by means of Christ's satisfaction is a deeply confused way of thinking. For it conflates two things that cannot both be true: it cannot be that Christ has paid the price for my sin or paid my debt, *and* that God has forgiven my sin, the debt I owe. Either he forgives the debt, or he requires its payment by Christ as my substitute. But both alternatives cannot be true.[5]

Of course, there is much biblical material that points to the notion of redemption from sin, and the fact that a price is paid for the remission of sin. But these passages Socinus understands to be metaphorical in nature, pointing to the way in which God's action liberates us from the debt of sin by forgiving us, not literally requiring some satisfaction for the sin we have committed.

On the constructive side of his argument, Socinus is clear that Christ's principle role is prophetic in nature. He reveals God's will in his teaching, which is a pattern for human beings to follow. His life, teaching, and death are an example and inspiration to incite us to respond accordingly, asking God for forgiveness for our sin. This forgiveness takes place upon our request but not because of any transaction between God and Christ, still less because of some mechanism by means of which Christ reconciles us to Godself. Rather, God is already disposed to forgive sin, and needs no satisfaction or atonement in order to do so. As Socinus puts it, "Christ takes

---

[5]See Socinus, *De Jesu Christo Servatore*, 3.2.343.

away sins because by the example of his most innocent life, he very readily draws all, who have not lost hope, to leave their sins and zealously to embrace righteousness and holiness."[6]

John Hick on atonement. John Hick's work on the atonement is, in many respects, a modern equivalent to the sort of moral exemplarism to be found in the work of Socinus, although he comes to his conclusions independently of Socinus. His work does not really take forward the previous discussion of the topic; it merely offers an accessible version of a moral exemplarism based on the work of previous thinkers, and especially theologians and philosophers like Kant, Schleiermacher, and Ritschl. Nevertheless, the way in which he casts his discussion in terms of the upshot of Enlightenment thinking and modern religious pluralism, and the need for an account of Christ's work that makes sense in a post-Christian world, means that his account is particularly salient for contemporary theology.

Hick maintains that language of the incarnation must be understood metaphorically, not literally. That is, Jesus of Nazareth was not literally God in human flesh. Rather, he embodied or lived out or "incarnated" certain moral values that set him apart as a uniquely important religious teacher alongside other great religious leaders in other traditions from Buddhism to Judaism. "We see in Jesus a human being extraordinarily open to God's influence and thus living to an extraordinary extent as God's agent on earth, 'incarnating' the divine purpose for human life," Hick writes. He goes on to say that "embodied within the circumstances of his time and place" Jesus as a kind of human ideal lived "in openness and response to God, and in doing so he 'incarnated' a love that reflects the divine love. This epoch-making life became the inspiration of a vast tradition which has for many centuries provided intellectual and moral guidance to Western civilization."[7]

Atonement, on his way of thinking, can be understood in either a narrow or broad sense. In the narrow sense, it has to do with the forgiveness of sin on the basis of an adequate act of satisfaction. It is analogous to a transaction that is needed in order to restore moral order. In the broader sense, atonement has to do with being in right relationship to God. Hick thinks that atonement

---

[6]Cited by L. W. Grensted, *A Short History of the Doctrine of the Atonement* (Manchester: Manchester University Press, 1920), 287.
[7]John Hick, *The Metaphor of God Incarnate. Second Edition* (1993; repr., Louisville, KY: Westminster John Knox Press, 2005), 12.

is usually identified with the narrow sense of the term and that this is a theological mistake that we must reject. It would be better to think of Christ's work as a contribution to the broader sense of atonement—here understood simply as a synonym for salvation, or being united to God.[8] Later in the book, Hick elaborates,

> The real meaning of Jesus' death was not that his blood was shed . . . but that he gave himself utterly to God in faith and trust. His cross was thus a powerful manifestation and continuing symbol of the divine kingdom in this present world, as a way of life in which one turns the other cheek, forgives one's enemies . . . trusts God even in the darkness of pain, horror and tragedy, and is continually raised again to the new life of faith.[9]

Clearly, it is the inspirational power of Christ's self-sacrifice that is the heart of the meaning of the cross, as far as Hick is concerned. Moral transformation may be consequent upon this, of course, as one seeks to align oneself with such a life and message. But it is not atoning in the narrow sense of the term; there is no mechanism in Christ's crucifixion by means of which human beings are reconciled to God.

TWO VERSIONS OF MORAL EXEMPLARISM

With this historical background in mind we may distinguish two versions of moral exemplarism that are often confused in discussion of this doctrine.

No-atonement moral exemplarism. The first version of moral exemplarism we shall call the *no-atonement doctrine of moral exemplarism* or just no-atonement exemplarism for short. This most clearly approximates to the views of Socinus and Hick. According to this version of the doctrine, the work of Christ is not a matter of atonement, strictly speaking, because (as the previous section demonstrated) it supplies no mechanism by means of which Christ's work reconciles fallen human beings to Godself. Such no-atonement exemplarist doctrines represent one way of understanding the work of Christ, including the events of his death and resurrection. But because such views have no place for a concept of human sin or reconciliation, they are not doctrines of atonement as such. (For, as we are using the term in this work,

---

[8]Hick, *Metaphor of God Incarnate*, ch. 11.
[9]Hick, *Metaphor of God Incarnate*, 132.

atonement is a concept that has to do with reconciliation.) Hence, the designation *no-atonement* moral exemplarism. The central idea conveyed by such doctrines is that Jesus of Nazareth provides a moral example to us of how we ought to live—a life of self-sacrifice culminating in the giving up of his own life in order to vindicate his message. This is certainly an aspect of Hick's presentation, and it ties in with his broader claim that Jesus of Nazareth is one among a constellation of great religious leaders in various world religious traditions all of whom provide examples of moral sainthood that may be emulated. Think of Muhammad, or Siddhartha Gautama who became the Buddha, or Moses—all these religious leaders have a similar function for Hick.[10] Understood in this way, Christ's work may show us a better way to live that might provide a kind of religious inspiration to live a life of greater moral and religious purity. It also shows us God's love made manifest in the life of Jesus. It may even elicit an appropriate response of love in us that leads to the pursuit of a moral life aligned with the ministry and teaching of Christ. But—importantly—on this way of thinking nothing about the life, work, and death of Jesus brings about some kind of reconciliation with God, some moral transformation needed in order to heal a putative moral breach in human relations with God brought about by human sin. Indeed, according to Hick's religiously pluralist version of moral exemplarism, Christ's life and work are not even unique in their moral or theological significance. Rather, Christ represents the life of a moral saint, one of many such great religious teachers, whose work is an inspiration that should be emulated.

This is significant for several reasons. First, it eviscerates the Christian gospel of much of its distinctive doctrinal content. For, on the no-atonement version of moral examplarism, what is theologically salient is the way in which Christ's example may influence or sway us, in order that we may live a more moral life. Morality here is understood in terms of the ethical teaching of Christ, summarized in his Sermon on the Mount. But such ethical teaching is denuded of all sorts of doctrinal trappings. It does not include the doctrine of the Trinity, or the two-natures doctrine of the incarnation, a distinctively Christian account of human sin, or even the need for atonement itself. It does

---

[10]Hick elaborates his theory of religions along these lines in his major work, *An Interpretation of Religion: Human Responses to the Transcendent. Second Edition* (1989; repr., London: Macmillan, 2004).

not require any eschatological hope either. It is a kind of bare moralism, by which I mean an approach to Christ's life and work that enjoins us to bring our lives in conformity to a set of moral principles because of Christ's example. But it requires little more than that, theologically speaking. That is a very thin account indeed, and one that seems almost unrecognizable as a species of specifically *Christian* theology.

This raises a second, and closely related point. As Hick's account intimates, the no-atonement version of moral exemplarism is a doctrine that does not require its advocates to be Christians at all. Suppose Smith is a professor of ethics with no clear religious affiliation. In her search for the good life, she reads the works of many different moral thinkers, and eventually alights upon the moral teaching of Christ as reported in the Sermon on the Mount in Matthew 5–7. Intrigued, she begins to read all four of the canonical Gospels, beginning with Matthew, and progressing through Mark to Luke and John. She finds herself deeply moved by the person of Christ as he appears in these narratives. His moral teaching on simplicity of life, and self-sacrificial love, and devotion to God and to the community, and especially to the poor and disadvantaged, is something that resonates deeply with her desire to find a comprehensive moral vision that may shape her own interior life. Upon reading about Christ's passion, she is struck by how he lives out a consistent ethic, even though it ultimately costs him everything, rather like Socrates. Yet here, in Christ, is an example of someone who sought not merely to teach the youth to be critical of authority, or to question everything, but who sought to provide a deep and consistent moral foundation upon which a person may grow and flourish. Nowhere is this more evident than in the manner in which Christ forgives his persecutors from the cross upon which he was crucified.

The effect upon Smith is profound. She reads and rereads the Gospels, Mark being her favorite because of its immediacy. The person of Christ jumps out of the page, arresting her with each new reading. Through this engagement with the text of Scripture, and deep reflection upon what she has been reading, Smith comes to see that Christ's work, teaching, and ultimately, his self-sacrifice for the principles that guided his life, presents an irresistible picture. He is a model of the good life, an exemplar like no other she has encountered in her research. For in the person of Christ, there is a combination of piety, devotion to duty, purpose, clear moral teaching of the highest order, and a ministry suffused with a desire to love others, and address their physical and spiritual needs, especially with respect to the poor and disadvantaged. Transfixed by the moral example of Christ and his self-sacrificial act of crucifixion, Smith vows to change her life in order that she may align herself and her religious convictions with the example of Christ as a model for the good life that is predicated upon the need to love other people in her community, and especially the poor and disadvantaged, in practical ways in order to bring about moral change.

Now, it is important to see from this story about Smith that the no-atonement version of moral exemplarism may involve a kind of *transformative experience*. By this, I mean an experience that brings about significant transformation that one could not necessarily anticipate prior to undergoing that experience.[11] It is just that the sort of transformative experience in question need not be a properly Christian one. It may well be religious in nature, as is the case with Smith. It may result in significant change to one's life, and a reorientation of what one thinks is important and the things that one prioritizes. It may do all these things, yet without requiring the person undergoing such a transformation to become a Christian. That is not insignificant. In fact, such change is potentially momentous, and may bring about great good as a consequence. Nevertheless, it is just as clearly not an example of a transformative encounter with the person and work of Christ that results in a person becoming a member of Christ's church and professing faith as a Christian. Missing from this picture, from the point of view of Christian theology, is a concept of sin, an adequate account of the doctrine of God, and, most importantly for our purposes, a recognition that Christ's life, death, and resurrection is a work of reconciliation brought about by some mechanism of atonement.

The Christian ethicist H. Richard Niebuhr once offered this famous excoriation of classical liberal theology: "A God without wrath brought men without sin into a kingdom without judgment through the ministrations of a Christ without a cross."[12] It would be unfair to our hypothetical Smith to say that she did not think the cross of Christ was important to her understanding of the good life, as one seeking to live a life in alignment with the teaching and example of Jesus of Nazareth presented in the canonical Gospels. Nevertheless,

---

[11]Such transformative experience has recently been the subject of philosophical scrutiny. See L. A. Paul, *Transformative Experience* (Oxford: Oxford University Press, 2014).

[12]H. Richard Niebuhr, *The Kingdom of God in America* (1932; repr., Middletown, CT: Wesleyan University Press, 1988), 193.

Niebuhr's characterization is not far from the truth, and does go some way to expressing some of the concerns an orthodox Christian theologian might have with the way in which Smith's transformative experience yields only a kind of mere moralism, rather than a theologically rich Christianity.

Atonement moral exemplarism. By contrast, the second version of moral exemplarism *is* a doctrine of atonement because it does provide a mechanism by means of which human beings may be reconciled with God, even though we might consider it to be conceptually "thin."[13] For this reason, let us call it *atonement moral exemplarism*, or just atonement exemplarism. The most significant difference between atonement exemplarism and no-atonement exemplarism is that in atonement exemplarism, the work of Christ, and his death in particular, is understood as a mechanism by means of which human beings may be reconciled to God. The mechanism in question is rather "thin," so to speak. Nevertheless, it is present, and does mean that this version of the view constitutes a doctrine of atonement, rather than merely a view about the life, ministry, and death of Christ, as was the case with respect to our fictitious case of the ethics professor Smith.

To see this, consider a second example. This involves Smith's friend, Jones, who is an ordinand. Jones has long held that Christ is a moral example whose life and work should form the moral foundation of a person's life. In fact, it was she who first suggested this to Smith, which set her off on her reading of the Gospels in her own quest for the good life. However, in her own theological formation, Jones has come to see that regarding Christ as merely a moral example is theologically insufficient. Only if Christ's example of love in his crucifixion is able to radically change a person, changing them from someone alienated from God's love and mired in sin, to someone living a life of self-sacrifice and ministry, especially ministry to the poor and disadvantaged, as a follower of Christ and member of the church, is his work sufficient. For, Jones thinks, the transformative work of Christ's loving example must bring us back into relationship with God. It must bring about not just a moral transformation but a spiritual reorientation and reconciliation with God.

Laurie Paul in her work on transformative experiences distinguishes between *epistemic transformation* and *personal transformation*.[14] An experience

---

[13]This is a point that Jordan Wessling impressed upon me in conversation.
[14]See Paul, *Transformative Experience*, chapter 2, "Transformative Choice."

is epistemically transformative if you can only know what it is like by undergoing the transformation yourself. For instance, seeing a particular color for the first time. A personal transformation is one in which your view on an issue fundamental to who you are is changed. For example, reading George Orwell's dystopian novel *1984* and having one's political views changed forever as a consequence. When a transformative experience includes both an epistemic and personal aspect it is truly transformative. A good example of this is becoming a parent. Those who have become parents often say that it is a transformative experience that they could not have prepared themselves for, and (often) did not fully understand, prior to actually having a child. Something about undergoing the experience of becoming a parent for oneself changes a person, in a way that no textbook could explain adequately. Both epistemic and personal dimensions of transformation are clearly present in this example.

Religious conversion is another paradigm of truly transformative experience because it too has both epistemic and personal aspects. Clearly, Jones's experience is transformative in this complete sense because it involves a kind of religious conversion. Through engagement with Christ's saving work, and especially his crucifixion, Jones comes to see that the love Christ displays is a divine love that should elicit a response of love from her. It should transform her so that she comes to see something new about God's love in Christ reconciling the world to Godself, as well as a personal transformation through such an encounter. This total transformation is at its core about bringing Jones back into alignment with the God from whom she has become estranged, by means of the love of Christ exemplified in his work on the cross. Clearly, Jones's transformation includes a thin doctrine of atonement; this is something missing from Smith's transformation. Yet Jones's account is still recognizably a version of moral exemplarism: Christ's moral example, and his display of divine love, motivate Jones in a way reminiscent of Abelard's doctrine, with which we began.

TWO OBJECTIONS TO MORAL EXEMPLARISM

There are a number of problems with moral exemplarism, several of which we have already touched upon in passing in this chapter. In this section, let us focus on two in particular, which I take to be the most serious objections faced by advocates of moral exemplarism. These are whether exemplarist views have an adequate account of the doctrine of sin, and whether exemplarists are guilty of condoning redemptive violence.

However, it is important to be clear before drawing attention to these potential shortcomings that the problems with the different versions of moral exemplarism are largely about the inadequacy of this way of approaching the doctrine of atonement, not with a mistaken conception of the nature of the atonement. This is an important consideration. For all extant accounts of the atonement incorporate some version of moral exemplarism. All Christian theologians think that Christ is a moral example to imitate and that his work on the cross is a supreme instance of divine love that should elicit from us a loving response. That much is a kind of conceptual minimum for any account of atonement. It is just that this claim is not sufficient as an understanding of the nature of the atoning work of Christ. It is, we might say, a necessary condition for a complete understanding of the atonement (for surely Christ's saving work is at least a work of love that should be imitated, and that should draw from us a similar, loving response). But it is not a sufficient condition. For most theologians working on the atonement, more needs to be said about the nature of Christ's reconciling work than can be provided by a version of moral exemplarism alone.

This brings us to the question of what is missing from the versions of moral exemplarism we have discussed. What more is needed to provide an adequate understanding of Christ's reconciling work? Often, it is a deficient doctrine of sin that is pointed to when this question is raised. This is particularly true of the no-atonement version of exemplarism. It is less clear that this is a problem for the atonement exemplarist position, however.

In the case of no-atonement exemplarism, the doctrine of sin does not really factor into the picture—at least, the version of the view sketched in our hypothetical scenario involving Smith. Sin is not relevant on this view because in order for Christ's moral example to be effective, no doctrine of sin needs to be taken into account. In one sense, that is the point of the Smith example: to show that someone could adopt such a version of exemplarism without commitment to doctrines that are peculiar to Christianity, such as, say, a doctrine of sin, let alone a doctrine of original sin. The fact that a no-atonement exemplarism doesn't require anything of its advocate that would identify her as a specifically *Christian* thinker (remember, Smith is an ethics professor of no particular religious affiliation, not a theologian or minister) indicates that there is something seriously theologically deficient about this way of understanding the work of Christ. A doctrine of sin is one important reason for such a shortcoming, because without a doctrine of sin it is not clear what it is that Christ's work saves a person from. But, of course, that is just to say that the no-atonement exemplarist is not interested in salvation from sin, but in a moral life lived in light of Christ's example and according to the tenets of his ethical teaching that can be gleaned from the Gospels.

Well, then, what about the atonement version of exemplarism? Does it fare any better with respect to the doctrine of sin? Perhaps it does. It is certainly less clear to me that it suffers from the same failings on this score as the no-atonement version of exemplarism. Much here depends on the nature of the transformative experience undergone by the fictional character of Jones. It certainly seems consistent with the story told above that Jones could, as part of her transformation, come to see that her own life is inadequate, alienated from God, and in need of divine love to renew and restore her to a spiritual and moral state in which she can appropriately love and serve God in return. It may be that coming to see that and being brought into a greater under-standing of God's desire to reconcile Jones to Godself through the loving work of Christ is, on this way of thinking, what it means for atonement to take place. Christ's work of love, and his sacrifice on the cross, transform Jones. At least part of that transformative experience includes seeing her own inad-equacy and the need for such transformation from an alienated state to a reconciled one. And if that is right, then an understanding of his alienated state prior to this transformative experience could include some doctrine of sin, even if it is not a full-blown doctrine of original sin.

That may not be sufficient for many theologians (depending on the theo-logical tradition to which the theologian in question belongs, and, as a con-sequence, the view of sin and original sin that the theologian in question holds[15]). But it is one important way in which the atonement version of exemplarism can be distinguished from no-atonement exemplarism.

---

[15]Not all Christians hold to a doctrine of original sin. The Eastern Orthodox prefer to speak of the ancestral sin that has damaged human nature, rather than of a moral corruption that is transmit-ted to all human beings after a primeval Fall. See John S. Romanides, *The Ancestral Sin* (Ridge-wood, NJ: Zephyr, 2002).

Let us turn now to another criticism of moral exemplarist accounts of Christ's work. This comes from a rather different direction, namely feminist theologians. Here the worry is that moral exemplarism condones violence (for God permits Jesus to die to display divine love) and valorizes suffering (the innocent Christ suffering on behalf of the guilty), which is morally and theologically unacceptable. We will consider the issue of redemptive violence more fully in chapter eight. However, it is worth raising the issue here because it highlights the rather surprising fact that moral exemplarist views are susceptible to a criticism that is usually leveled at defenders of satisfaction and penal substitution doctrines of atonement. Does moral exemplarism condone violence? Does this view valorize suffering? It is not obvious that either objection is fatal to the careful defender of moral exemplarism.

On the question of condoning violence, the exemplarist can claim that Christ's death, though violent, is not necessarily something that is condoned by God. It might be that God's act of love in Christ generates an adverse reaction in those who are troubled or threatened by his messianic ministry, which leads to his death. On this way of thinking, Christ's crucifixion is the upshot of human reaction to the message of love Christ brings in his ethical teaching. God is not necessarily morally or even causally responsible for that reaction. That would need to be argued for, and it is no part of the exemplarist position that God must be morally or causally responsible for the death of Christ.

On the matter of valorizing suffering, the exemplarist can respond by saying that suffering may be thought valuable and, in some sense, productive if it brings about a state of affairs in which greater love is made manifest—a value that would not have been brought about without such suffering. An example of this is childbirth. The suffering undergone by a mother in giving birth is productive because it brings about a state of affairs—the birth of the child—in which a great good is brought about, one that manifests or makes possible a greater amount of love than would have been the case without the birth of the child in question. Although Christ's suffering is not productive in this direct manner, it may be that he suffers in a way that does bring about a better, and more valuable state of affairs,[16] namely, one in which God's love is diffused more widely, and received more generally as a consequence. That

---

[16]In this context I just mean "more valuable" in the sense of axiologically more valuable, that is, more valuable according to some objective scale of value.

is a great good, and should be greatly valued. It may be that God has good reasons for bringing about a world where such suffering occurs to Christ, even if God does not directly cause that suffering. He may have reasons for permitting it, even if those reasons are not always accessible to us. There is much more to be said on these matters, but we shall return to them in the discussion of atoning violence in chapter eight. I trust that enough has been said here to see that the defender of some version of moral exemplarism has conceptual resources on which to draw in order to meet these objections and attempt to turn them back.

CONCLUSION

We began by trying to dispel the common misunderstanding that moral exemplarism originates with, or at least, is strongly associated with, the theology of Peter Abelard. It is not at all clear that Abelard was a moral exemplarist as we understand the term today. He held to a version of satisfaction. The sixteenth-century theologian Faustus Socinus is a good candidate for the first explicit moral exemplarist, however. He provides perhaps the first, and one of the clearest, defenses of moral exemplarism. Although his views are not often discussed in detail, they have been very influential on later theology. Finally, we considered the modern exemplarist John Hick. His version of moral exemplarism, coupled with his advocacy for religious pluralism, and his awareness of questions concerning religious diversity in the world today, make him a good example of a modern exemplarism, and, to some extent, an inheritor of Socinus' project. We have seen that there are different versions of the moral exemplar view. Some popular versions of the view do not amount to a doctrine of atonement because they offer no mechanism by means of which Christ reconciles fallen humanity to Godself. These we have placed under the designation *no-atonement exemplarism*. Such views are accounts of the work of Christ that are not doctrines of atonement, strictly speaking. However, there are some versions of the view that do constitute doctrines of atonement because they include a conceptually thin version of a mechanism for atonement. Such doctrines we have called *atonement exemplarism*. Nevertheless, versions of moral exemplarism that are doctrines of atonement seem to presume an inadequate understanding of human sin. They also appear to valorize violence and suffering in way that is problematic.

Consequently, if it is taken as a distinct account of the reconciling work of Christ the moral exemplar view may be insufficient. But the notion that Christ is a moral example is a common feature of atonement theology where it often appears as one facet of more fulsome, conceptually "thicker" ways of understanding the atonement. For instance, it could be that Christ's act of satisfaction should elicit a response of gratitude and love that is modeled on the example Christ sets, and Christ's atonement could be a moral example of how fallen human beings should live in addition to which it is also a ransom that purchases the salvation of fallen humanity, and so on. It may be that moral exemplarism is best understood in this way as ancillary to other, more developed ways of thinking about the reconciling work of Christ.

FURTHER READING

Abelard, Peter. *Commentary on the Epistle to the Romans*. Fathers of the Church Medieval Continuations Series. Translated by Stephen R. Cartwright. Washington, DC: Catholic University of America Press, 2011.

Boersma, Hans. *Violence, Hospitality, and the Cross: Reappropriating the Atonement Tradition*. Grand Rapids: Baker Academic, 2004.

Gomes, Alan W. "*De Jesu Christo Servatore*: Faustus Socinus on the Satisfaction of Christ." *Westminster Theological Journal* 55 (1993): 209-31.

Grensted, L. W. *A Short History of the Doctrine of the Atonement*. Manchester: Manchester University Press, 1920.

Hick, John. *An Interpretation of Religion: Human Responses to the Transcendent*. 2nd edition. 1989. Reprint, London: Macmillan, 2004.

——. *The Metaphor of God Incarnate*. 2nd edition. 1993. Reprint, Louisville, KY: Westminster John Knox Press, 2005.

McGrath, Alister E. "The Moral Theory of the Atonement: An Historical and Theological Critique." *Scottish Journal of Theology* 38 (1985): 205-20.

Niebuhr, H. Richard. *The Kingdom of God in America*. 1932. Reprint, Middletown, CT: Wesleyan University Press, 1988.

Paul, L. A. *Transformative Experience*. Oxford: Oxford University Press, 2014.

Quinn, Philip. "Abelard on Atonement: Nothing Unintelligible, Arbitrary, Illogical, or Immoral About It." In *A Reader in Philosophical Theology*, ed. Oliver D. Crisp, 335-53. London: Bloomsbury, 2009.

Rashdall, Hastings. *The Idea of Atonement in Christian Theology, Being the Bampton Lectures for 1915*. London: Macmillan and Co., 1919.

Rees, Thomas, trans. *The Racovian Catechism, with notes and illustrations; translated from the Latin, etc.* 1605. Reprint, London: Longman, Hurst, Rees, Orme, and Brown, 1818.

Ritschl, Abrecht. *The Christian Doctrine of Justification and Reconciliation.* 2nd ed. Translated by H. R. MacIntosh and A. B. Macaulay. Edinburgh: T&T Clark, 1902.

Romanides, John S. *The Ancestral Sin.* Ridgewood, NJ: Zephyr, 2002.

Schleiermacher, Friedrich. *The Christian Faith.* Edited by H. R. MacIntosh and J. R. Stewart. Edinburgh: T&T Clark, 1928.

Socinus, Faustus. *De Jesu Christo Servatore, Part III.* Translated by Alan W. Gomes. PhD dissertation, Fuller Theological Seminary, 1990.

Weingart, Richard E. *The Logic of Divine Love: A Critical Analysis of the Soteriology of Peter Abailard.* Oxford: Oxford University Press, 1970.

Williams, Thomas. "Sin, Grace, and Redemption." In *The Cambridge Companion to Abelard*, ed. Jeffrey E. Brower and Kevin Guilfoy, 258-78. Cambridge: Cambridge University Press, 2004.

6

PENAL SUBSTITUTIONARY
ATONEMENT

In recent times no doctrine of atonement has been so maligned as penal substitution. Paradoxically, perhaps, no doctrine of atonement has had such a grip on the popular imagination of many Christians, particularly those from evangelical and Pentecostal backgrounds. Books continue to appear to defend the doctrine,[1] and academic tomes continue to be written, many critical of it in some way or other.[2]

We have already encountered penal substitution in passing in previous chapters, and more substantively in considering its relationship to satisfaction in chapter four. There are a number of ways in which Christ's work can be said to include a substitutionary element, and satisfaction may be one such way. Ransom also includes some sort of substitution, of Christ to ransom those he comes to save, as we noted in chapter three. And, as we shall see in the next chapter, there are still other views that share a family resemblance to penal substitution, including a substitutionary component, though they have different understandings of the means by which Christ's work reconciles human beings to God. So, although it may be a necessary condition for penal substitution, a substitutionary component is not sufficient to distinguish it from other approaches to the atonement. The substitution in question has to be of a particular sort. Specifically, it has to be the substitution of Christ for fallen humanity, with Christ taking upon himself the penalty for sin, which is due to Adam's race on account of sin. So the substitution in view must be

---

[1]The latest of these is William Lane Craig, *The Atonement* (Cambridge: Cambridge University Press, 2018).

[2]There are many such volumes. A good place to start is Derek Tidball, David Hilborn, and Justin Thaker, eds., *The Atonement Debate* (Grand Rapids: Zondervan, 2008).

penal in nature. That is, it must be related to punishment under the law, in this case, the moral law of God. Putting these elements together, we may say that penal substitution is the doctrine of atonement that claims Christ's reconciling work has to do with his suffering the penalty of sin in place of human sinners. He takes upon himself the penal or legal penalty for our sin. Because he suffers in place of fallen human beings, satisfying the requirements of the divine moral law, we do not need to be punished for our sin provided we are united to the benefits of Christ's work by faith. This, in short, is the heart of the penal substitutionary account of atonement.

But it is important to note an ambiguity here. The ambiguity has to do with whether Christ is *actually punished*, suffering my penalty for sin, or whether he merely takes upon himself the *penal consequences* of my sin. The difference is an important one, as we shall see later in the chapter. If one person receives the punishment of another, then they are treated as if they were the guilty party, being (somehow) punished in place of the other. However, if someone merely takes on himself the penal consequences of another person's sin, then he is not punished as the guilty party, but rather accepts the harsh treatment that would be a punishment if it were served on the guilty party. In taking upon himself the penal consequences of sin, the substitute pays the legal debt but does not suffer a punishment, strictly speaking. We have already encountered an analog to this in the chapter on satisfaction. This is the paying of a parking ticket by a friend. In paying the ticket the friend accepts the liability for the debt, but not the guilt of the person who got the ticket in the first place. So there are important variations within the doctrine of penal substitution that lead some to speak of a "family" of penal substitution views rather than a single doctrine.

A good biblical case can be made for some sort of penal substitution. The animal sacrifices in the Old Testament prescribe how (amongst other things) they should be used as cultic substitutes for the people. The claim that "the life is in the blood," and the injunction that it has been given "to make atonement for yourselves on the altar; it is the blood that makes atonement for one's life" (Leviticus 17:11) reinforces this. Similarly, in Leviticus 16:21-22, Aaron is instructed to lay hands on the scapegoat that has transferred to it (whether symbolically or really) the sins of the people, whereupon it is released into a solitary place in the desert. This action is said to carry away the sins of the people. Isaiah 53 is usually cited by defenders of penal substitution as a key Old Testament text that prefigures Christ's reconciling work in the person of the suffering servant. Verses 4–6 are the heart of the matter:

> Surely he took up our pain and bore our suffering, yet we considered him punished by God, stricken by him, and afflicted. But he was pierced for our transgressions, he was crushed for our iniquities; the punishment that brought us peace was on him, and by his wounds we are healed. We all, like sheep, have gone astray, each of us has turned to our own way; and the Lord has laid on him the iniquity of us all.

In the New Testament, Romans 3:21-26 is an important passage that is said to support penal substitution, which we have already encountered in chapter one. Verses 25–26 state,

> God presented Christ as a sacrifice of atonement, through the shedding of his blood—to be received by faith. He did this to demonstrate his righteousness, because in his forbearance he had left the sins committed beforehand unpunished—he did it to demonstrate his righteousness at the present time, so as to be just and the one who justifies those who have faith in Jesus.

Much scholarly ink has been spilt arguing over whether Paul has in mind the expiation of sin in Christ's sacrifice of atonement, or whether he means to suggest that God is propitiated by Christ's work. Recall that, whereas expiation has to do with reparation for sin, propitiation connotes the idea of placating divine wrath. Although there is a significant difference of biblical interpretation between saying Christ suffers a penalty to expiate human sin, or Christ is punished to propitiate God's wrath, we can set it to one side for present purposes. The reason for this is that an argument for penal substitution can be had irrespective of whether Christ is said to suffer a penalty for human sin in an act of expiation, or (in addition) is said to be punished in order to propitiate God's wrath. Whether his punishment placates God in addition to expiating sin is an important matter, but it does not alter the mechanism of atonement involved—which is what we are after. Both of these ways of understanding Paul's meaning in Romans 3 are consistent with a penal substitution in which Christ takes upon himself the penalty for human sin.

This is an important point because some recent critics of penal substitution have queried the understanding of divine wrath that it presumes, worrying that it ascribes a kind of emotional life to God that would seem abusive in a human being. That is, the doctrine seems to imply God is "wroth with sin" and requires Christ's death in order to be placated like some kind of tyrant. My point here is that even if passages like Romans 3 deal only with expiation, or the expunging of human sin, and not propitiation, or the placating of a wrathful deity, a penal substitution argument can still be run on that basis. It would be a more moderate version of penal substitution, in which the focus is expiating sin rather than propitiating God. But this change of focus would not damage the structure or logic of penal substitution, so to speak. It would be like swapping out one power source for another in order to use a particular piece of machinery. Such an argument would be rather different from some versions of the doctrine, to be sure, for many of them do think of Christ's work as a penal substitute as a propitiation of divine wrath. Nevertheless, penal substitution can be had without propitiation-language, using only the terms required by the expiation or expunging of human sin.

Some recent defenders of the doctrine claim that it is also an understanding of the atonement that can incorporate many of the other motifs of atonement we have already encountered. In this way, penal substitution acts as a sort of master-argument, with these other themes as tributaries that empty out into the larger argument of penal substitution, rather like smaller streams that feed into a larger river.[3] Christ's penal substitutionary work is a ransom, for Christ buys us back at great cost from the sin to which we have become enslaved. His work is an example to us of divine love and condescension that should stir us up, and galvanize us to live in a similarly selfless manner. It is an act that satisfies God because punishment is meted out so that his justice is upheld. It is the means by which Christ is able to heal our fallen human natures in the expiation of our sins; and so on. Some defenders of penal substitution regard this as a reason for thinking that penal substitution is the one atonement doctrine "to rule them all," like the One Ring in J. R. R. Tolkien's Middle Earth. This is an important consideration. If its defenders are right about this, then penal substitution has an advantage over at least some other atonement themes and motifs because it is able to provide a more comprehensive understanding of Christ's reconciling work, in which

---

[3]Thus, e.g., J. I. Packer in "What Did the Cross Achieve? The Logic of Penal Substitution" *Tyndale Bulletin* 25 (1974): 3-45.

these other notions feature as component parts. However, this potential advantage must be weighed against the objections to the doctrine that have been brought against it, several of which are very serious indeed. In the next section we turn to the consideration of these objections, before offering an assessment of them at the end of the chapter.

OBJECTIONS TO PENAL SUBSTITUTION

There are more objections to penal substitution than we can attend to here. Instead of trying to do justice to all the concerns that have been raised in the literature, let us focus in on a handful of really hard objections, with a view to ascertaining whether the defender of penal substitution can meet these concerns. The worries in question are: the problem of divine violence and "divine child abuse," the problem of forgiveness and punishment, the problem of "punishing" an innocent, and the problem of transferred sin and guilt. Here as in previous chapters, we begin with objections that are somewhat easier to meet, proceeding to those that seem to present more difficult conceptual problems for penal substitution.

The problem of divine violence and "divine child abuse." Like the satisfaction doctrine, as well as (to some extent) the ransom view, penal substitution seems to valorize divine violence. Feminist critics of atonement doctrines have argued that traditional atonement doctrines (not just penal substitution) depict a kind of "'divine child abuse'—God the Father demanding and carrying out the suffering and death of his own son."[4] A full assessment of problems with atoning violence must wait until chapter eight. However, the "divine child abuse" criticism has been leveled against defenders of penal substitution in particular in recent years, so it behooves us to consider it here.

The first thing that should be said is that there is a real problem with the issue of divine violence as it is portrayed in many popular accounts of the atonement, especially in respect to penal substitution. The wrath of God being visited upon his Son and his anger being poured out upon Christ, as well as the suffering of Christ's soul and body, and the extinguishing of his human life with the cry of dereliction indicating that God the Father had

---

[4]Joanna Carlson Brown and Rebecca Parker, "For God So Loved the World?" in *Christianity, Patriarchy, and Abuse: A Feminist Critique*, ed. Joanne Carlson Brown and Carole R. Bohn (New York: The Pilgrim Press, 1989), 26.

turned his back on Christ—these are images familiar to many Christians. They are also deeply ingrained in the rhetoric of popular historic Christian thought. So these are no superficial or trivial worries. If God is violent and wrathful, what does that say about the divine nature? Does his emotional life swing from one extreme to another? Does he act whimsically? Does he crush his Son in his rage?

No sensible Christian, let alone sensible defender of penal substitution, would own such a grotesque caricature of the life of God.[5] But even if we set aside the extremity of language and try to focus instead upon the notion of divine violence itself, there are concerns that thoughtful Christians will surely see the need to address. For on the face of it, it does look like God acts violently in the atonement.

Let us begin by dealing with the problem of the heat generated by the rhetoric of "divine child abuse." This is actually not as serious an objection to the doctrine of atonement in general, or to penal substitution in particular, as it might appear at first glance. This is because one would have to be willing to give up the doctrine of the Trinity for the objection to have any traction. But clearly no Christian is going to give up the Trinity, so the objection fails to get off the ground.

Here is why: in many cases, child abuse occurs where a parent harms a child. Now, the parent is numerically distinct from the child. They are separate individuals, which is part of the reason why abusive acts of this nature are so terrible. It involves the violation of one vulnerable individual by another in a position of power and responsibility. However, once this much is plain it should also be clear that there is a real problem with attempting to transpose the case of human child abuse onto the Trinity. For the divine persons of the Godhead are not individuals in a familial relationship. The Father and the Son are *one entity* in a very strong sense; after all Christianity is a species of monotheism. Whatever model of the Trinity one adopts (and there are a number of models to choose from), what is non-negotiable about the doctrine of the Trinity is that God is one in essence and yet three persons. As the Athanasian Creed puts it, the catholic faith that all Christians hold is that

---

[5]Note, I do not say there are *no* such people as such. I say only that no *sensible* defender of penal substitution would recognize this caricature as the view they defend.

we worship one God in trinity and the trinity in unity, neither blending their persons nor dividing their essence. For the person of the Father is a distinct person, the person of the Son is another, and that of the Holy Spirit still another. But the divinity of the Father, Son, and Holy Spirit is one, their glory equal, their majesty coeternal.

Later, it says, "Thus the Father is God, the Son is God, the Holy Spirit is God. Yet there are not three gods; there is but one God."

Moreover, as this excerpt from the Athanasian Creed demonstrates, the doctrine of the Trinity entails the denial of the claim that there are numerically distinct individuals in the Godhead, as if the Father, Son and Holy Spirit were like the three Greek gods Zeus, Poseidon, and Hades. Given these considerations, it should be clear that the "divine child abuse" accusation fails. The Father is not abusing the Son, acting violently towards him as sometimes happens in human father-son relationships. Instead, the Father and Son compact together with the Holy Spirit as coequal and coeternal members of the one Godhead to bring about human salvation in the knowledge that without divine grace human beings cannot save themselves. This is true of many traditional atonement doctrines, not just penal substitution. But the worry with penal substitution in particular is that it throws these concerns into sharp relief. However, since defenders of penal substitution also defend the doctrine of the Trinity, it should be clear that it is not a doctrine that can entail "divine child abuse" because only one divine entity is in view.

That said, the deeper worry about divine violence is harder to turn back. Many of those who defend penal substitution agree that Scripture speaks in manifold ways about God's wrath and anger with sin and about his punishment of it (e.g., Rom 1:18). Yet many of these same theologians would also agree with a classical picture of the divine nature, where God is loving or benevolent, immutable or unchangeable, and just. These divine attributes appear to be pulling in different directions. We associate wrath and anger with a change of emotional state, which is temporary. The parent is angry with his child for stealing the cookie, or the manager is angry with the administrative assistant for sending the letter to the wrong person. The examples of mundane expressions of human anger could be multiplied. But if God is loving and unchangeable in his very nature, then it seems that he cannot have such changing emotional states. His "emotional" life, if we may speak of it as such, is infinitely more stable than that of human beings. For he is not subject to whims, frustrations, irritations, and the like. No creaturely action can alter the inner life of God if his is immutable in a strong sense.

A large part of the problem here has to do with what is usually called *anthropomorphism*. This is when we ascribe human characteristics to some non-human object or entity. There is much anthropomorphism in Scripture. For instance, we read of the outstretched arm of the Lord saving the Israelites (Exodus 6:6), of the eyes of the Lord ranging over the whole earth (2 Chronicles 16:9), and so on. But apart from the incarnation, God has no body. These are human attempts to speak about God in anthropomorphic language. Scripture speaks of the wrath of God, and of his anger. But how can God be said to be wrathful *in his nature* if God is love, as the Apostle John tells us (1 John 4:8)? He cannot change in his nature on this way of thinking (James 1:17), so he cannot begin to be wrathful, or stop being wrathful. Yet it seems strange to think that he can be both wrathful and loving simultaneously. And, clearly, the inner life of God is characterized by love not wrath (for God is not conflicted in his inner life).

There are at least two ways of dealing with this difficulty. The first is to suggest that God's wrath is an expression of his love as it is mediated by his justice. On this way of thinking, when Paul says in Romans 1:18 that "the wrath of God is being revealed from heaven" against those who suppress the truth by their wickedness, he has in mind something like the idea that God's love for holiness, goodness, and truth, which is frustrated by human wickedness, results in the exercise of divine justice in punishment that is an expression of God's wrath. In human relationships we think of wrath as a kind of extreme anger. But this is a poor analog for what is going on in the divine nature. God is not in an uncontrollable rage with sin. Rather, his love expressed via his justice against the wickedness of human sin is received as the visitation of his wrath in punishment. This is a just anger, much as one might be justly angry with the perpetrator of child abuse in a human relationship, and desire justice.

However, although this way of approaching the problem does something to ameliorate the problem of divine wrath, some will worry that it doesn't really adequately address the deep concern about violence and atonement. So maybe we could consider a second way to deal with the apparent tension between divine wrath and divine love. Perhaps, as I indicated at the beginning of this chapter, language of divine wrath is really a way of expressing the human reception of certain divine acts of justice as they are distributed to his creatures, for Scripture does say God is just in all his ways (Deut 32:4).

On this second way of thinking about this problem, God's punishment of Christ in place of fallen human beings is not an act of violence or anger. Rather, it is an act of love and condescension, the love that God has had from eternity for the works of his hands expressed in condescending to become human in order to provide an atonement for human sin. This act is also an exercise of divine justice, because God is just and must ensure that sin is dealt with in a manner consistent with his just nature. For those defenders of penal substitution who, like Anselm, think God cannot forgive sin, God's justice is exercised as an expression of his nature, and God the Son voluntarily takes upon himself the task of meeting the requirements of divine justice by suffering the penalty of human sin in a vicarious act of salvation on the cross. Since death is the penalty for sin, he pays that price. For those defenders of penal substitution who think God may forgive sin, God's justice is exercised because, say, it is important that his fallen creatures see the moral seriousness of their condition, and their need for salvation. Christ's substitutionary work demonstrates this to us.

How does this help with the problem of divine violence? By attending to the doctrine of God that informs traditional accounts of penal substitution, we can see that a plausible reconstruction of penal substitution is able to explain that God is not an emotionally mercurial deity, visiting his wrath in moments of anger like Thor or Odin. He is constant in his nature, which is unchanging. The language of "wrath" and "anger" may be understood as anthropomorphic ways of getting at the expression of his justice. But this in turn is rooted in a character that is essentially loving. Far from being an episode of divine violence, on this way of thinking the cross is the supreme expression of God's love for us. As 1 John 3:16 famously puts it, "This is how we know what love is: Jesus Christ laid down his life for us. And we ought to lay down our lives for our brothers and sisters."

The problem of forgiveness and punishment. When we considered the doctrine of satisfaction, we saw that Anselm claimed God cannot forgive sin without punishment. Often this claim is repeated by defenders of penal substitution. Sometimes the idea is that God cannot forgive sin because his justice is inexorable and must be meted out, whereas his grace and mercy are discretionary, and distributed only to those upon whom his favor rests. We have already dealt with the problems attending this sort of view in chapter one. In fact, both the defender of satisfaction as well as the defender of penal substitution may make the weaker claim that God may, rather than must punish sin. In one respect, this makes the question of divine justice easier to address for then God may forgive sin like human beings do. He may forego punishment if he so desires. However, in another sense, it makes matters harder, because then some explanation is required to account for why God doesn't simply forgive *all* sin without atonement.

As we noted in the previous section, one response to this sort of concern is to say that God may set aside punishment in many cases, but that there may be good moral reasons for punishing sin in at least some cases. The idea here is that failing to treat a sin with sufficient moral seriousness—making light of it, as if it can simply be forgiven without reparation—does not help us to see the real heinousness of sin. It would be like forgiving the naughty child every time she did something wrong irrespective of how grave it was. It seems reasonable to think that pursuing such a parenting policy would not, in the end, be for the good of the child. She would not come to see the gravity of certain actions, and would not develop appropriate moral discernment about the propriety of certain action in certain circumstances. For if she is simply forgiven without punishment every time she does something wrong, how is she to understand the moral consequences of her actions? So it may be that the defender of penal substitution can opt for the claim that God *may*, but not *must*, punish sin instead of the stronger claim that he simply must punish sin, which is tantamount to Anselm's view. But—importantly for our purposes—both of these views about the nature of atonement are consistent with penal substitution.

The problem of "punishing" an innocent. Let us turn to our next problem, having to do with the "punishment" of an innocent person, which, in the case of atonement, is Christ. Consider these words from twentieth-century Dutch Reformed theologian Louis Berkhof:

> All those who advocate a subjective theory of the atonement raise a formidable objection to the idea of vicarious atonement. They consider it unthinkable that

a just God should transfer His wrath against moral offenders to a perfectly innocent party, and should treat the innocent judicially as if he were guilty. There is undoubtedly a real difficulty here, especially in view of the fact that this seems to be contrary to all human analogy.[6]

This is a significant admission coming from a theologian sympathetic to a doctrine of penal substitution. If a person is innocent of a crime, that person cannot be punished for the crime. Punishment is the imposition of some kind of hardship for an offense. But where a person has committed no offense, no penalty can be applied. Suppose a referee in a football game called a penalty when there was no infraction of the rules, stopping play for no good reason. At least part of the anger and frustration such a decision would cause has to do with the fact that the referee cannot apply a penalty when no offense has taken place.

Transpose this to the case of the atonement. According to the structure of the argument for penal substitution, Christ, an innocent, is punished in place of human beings guilty of sin. He willingly takes upon himself the penalty for our sin. But if an innocent person cannot be punished because she or he cannot have the requisite penalty applied to them—for an innocent person is, by definition, *blameless*—then it looks like defenders of penal substitution are committed to a doctrine that has a serious moral problem. Rather than offering a way of explaining how Christ's may take upon himself our punishment, it offers an account of the atonement at the heart of which is a travesty of justice. It makes no legal difference that Christ voluntarily takes upon himself this role. For even if an innocent person were to agree to take on the punishment due to another, what would be meted out to the innocent person would not be punishment. It would simply be harsh treatment of a blameless person, which is unjust. Yet, God cannot act unjustly. In which case, this cannot be an adequate account of the atonement.

Unsurprisingly, perhaps, the defender of penal substitution is not without response to this objection. One way of meeting this concern involves pointing out that human beings appear to be in two minds about penal substitution when it comes to merely human legal arrangements. In some cases, we do permit penal substitution to take place. In other instances, we do not.

---

[6]Louis Berkhof, *Systematic Theology* (1939; repr., Edinburgh: Banner of Truth, 1988), 376.

Consider the case of the person paying a parking fine, a case we have already encountered in discussing the doctrine of satisfaction. There we used it to illustrate the satisfaction of a penalty by someone other than the guilty party. Here we can press the example a little further. Where the person guilty of incurring the parking fine is unable to pay, a wealthy friend can step in and cover the cost. On the face of it, this looks like a case of penal substitution. One person stands in for another, taking upon herself the penal consequences of her friend's fine.

However, it is not clear that this is a case of penal substitution, for several reasons. First, consider the fact that the wealthy friend is innocent of the fine. She *does* take upon herself the penal consequence of paying the fine—that much is true. The law only requires that the fine is paid. However, it does not require that the person *guilty of incurring the fine* be the person who pays the fine. So the wealthy friend is able to pay the fine in place of the one guilty of incurring the fine. Clearly, the wealthy friend is not the guilty party. Moreover, in paying the fine she does not *become* the guilty party; she does not take upon herself any guilt for the crime committed. She merely pays the fine on behalf of the guilty party.

Second, consider the fact that the wealthy friend is not *punished* by paying the fine; in fact, strictly speaking, no punishment takes place. This is true even if the fine is a substantial sum of money, which would cause the person guilty of incurring the fine great financial difficulty. For notice that in paying the fine, the wealthy friend is not punished; she is simply paying what is legally required, that is, the penalty, yet without any admission of guilt, and without blameworthiness being ascribed to her. It is not just that she is not the guilty party. It is that the question of guilt in the case of the parking fine is not legally salient. The law is "blind" to the question of which party is guilty of the crime. All that matters for the purposes of resolving the matter legally is that the debt is paid. There is, then, a kind of legal relaxation of the question of guilt in the case of the fine; it is not taken into consideration in the paying of the penalty due.

So, in the case of the wealthy friend paying the fine, an innocent person provides the money to settle the penalty on behalf of another. Yet the innocent is not punished in place of the guilty party. If there is a substitution of a sort in this case, it is of a rather "thin" sort, namely, the payment of the penalty by the wealthy friend. But it is not a substitution of the sort needed by defenders of the theological version of penal substitution because the innocent wealthy friend is not punished in paying the fine instead of the friend that has incurred the fine. No punishment takes place. All that takes place is the payment of the penalty due. We might say that the wealthy friend takes upon herself the penal consequences of the fine (the financial penalty), but in so doing is not punished in place of one that has incurred the fine. So, it looks like this is actually a case of satisfaction and not penal substitution after all. Some defenders of the theological doctrine of penal substitution point to cases like this one as examples of what is sometimes called *pecuniary penal substitution,* because the substitution in question is of a financial nature. But it looks like this rests on a mistake, for the substitution in question boils down to a case of satisfaction: the paying of a penalty, not the meting out of punishment.

But this example of the parking fine suggests an alternative response to this objection, which is open to the defender of penal substitution. This is to claim that Christ is not punished for our sin, strictly speaking. Instead, he takes upon himself the harsh treatment that we would have to endure if we were to be punished. In taking this harsh treatment upon himself, Christ takes upon himself the penal consequences of our sin. But he is not thereby punished because he is innocent. This way of addressing the problem of "punishing" the innocent Christ involves amending an important feature of many traditional accounts of penal substitution that do speak of Christ's work in terms of his taking upon himself our punishment in our place. But the cost may be worth the benefit. If the defender of penal substitution is committed only to this weaker claim that Christ suffers the penal consequence of human sin, then he is not an innocent being punished in place of the guilty after all, and the objection folds. Instead, he is one who voluntarily takes upon himself the harsh treatment that would be punishment if we were to endure it. Although it does address the question of "punishing" the innocent, this solution does leave some important questions unresolved. For instance, on this revised view it still seems that the innocent Christ suffers harsh treatment that he is not due. And normally we would think that is unjust. A child who takes the harsh treatment that is due to his brother because he doesn't want his brother to suffer may do a noble thing. Nevertheless, we would still think that the suffering he endures is unjust and inappropriate. It is more difficult to see how the defender of penal substitution can address this particular concern.

The problem of transferred sin and guilt. Earlier I said that one strategy for defending penal substitution against the objection that one cannot punish an innocent person is to point out that in human legal transactions we are in two minds about penal substitution. Yet if the case of the parking fine is on target, then that will not do as an example of such conflicted thinking because it is not a clear case of penal substitution. Suppose we lay this to one side. It would appear that the sort of penal substitution envisaged by theologians is much more like a felony, or serious crime, than like a misdemeanor, or minor wrongdoing. Yet in the case of felonies, the question of guilt does become legally salient. Take the example of a murderer. It matters that the person punished for the murder is the murderer, not some substitute, because we think that the guilt for this crime is bound up with the one who has committed it. It "attaches" to that person; it cannot be transferred to another. In other words, it is an inalienable characteristic of those to whom it applies. If a friend were to agree to be "punished" in place of the murderer, no judge would agree to this arrangement because this would actually constitute a failure to carry out the punishment due. It would be a failure to carry out the punishment because (a) the substitute is not the guilty party, (b) guilt is legally salient so that the penalty for the crime must be meted out to the guilty party in order for punishment to be served, (c) guilt is an inalienable quality of the person guilty of the crime, and (d) no punishment can be meted out where the person suffering the harsh treatment is innocent of the crime committed.

In older theological textbooks a distinction is often made between the aspect of guilt that attaches to a person, that is, the blameworthiness or culpability of the guilty person, and that aspect of guilt that has to do with punishment. Guilt may be expunged by punishment, and yet the person concerned remains the one guilty of having committed the crime. A murderer is still a murderer even if he has served his time in prison and can no longer be punished for his crime.

This distinction only underlines a further problem for defenders of penal substitution. Suppose human sin is indeed as serious as defenders of penal substitution suppose. It is like a felony. Guilt in such cases is normally legally salient, at least in human law. So the sinner should pay the penalty for her or his sin, for she or he is the guilty party. How can the sin and guilt of fallen human beings be transferred to Christ, an innocent person? This is not the same problem as the harsh treatment ("punishment") of an innocent person. This related worry has to do with the transfer of sin and guilt from a guilty party to an innocent one. Some defenders of penal substitution maintain that what is transferred to Christ is the aspect of guilt that is punishable. The sinner always remains the one guilty of having committed the sin; the issue is whether someone else can have transferred to them the punishable aspect of that guilt. The idea here is that Christ can take upon himself this task, being punished in place of the sinner and taking upon himself that aspect of the sinner's guilt that is liable to punishment. So punishment can be transferred.

Then there are biblical passages such as 2 Corinthians 5:21, which says "God made him who had no sin to be sin for us, so that in him we might become the righteousness of God." Some defenders of penal substitution, wishing to take this Pauline claim seriously, maintain that in suffering our punishment on the cross Christ "becomes sin" for us. That is, he has imputed or ascribed to him our sin as well as our guilt because "he was pierced for our transgressions, he was crushed for our iniquities" so that "the punishment that brought us peace was on him" (Isaiah 53:5). This is a very strong claim indeed. It is tantamount to saying that the atonement involves Christ taking upon himself the sin and guilt of fallen humanity so that their sin and guilt are imputed to him, in order that he may be punished in place of fallen human beings. He in some very strong sense becomes the sin-bearer and the guilt-bearer.

But can sin and guilt be transferred like this? It seems that they cannot—at least, not normally in the case of felonies like murder. And, as we have already intimated, our sin is much more like such a felony than it is like a financial debt. Defenders of penal substitution often claim that although Christ is indeed innocent of sin and guilt, our sin and guilt is imputed or ascribed to him by God. This is a kind of legal fiction, whereby God treats Christ *as if* he were the one guilty of sin, though he is in fact innocent of any sin. His "punishment" is numerically distinct from my punishment. So the idea must be that in suffering the penal consequences of my sin Christ suffers in a qualitatively similar manner, that is, in a manner that is similar in quality to the punishment that would be suffered by the sinner if she or he were punished instead of Christ. But having someone other than the felon suffer qualitatively similar penal consequences for the crime committed by the felon, ascribing to the substitute the sin and guilt of the felon, would hardly constitute an example of human justice. It would, in fact, be a miscarriage of justice. We would not consent to such an arrangement in the case of a felony like murder. What about the theological application of penal substitution means an exception can be made in the case of Christ, which is not a traducing of justice? This, it must be said, is a deep theological problem that defenders of penal substitution must address.

One way to meet this worry involves appealing to the notion of legal relaxation once again. The idea is that God may "relax" the strict requirement of the moral law so that a legal substitute (Christ) may take upon himself the penal consequence of human sin, suffering the penalty that would be punishment if it were served upon fallen human beings. On this way of thinking Christ accepts and pays the debt of human sin, but he does not thereby incur or have attributed to him the guilt of human sin. This may be a way of responding to this worry if there is a purely legal sense in which Christ can act on behalf of fallen humans without incurring guilt or having guilt ascribed to him. Nevertheless, it is an odd arrangement where the guilty party is not punished, but an innocent party pays the debt due in abstraction, as it were, from any claim about culpability for sin. Yet this is one route that a defender of penal substitution might take.

AN ASSESSMENT OF PENAL SUBSTITUTION

We have seen that there are real conceptual problems with penal substitution, some of which strike at the very heart of the doctrine. For some recent theologians this is a reason for thinking that it is an account of the atonement that has outlived its usefulness, and should be replaced by other, more helpful ways of thinking about Christ's reconciling work. However, even if one thinks that no single atonement doctrine captures all that needs to be said about the atonement, and even if one is skeptical that any given atonement doctrine can provide an all-encompassing account of the atonement, such doctrines are surely truth-apt and truth-aimed. So setting aside one particular understanding of the atonement because it seems less helpful than other potential candidates needs to be understood not merely as a preferential claim, but as a claim about the extent to which penal substitution captures or expresses something of the truth of the atonement, relative to other candidate doctrines. If it turns out that other approaches to the atonement do a better job of expressing the mechanism of atonement, then so much the worse for penal substitution. But let us not make the mistake of thinking that the issue is something other than proximity to the truth of the matter, as witnessed to by Scripture and the Christian tradition.

We have seen that defenders of penal substitution are faced with deep conceptual difficulties having to do with the harsh treatment of an innocent person "punished" in place of guilty sinners, and the ascription of sin and guilt from these sinners to the blameless person of Christ. Although these are significant problems, they are not necessarily insurmountable. The doctrine can be defended, given certain assumptions. But perhaps much of the content of the doctrine of penal substitution can be transposed into a slightly different context, in which some explanation can be given of Christ's union with fallen humanity in his incarnation, life, death, and resurrection that addresses these issues in a rather different, and perhaps more helpful, way— one that doesn't raise some of the same problems in quite the same manner. This we shall attempt to provide in chapter ten.

FURTHER READING

Berkhof, Louis. *Systematic Theology*. 1939. Reprint, Edinburgh: Banner of Truth, 1988.

Boersma, Hans. *Violence, Hospitality, and the Cross: Reappropriating the Atonement Tradition*. Grand Rapids: Baker Academic, 2004.

Brown, Joanna Carlson, and Rebecca Parker, "For God So Loved the World?" In *Christianity, Patriarchy, and Abuse: A Feminist Critique*, ed. Joanne Carlson Brown and Carole R. Bohn, 1-30. New York: The Pilgrim Press, 1989.

Calvin, John. *Institutes of the Christian Religion*. Book 2, chapter 16. Edited by John T. McNeil. Translated by Ford Lewis Battles. 1559. Reprint, Philadelphia: Westminster Press, 1960.

Craig, William Lane. *The Atonement*. Cambridge Elements. Cambridge: Cambridge University Press, 2018.

Crisp, Oliver D. "The Logic of Penal Substitution Revisited" In *The Atonement Debate: Papers from the London Symposium on the Theology of Atonement*, ed. Derek Tidball, David Holborn, and Justin Thacker, 208-27. Grand Rapids: Zondervan, 2008.

Gathercole, Simon. *Defending Substitution: An Essay on Atonement in Paul.* Grand Rapids: Baker Academic, 2015.

Hodge, A. A. *The Atonement.* Philadelphia: Presbyterian Board of Publication, 1867.

Holmes, Stephen R. "Penal Substitution." In *T&T Clark Companion to Atonement,* ed. Adam J. Johnson, 295-314. London: Bloomsbury, 2017.

Lewis, David. "Do We Believe in Penal Substitution?" *Philosophical Papers* 26, no. 3 (1997): 203-9.

Packer, James I. "What Did The Cross Achieve? The Logic of Penal Substitution." *Tyndale Bulletin* 25 (1974): 3-45.

Thurow, Joshua. "Communal Substitutionary Atonement." *Journal of Analytic Theology* 3 (2015): 47-69.

Williams, Garry J. "Penal Substitution: A Response to Recent Criticisms." *Journal of the Evangelical Theological Society* 50, no. 1 (2007): 71-86.

GOVERNMENTAL AND VICARIOUS PENITENCE DOCTRINES OF ATONEMENT

Several of the accounts of the atonement we have considered thus far have at their core some notion of substitution, even if it is a rather thin one. Thus, Christ is said by some theologians to be a ransom for our sin; by others Christ is said to satisfy divine honor so that we are not punished; according to others Christ is said to be punished in our place. But there are variations on a substitution-theme distinct from these views that are the subject matter of this chapter. These doctrines are not as well-known as satisfaction, ransom, or penal substitution. Nor are they often discussed in recent surveys of the atonement. Yet they offer important approaches to the reconciling work of Christ that provide alternative ways of thinking about the notion of substitution, without being versions of penal substitution, or ransom, or some sort of satisfaction doctrine. Because they are not widely discussed in contemporary theological literature, it is worth beginning with a brief account of the historical background to these two doctrines, before exploring them in more detail.

HISTORICAL BACKGROUND

The first of these two doctrines emphasizes the idea that Christ reconciles us by becoming a penal example, or by means of penal non-substitution, as I have called it elsewhere. The central idea here is that God makes Christ an example of what would happen to fallen human beings if he were to punish them for their sins as they deserve. Christ suffers as a kind of deterrent, and so that God's moral government of the universe is upheld (by displaying what would happen to sin without his deterrent example). So his role is a penal one, pertaining to the divine moral government of the cosmos, and the exercise of God's moral law. But it is not strictly speaking a role that involves him as a substitute for human sin. In textbooks of theology this view is usually called the governmental doctrine of atonement, since it is God's rectoral role, that is, his role in the moral government of humanity, that is its focus. It is often thought to have originated with the Dutch lawyer Hugo Grotius (AD 1583–1645), who wrote a work on the atonement in response to the criticisms of penal substitution by the Socinians in the sixteenth century. This was entitled *A Defense of the Catholic Faith Concerning the Satisfaction of Christ* (*Defensio fidei catholicae de satisfactione Christi*), and was first published in 1617. Grotius's legal training enabled him to find a way of conceiving the atonement that elided the objections being brought against the Reformation doctrine of vicarious satisfaction by Faustus Socinus (several of which we considered in the last chapter). However, it is not clear that Grotius thought of his own work as an attempt to produce a new account of the atonement. Rather, he thought he was defending the views of the Reformation, shoring them up with new ways of thinking about how the notion of God's moral government could be brought to bear upon the atonement so as to meet the criticisms of Socinus. Whether Grotius was right about this is another matter. It is certainly the case that the governmental doctrine of atonement represents an account of Christ's reconciling work that is distinct from penal substitution, even if it was not Grotius's intention to develop a different view.

Grotius was an Arminian by theological persuasion. For this reason, the governmental account became popular in later Arminian and Wesleyan circles, and several nineteenth century American Methodist theologians of note offered sophisticated versions of this doctrine—the best known of these being the version of the doctrine penned by John Miley (AD 1813–1895). However, what is less well-known is that there is also a Calvinist version of the doctrine that was developed by the disciples of Jonathan Edwards in the eighteenth century in the theological movement known as the New Divinity. So this way of thinking about the atonement has had some influence, in both European and American theology of the past.

The second doctrine we shall consider in this chapter maintains that Christ brings about human reconciliation by an act of vicarious penitence, or what I have called elsewhere an act of non-penal substitution. The core idea here is that Christ does perform a substitutionary act in bringing about human reconciliation, but not one that is penal in nature. Hence, *non-penal* substitution. Instead, his vicarious action is *penitential* in nature. That is, he offers up his life and ultimately his death as an act of penitence or repentance on behalf of fallen human beings. This doctrine was developed in the nineteenth century by the Scottish Presbyterian minister John McLeod Campbell (1800– 1872). Strangely enough, he came across the idea in his reading of Jonathan Edwards, who, in a throwaway remark at one point in his voluminous writings, observed that atonement could have been made by a perfect penitential act on behalf of humanity.[1]

This struck Campbell as an idea worth pursuing, and the result was the vicarious penitence doctrine of atonement that he set forth in his work on the subject, *The Nature of the Atonement and its Relation to Remission of Sins and Eternal Life* (1856). Other, similar views were put forward in the early twentieth century by J. K. Mozley in particular. But it was not until later in the twentieth century when Campbell's views were championed by the Scottish theologians Thomas F. Torrance and James Torrance that this doctrine of atonement came to the fore once more.[2]

In the remainder of this chapter we will explore these two views in turn, offering some criticism of each, before drawing the different threads of doctrine together in an assessment of these two accounts of atonement to conclude.

THE GOVERNMENTAL DOCTRINE OF ATONEMENT

The biblical basis for the governmental view is connected to those passages of Scripture that speak of Christ's work as the righteous exercise of divine justice in the government of the world, and the requirement for the fulfillment of the moral law. For instance, in Romans 3:24-26 we read that

---

[1] See Jonathan Edwards, *The Works of Jonathan Edwards, Vol. II*, ed. Edward Hickman (1834; repr., Edinburgh: Banner of Truth, 1974), 565.

[2] For a recent sympathetic overview of McLeod Campbell's views, see Andrew Purves, *Exploring Christology and Atonement: Conversations with John McLeod Campbell, H. R. Mackintosh and T. F. Torrance* (Downers Grove, IL: IVP Academic, 2015).

all are justified freely by his grace through the redemption that came by Christ Jesus. God presented Christ as a sacrifice of atonement, through the shedding of his blood—to be received by faith. He did this to demonstrate his righteousness, because in his forbearance he had left the sins committed beforehand unpunished—he did it to demonstrate his righteousness at the present time, so as to be just and the one who justifies those who have faith in Jesus.

From the point of view of the defender of the governmental view, this passage indicates that God as a moral governor of the world must act righteously in dealing with sin, and that Christ is the means appointed to that end. In his letter to the Galatians Paul says, "Christ redeemed us from the curse of the law by becoming a curse for us, for it is written: 'Cursed is everyone who is hung on a pole'" (Gal 3:13). Here, the advocate of the governmental view can say that Christ has indeed become accursed for us as our penal example—the one who takes on what would have been our punishment if God had meted out to us the penalty for our sin instead of making Christ an example. Later in the New Testament, the writer to the Hebrews says, "For this reason Christ is the mediator of a new covenant, that those who are called may receive the promised eternal inheritance—now that he has died as a ransom to set them free from the sins committed under the first covenant. . . . In fact, the law requires that nearly everything be cleansed with blood, and without the shedding of blood there is no forgiveness" (Heb 9:15, 22). The defender of the governmental view can take up the ransom language here and adapt it. Christ is a ransom. He does pay what would be the penalty due for human sin if it were visited upon us. For this reason he does release us from the requirements of the moral law by taking upon himself what would be the penal consequences of our sin as our penal example. For without the shedding of blood God cannot forgive us. Hence, Christ had to act on our behalf as our penal example.

As has already been mentioned in introducing this doctrine, it emphasizes the rectoral, rather than retributive, justice of God. Rectoral justice is the justice by means of which God rightly governs the cosmos according to his holy law. By contrast, retributive justice has to do with the way in which God ensures that sin is appropriately punished, where there must be a fit between the crime committed and the penalty incurred. According to defenders of the governmental account of atonement, divine rectoral justice is, in one sense, more fundamental than divine retributive justice. For God is a moral governor through-and-through. He cannot cease to act in a way consistent with his holy character, and he cannot refrain from exercising his moral government over creation without ceasing to act in a way consistent with his holy character. God cannot act in a way inconsistent with his holy character. Hence, he must act in way consistent with his role as moral governor of the world he has created. We might say that his rectoral justice—that is, the aspect of his justice that has to do with the moral governance of the world—must be satisfied. It cannot be set aside. By contrast, God's retributive justice—that is, the aspect of justice that has to do with just deserts for sin, and the fit between crime and punishment—may be "relaxed" in order to save fallen human beings. The notion of legal relaxation at work here has to do with allowing a certain leeway, so that the strict letter of the law is not executed, though its spirit is still carried out. Strictly speaking, in the governmental view, God allows that the punishment that should be visited upon fallen human beings can be set to one side provided there is some appropriate act performed by Christ that has a deterrent effect upon fallen human beings. It is as if God says, "I'm not going to punish you, Sinner, for your sins as they deserve. Instead, I'm going to show you what would happen if I did punish your sins as they deserve. I'm going to set Christ before you as a penal example. His death will show you the gravity of your sin, and what it should lead to if I were to punish you. However, if Christ performs this deterrent action by becoming a penal example to you, then I do not need to punish you. My moral government of the universe will be upheld because Christ will have shown you what would happen to human sin. His atoning work means that I am able to relax the need to visit retribution upon you. Instead, I may forgive you your sins."

In the context of post-Reformation debate about the atonement, and particularly in light of the attacks upon the Reformation doctrine of vicarious substitution mounted by the Socinians, the governmental view made certain concessions to the opponents of the Reformation doctrine of atonement in order to safeguard some of its core ideas. Here we can enumerate four of these that are particularly important in order to understand the governmental doctrine. First, the Socinians had argued that sin cannot be transferred from one person to another, nor can guilt. This, as we saw in the previous chapter, is a key objection to penal substitutionary accounts of atonement. The governmental doctrine avoids this worry by stipulating that no such transfer of sin and guilt is required in atonement. Christ does not take upon himself our sin or guilt. He might be said to take on himself the penal consequences that would be ours if God were to visit punishment upon us. But that is not the same as him taking on our sin and guilt.

Second, the Socinians had claimed that retribution seems unjust. If God can forgive sin without punishment—as appears to be the case in the New Testament (Mt 9:5; Mk 2:5; Lk 5:20; 7:48)—then why *must* he punish us for our sins? The defender of the governmental view can say in response to this worry that God does not have to punish sin at all. By making a distinction between rectoral justice and retributive justice, and by arguing that rectoral justice is fundamental to God's nature whereas retribution is not, the defender of the governmental view can reason that God may relax retribution and yet still preserve his rectoral justice. If Christ is a deterrent to sin, and a penal example of what God would do if he did visit his retributive justice upon us, the way is open for God to forgive sin as the Socinians envisaged.

Third, the Socinians worried about how Christ could act as a substitute for sinful human beings. How can an innocent person stand-in for sinful people, taking upon himself the punishment due to the sinners? This seems unjust. By removing the notion of penal substitution, and replacing it with a penal example, the defender of the governmental view can elide this objection altogether. For as we have seen, Christ is not a substitute at all on the governmental account.

The fourth issue to which the Socinians addressed themselves was the matter of the value of Christ's atoning work. How can Christ's work be of equivalent value to the punishment that would be visited upon fallen human beings without atonement? Although Christ's suffering on the cross is no doubt exquisite, it is nevertheless finite. It lasts from midday to 3 p.m. in the afternoon, according to the canonical Gospels. By contrast, punishment in hell is supposed to be everlasting. It has a first moment but no last moment. So there seems to be a significant disparity between the length of time Christ suffers and the length of time that sinners in hell suffer. But also, Christ's suffering is qualitatively different from that of the damned in hell. They suffer everlastingly the awful miseries of the damned; he suffers for a finite period the privations of the cross. Although the cross is dreadful, it does not seem to be as awful as the terror of the damned, which has no end. So how can

Christ's atonement be equivalent to the suffering of those cut off from God's grace in the life to come?

Here the advocates of the governmental account of atonement made a distinction between different sorts of values attaching to different actions. Some actions are of more value than others. For instance, helping someone across the road has some positive value; but saving someone from being run over and killed by a car has greater positive value. In the case of Christ's work, the value of his atonement does not have to be *exactly equivalent* to the disvalue of the suffering of the damned. All that is required for atonement, so the advocates of the governmental view averred, is that Christ's saving work be a *suitable equivalent* (*solutio tantidem*) to the disvalue of human sin. In other words, Christ's atonement is of suitably equivalent moral value sufficient such that God may use it as a penal example of what would happen to sinners if they were punished for their sins. Consider an example of this. Suppose that Jack owes Jane a sum of money—say, a thousand dollars. Jane may require the exact sum from Jack in payment. That would be payment of an exact equivalent to the amount of money he borrowed from her. Alternatively, Jane may allow Jack to pay her something in kind, that is, some alternative to the exact amount he owes. This kind payment may not be an exact equivalent to the monetary amount Jack owes Jane. But Jane may be willing to treat it as a suitable equivalent to the exact amount owed. Perhaps Jane suggests Jack provides her with one of his portrait paintings instead of the money. This would be a suitable equivalent that would settle the debt between them despite the fact that the value of the painting is not strictly equivalent to the financial debt owed. Something like this sort of arrangement is envisaged in the case of the value of Christ's atoning work according to the defenders of the governmental view, at least in part in order to rebut the worry about the value of Christ's work raised by the Socinians.

OBJECTIONS TO THE GOVERNMENTAL DOCTRINE OF ATONEMENT

Although the governmental doctrine of atonement offers a sophisticated account of the reconciling work of Christ that does not suffer from some of the perceived shortcomings of penal substitution, it is not without difficulties. Here are three of the more serious concerns.

First, on the face of it, the governmental view appears to make atonement superfluous as a mechanism of salvation. For, on this way of thinking, Christ's work is not to bring about the reconciliation of fallen human beings. Rather, it is about him acting as an example of what God would have had to do to human beings without Christ's intervention.

An example will make this clearer. Imagine a teacher coming into a classroom and finding that some prankster has drawn a cartoon of her on the board with some rude caption written underneath. The teacher wants to know who has done this and will punish the wrongdoer. But no one owns up to drawing the cartoon. So she picks the best-behaved child in the class (and the person least likely to have done the drawing) and ensures he receives the harsh treatment that would be meted out to the guilty party. The teacher does this to provide an example to the class. "Let this be a lesson to you!" she says. "I will not permit students to flout school rules in this way by making a mockery of me." The intention is to deter similar insubordinate behavior in future. Although the student receiving the harsh treatment is not the perpetrator (let us suppose), he stands in for the perpetrator, taking the penalty instead.

Now, whatever else we think about this classroom example, it is clear that the well-behaved pupil suffering the harsh treatment that should have been meted out to the one guilty of drawing the cartoon is not in any way taking punishment upon himself. Nor is he providing some action that atones for the one guilty of having drawn the cartoon on the board. This would be the case even if the pupil volunteered to take the harsh treatment, and happily accepted the harsh treatment on behalf of the one who was guilty of drawing the cartoon. The action of standing in for the guilty student and receiving the harsh treatment that the guilty student should receive does no work in atoning for that action. It does no work in reconciling the guilty student with the teacher. And it does no work in removing the culpability of the pupil who has done the drawing on the board. In other words, the example made of the innocent student cannot be an atonement because it is not the right sort of action; it does not provide an appropriate mechanism for bringing about reconciliation. The reason for this is twofold: the well-behaved student is not the one guilty of having drawn the cartoon in the first place, so he cannot be an appropriate subject of atonement; and the harsh treatment he receives is not appropriately connected to the guilty party or the teacher in order to bring about reconciliation.

This raises a broader concern about conceiving of the atonement principally in the language of deterrence. One of the shortcomings of deterrence accounts of punishment is that they do not require there to be a connection between the crime or sin committed and the penalty meted out. On the deterrence view it is possible for an innocent person to suffer the harsh treatment that is due to the criminal provided it has the appropriate effect on the broader population, which is to deter them from the prohibited action. For deterrence is primarily concerned with the consequences of punishment. But then, it is possible for an innocent person to receive the harsh treatment in question (like our example of the well-behaved pupil in the classroom) since whether the person receiving the harsh treatment is the one guilty of the crime is not necessarily salient for the purposes of deterring others. Yet, far from being a reason for commending deterrence as a way of thinking about punishment, this seems monstrous—a miscarriage of justice. Yet just such an arrangement is in view in the example of the well-behaved student in the classroom, as well as in the case of Christ's work according to the governmental understanding of the atonement.

Second, and closely related to this first point, the governmental view means that an innocent (i.e., Christ) is treated harshly instead of the guilty (i.e., fallen human beings). But that seems unjust and for similar reasons to those we encountered when dealing with penal substitution in the previous chapter. There we saw that an innocent person cannot be punished because an innocent person is not culpable or blameworthy for the crime or sin committed. The innocent person does not have the relevant relation to guilt. Indeed, that is what it means for a person to be innocent of a crime that has been committed. Although the governmental view denies that Christ is punished for human sin, it still has an innocent person suffering the harsh treatment that should be meted out to the guilty, and that, on the face of it, seems to be a travesty of justice.

Third, and arising from consideration of the two previous worries, we may wonder whether the governmental account of atonement is really a doctrine of *atonement* at all. For if Christ is merely a penal example to fallen human beings then it appears that Christ's work does not atone for anyone, strictly speaking. In response to this worry, defenders of the governmental view could claim that Christ's work makes it possible for God to forgive human sin, so it does bring about reconciliation with God. This is true even if it is not the means by which reconciliation is made, strictly speaking, but rather the means by which an obstacle to God forgiving fallen human beings is removed. That much seems right. Nevertheless, it is still true that on this way of thinking Christ's work is not the actual means of reconciling us to God. And that is the concern here: the work of Christ is not a work of reconciliation on the governmental view. Rather, it is a means of removing an obstacle to reconciliation. It is the difference between two people communicating by means of a telephone (the telephone being the *medium* by means of which they communicate), and two partially deaf people switching on their hearing aids so that they can hear another person. In the first case, the telephone, like the atonement, is the mechanism by means of which the two persons are able to communicate with each other. In the second case the non-functional hearing aid needs to be switched on in order to remove an obstacle to effective communication. Clearly, removing an obstacle to reconciliation obtaining is not the same as providing the means by which reconciliation takes place. It appears that the governmental view only does the former, not the latter. But traditionally, the atonement is about reconciling fallen human beings with God, not merely removing an obstacle to such reconciliation. It does *include* removing an obstacle, namely, sin. But it is not *merely* the removing of an obstacle, but *in addition to this*, the action by means of which reconciliation takes place.

These represent some of the most serious shortcomings of traditional governmental views of the atonement. However, it should be pointed out that some of the most sophisticated defenders of this view (such as the nineteenth century American Methodist theologian, John Miley) do attempt to address most of these concerns. It may be that a sophisticated version of the view is able to rebut all or almost all these concerns. If that is the case, then the governmental view does represent an important alternative to penal substitution and one that may have more merit than it has been given in recent discussion of atonement.

THE VICARIOUS PENITENCE DOCTRINE OF ATONEMENT

The biblical basis for the vicarious penitence view is focused on the penitential aspect of Christ's high priesthood outlined in Hebrews 5:1-10. There we read the following:

During the days of Jesus' life on earth, he offered up prayers and petitions with fervent cries and tears to the one who could save him from death, and he was heard because of his reverent submission. Son though he was, he learned obedience from what he suffered and, once made perfect, he became the source of eternal salvation for all who obey him and was designated by God to be high priest in the order of Melchizedek. (Heb 5:7-10)

John McLeod Campbell took up these remarks about the penitential aspect of Christ's reconciling work in his own research. Writing as a minister in the context of the Scottish Presbyterian Calvinism of the nineteenth century, where many parishioners were unsure whether they were among God's elect, he sought to offer a better basis for assurance to his congregants—one rooted in a rather different account of atonement. On his diagnosis, the source of the problem with Victorian Scottish theology lay in the high Reformed Orthodox doctrine of God that Scots theologians had imbibed from the works of Puritan luminaries like Jonathan Edwards and John Owen. Their doctrine of a God who arbitrarily decrees the election of some and damnation of others he found abhorrent, along with their emphasis upon divine wrath in judgment for sin. For it reduced atonement to the purchase of forgiveness via the exercise of retribution in punishing Christ in place of the elect so that they may be saved. Campbell's doctrine of atonement sought to present a gentler face to God. For, as Campbell put it, "the Atonement . . . presumes there is forgiveness in God."[3] Yet, paradoxically (as we mentioned in the introduction to this chapter), he found the inspiration for his account in some remarks by Edwards on the nature of atonement. Edwards observed,

> It is requisite that God should punish all sin with infinite punishment; because all sin, as it is against God, is infinitely heinous, and has infinite demerit, is justly infinitely hateful to him, and so stirs up infinite abhorrence and indignation in him. Therefore, by what was before granted, it is requisite that God should punish it, unless there be something in some measure to balance this desert; either some answerable repentance and sorrow for it, or some other compensation.[4]

No *mere* human being could offer the requisite "answerable repentance and sorrow" for sin, thought Edwards. But perhaps one who is fully but not merely

---

[3]John McLeod Campbell, *The Nature of the Atonement*, 6th ed. (1856; repr., London: Macmillan, 1895), 17.
[4]Jonathan Edwards, "Miscellaneous Remarks on Satisfaction for Sin," 565.

human might be able to do this—one who is both God and human. It was this insight that stimulated Campbell's reflections on vicarious penitence.

In contrast (as he saw it) to Edward and Owen, Campbell placed God's love at the center of his doctrine. On his way of thinking, the reconciling work of Christ comprises his incarnate life of obedience to the will of the Father, including his public ministry and teaching, which culminates in his action of penitence on the cross. All of this expresses God's condescension towards us. Christ's life and death are, in a sense, one whole act of repentance and apology on behalf of fallen humanity, by means of which Christ is able to offer up the requisite "penitence and sorrow" that Edwards had speculated only the God-man could perform adequately on behalf of sinners. It is a bold theologian who characterizes even the cross of Christ as essentially a penitential act. Yet that was Campbell's conclusion: Christ does act vicariously on our behalf; he is a substitute standing in our place. That much the high Reformed theologians of his own tradition had gotten right. But the kind of substitutionary act that Christ performs is not what Edwards and Owen and their ilk had thought it was. Rather than being an act that atones for human sin by absorbing the wrath of God in being punished in place of human sinners (as with many versions of penal substitution), Christ's death is the culmination of a life of vicarious penitence—one long act of apology, if you will, that is offered as reparation on behalf of fallen humanity.

According to Campbell, this act of atonement has a backward-looking or retrospective aspect and a forward-looking or prospective aspect. The backward-looking aspect has to do with deliverance from sin, which is what Christ's reconciling work achieves. The forward-looking aspect has to do with the good things Christ's work brings to the sinner, especially reconciliation with God and the renewing work of the Holy Spirit. The deliverance from sin that constitutes the backward-looking component of Christ's work has two aspects, on Campbell's way of thinking: there is the way in which Christ deals with fallen human beings on behalf of God, and then there is the way in which Christ deals with God on behalf of fallen human beings. He is a kind of interface between God and humanity in this respect. In a memorable passage explaining the heart of his view, Campbell writes, "That oneness of mind with the Father, which towards men took the form of condemnation of sin, would in the Son's dealing with the Father in relation to our sins, take the form of a perfect confession of our sins. This confession, as to its own nature, must have been *a perfect Amen in humanity to the judgement of God on the sin of man*."[5] In a later passage he goes on to say this:

> That response [i.e., Christ's] has all the elements of a perfect repentance in humanity for all of the sin of man,—a perfect sorrow—a perfect contrition—all the elements of such a repentance, and that in absolute perfection, all—excepting the personal consciousness of sin;—and by that perfect response in Amen to the mind of God in relation to sin is the wrath of God rightly met, and that is accorded to divine justice which is its due, and could alone satisfy it.[6]

The idea is this: Christ takes upon himself the task of offering a perfect penitential act on behalf of estranged humanity. We are incapable of such an act because we are sinful; but he is without sin, and can therefore act on our behalf. The perfect life, ministry, and death of Christ constitute this act of penitence. It involves confession on our behalf, and a perfect sorrow and contrition for human sin. This Christ does for us, and God accepts this vicarious penitence on behalf of sinful humanity, in place of the penitence and confession we are incapable of making. In accepting this substitutionary penitence on our behalf, God is able to release us from the debt we owe. He treats Christ's confession and penitence as if it were our penitence, and he ascribes it to us in order that he may be merciful to us instead.

OBJECTIONS TO THE VICARIOUS PENITENCE DOCTRINE OF ATONEMENT

We come to objections to the vicarious penitence doctrine of atonement. Let us consider three. The first we have already touched upon in connection with the governmental view. It is this: How can a guiltless Christ offer vicarious penitence? It would seem that a penitential act requires the person performing it to be in need of penitence. But Christ is not in need of penitence; he has nothing to apologize for or repent of, because he is without sin (Heb 4:15) being God the Son incarnate. He cannot say to God, "I am the guilty party; I am the one worthy of punishment for my sin. May this act of penitence suffice to atone for my sinfulness." For he cannot own our guilt.

---

[5]Campbell, *The Nature of the Atonement*, 116-17, emphasis original.
[6]Campbell, *The Nature of the Atonement*, 117-18.

Although we do apologize on behalf of others (for example, our own naughty children) in such circumstances we do not take on the guilt of our misbehaving offspring. The apology offered is a kind of convention, a feature of human social interaction that is meant to excuse the behavior of one who is not fully responsible for their own actions. There are other more serious instances of public apology on behalf of others, however. Sometimes government representatives offer apologies for wrongs done by previous generations (such as wartime atrocities). Perhaps the defender of non-penal substitution can claim that such conventions provide some plausibility for the claim that Christ does something analogous in the atonement. Then, God treats Christ as an appropriate representative of fallen humanity rather like the government representative stands in for the whole government when making the apology for atrocities in the past. Admittedly, this way of thinking trades on a kind of legal or moral fiction, as does penal substitution. God treats Christ "as if" he is guilty; he treats us "as if" we are acting in Christ; and so on. But there appear to be mundane analogs to this, and we have something similar in legal cases of fictional imputation—such as treating the assets of a company for the purposes of prosecution as one corporate body, though the buildings, bank accounts, vehicles, and sundry other effects of the company are not *really* one entity. Perhaps the defender of non-penal substitution can appeal to this sort of legal precedent as a reason for thinking God may endorse this kind of arrangement after all.

A second objection concerns the necessity of the atonement on the vicarious penitence view. On the face of it, it seems like the vicarious penitence view denies that the cross is necessary for the atonement. If what is non-negotiable, as far as the reconciliation of human beings with God is concerned, is that Christ offers up some "answerable repentance and sorrow" for the heinousness of human sin (as Edwards maintained he could), then why does this have to include Christ's death? And in any case, isn't it rather odd to think of a person's death as a penitential act on behalf of someone else? But suppose that what is required in order for Christ's vicarious act of penitence to be effectual is that he offer up a perfect confession at each stage of human existence, culminating in a final act of penitence in a death freely offered instead of the death that fallen human beings would have to endure without his atonement. Perhaps, as the writer to the Hebrews puts it, Christ "learned obedience from what he suffered and, once made perfect . . . became the source of eternal salvation for all who obey him" (Heb 5:8-9). Perhaps that suffering culminated in the cross in order that he might offer reparation for human sin. The Christian philosopher Richard Swinburne characterizes atonement as including four elements: repentance, apology, reparation, and penance.[7] If we were to finesse Campbell's account with elements borrowed from Swinburne, we might say that Christ's life is a perfect act of repentance and apology offered as reparation to God. But, as Swinburne sees it, in cases of serious sin we need to perform some act of penance, that is, an act that demonstrates we are serious about making amends and seeking restitution. Perhaps the defender of a Campbell-like doctrine could think of Christ's work on the cross in this fashion: as an act of restitution, making amends between God and humanity, the culminating act in his lifelong vicarious penitence on behalf of fallen humanity.

A third objection to Campbell's doctrine is this: Can vicarious penitence atone for sin? Here we should distinguish between *the nature of the atoning act,* and *the nature of what is atoned for* by the act in question. We have seen that according to Campbell's doctrine, Christ's atoning act is substitutionary, but not penal in nature. That is, it is not primarily aimed at dealing with the legal or forensic consequences of human sin—the punishment that ought to be meted out for human sin and the fit between the sin of human beings and the punishment they must endure as a consequence. Instead, Christ's atonement is penitential. So at the outset, one must be willing to allow a broader range of actions to "count" as atonement than defenders of a traditional penal substitutionary or satisfaction view might permit. For they want atonement to be about retributive justice, whereas Campbell's account appears to be aimed more at reparation. That is, it is more about making amends in some other way than by punishment or the suffering of the penal consequences that would be punishment if it were visited upon guilty fallen human beings. So we might say that the nature of the atoning act according to Campbell is penitential not penal, and reparative rather than retributive in nature. Nevertheless, it is human sin that is atoned for by Christ. His vicarious penitence makes it possible for fallen human beings to be reconciled to Godself, and that penitence culminates in his death on the cross.

---

[7]Richard Swinburne, *Responsibility and Atonement* (Oxford: Oxford University Press, 1989).

ASSESSING THE GOVERNMENTAL AND VICARIOUS PENITENCE DOCTRINES

The governmental and vicarious penitence doctrines of atonement represent creative ways in which theologians in the Arminian and Reformed streams of Protestant thought sought to meet various objections to versions of vicarious substitution doctrine, especially that of the Reformation doctrine of penal substitution. Each view has its merits, and does manage to work around some of the most intractable problems of penal substitution doctrines, many of which are still worries raised in contemporary accounts of atonement. Nevertheless, as we have seen, there are various costs associated with each of these approaches to the atonement. Today neither of these views has many defenders, although there are some theologians influenced by Scottish Torrancean theology, or by the work of other theologians sympathetic to Campbell's account, like P. T. Forsyth, for whom Campbell's doctrine has merit. But even if one does not adopt one of either non-penal substitution or penal non-substitution wholesale, there are ways in which elements of these two accounts of the atonement may yet be taken up and refurbished in newer ways of thinking about Christ's reconciling work that find their alternative mechanisms of atonement conducive to theological construction today.

FURTHER READING

Campbell, John McLeod. *The Nature of the Atonement*. 1856. Reprint, Grand Rapids: Eerdmans, 1996.

Crisp, Oliver D. "John McLeod Campbell and Non-penal Substitution." In Oliver D. Crisp, *Retrieving Doctrine: Essays in Reformed Theology*, 92-115. Downers Grove, IL: IVP Academic, 2011.

———. "Penal Non-substitution." In *A Reader in Philosophical Theology*, ed. Oliver Crisp, 299-327. London: T&T Clark, 2009.

Edwards, Jonathan. *The Works of Jonathan Edwards, Vol. II*. Edited by Edward Hickman. 1834. Reprint, Edinburgh: Banner of Truth, 1974.

Grotius, Hugo. *A Defense of the Catholic Faith Concerning the Satisfaction of Christ Against Fausus Socinus*. Translated by Frank Hugh Foster. 1617. Reprint, Andover: Warren F. Draper, 1889.

Miley, John. *The Atonement in Christ*. New York: Philips and Hunt, 1879.

Mozley, J. K. *The Doctrine of the Atonement.* New York: Charles Scribner's Sons, 1916.

Purves, Andrew. *Exploring Christology and Atonement: Conversations with John McLeod Campbell, H. R. Mackintosh and T. F. Torrance.* Downers Grove, IL: IVP Academic, 2015.

THE PROBLEM OF
ATONING VIOLENCE

In a number of previous chapters, we have mentioned the problem of atoning violence, even discussing aspects of it, such as the issue of "divine child abuse," in chapter six. Yet it is only now that we tackle the problem head on. Why wait until the eighth chapter in order to do so? The reason is that it is important to see what the problem amounts to, and in order to do that, we needed to give some account of the traditional ways of thinking about the atonement that have informed the literature on the problem of atoning violence before tackling the problem itself. It is like saying we need to know something about the reasons that inform the doctor's diagnosis of a disease before embarking on a course of treatment to combat the causes of the disease in the patient's body. We are now in possession of some of the main reasons why many contemporary theologians of various different stripes such as some feminist thinkers, liberation theologians, and Mennonite theologians, have taken issue with traditional atonement doctrine, focusing on the valorization of violence that these different models and motifs seem to entail. So we are now better prepared to tackle the problem of atoning violence in earnest.

Well then, what is the problem of atoning violence? At its most general, it is the idea that violent acts are morally objectionable, so that bringing about reconciliation or atonement through violent means is morally unsustainable. As we have seen in previous chapters, many defenders of traditional atonement theology maintain that God brings about human reconciliation with Godself by means of (what appears to be) atoning violence. In which case, it looks like God acts in an immoral manner in bringing about human reconciliation with Godself via atoning violence. But surely God cannot act in an immoral manner. Hence, the Deity would not use atoning violence in bringing about human reconciliation with Godself. If we were to sum up the problem in a principle, we could put it like this: *Violence cannot bring about atonement.* To think otherwise, so critics of atoning violence aver, is to conflate two incommensurate things, namely, atonement, which is an act of divine reconciliation, with violence, which involves actions that are intended to harm rather than heal. The result of such conflation is a kind of theological oxymoron, like an "open secret" or, "the living dead."

In this chapter, we will consider what I take to be the most serious version of the problem of atoning violence for doctrines of atonement. We will see that there are, in fact, several different aspects to the problem that will need to be teased out as we go. To begin, we will consider a common attempt to turn back the problem, which is, in fact, an insufficient response. This is the rhetorical flourish response that claims the crucifixion is inherently violent, so that the attempt to remove language of violence from the Christian doctrine of atonement is itself a kind of violence, because it entails removing something integral to Christian doctrine. Although this is not a sufficient response to the problem of atoning violence, it does raise a real problem having to do with the character of God. For how can God be involved in acts of violence? This leads us in a second section to consider three further responses to the problem of atoning violence. The first is really a recap of the "divine child abuse" material we covered in chapter six. Then, we will consider two further options. These are the redemptive violence response and the double effect response. Although the redemptive violence response raises some important issues about the nature of what counts as violence, it also confuses matters and is ultimately not a successful response to the problem. However, the double effect response may succeed where the redemptive violence response fails. Borrowing the notion of the doctrine of double effect from medical ethics, it distinguishes between God's intention in atonement, and his bringing about of violence as a means to that end. We conclude the chapter with a summation of our findings.

It may seem odd to have a whole chapter devoted to the consideration of one sort of objection to traditional atonement theology. Why single out this particular concern amongst others? The reason is twofold. First, recent criticisms of atoning violence have raised serious problems for atonement theology that need to be addressed. Second, and relatedly, these concerns have shaped contemporary atonement theology in important respects. It is no longer possible to ignore or avoid discussing them when presenting a case for atonement. With this in mind, let us begin by setting out some of the versions of the problem of atoning violence.

THE RHETORICAL FLOURISH RESPONSE TO THE PROBLEM OF ATONING VIOLENCE

To begin with, we need to motivate the concern. To put it another way, why would we be worried about the claim that the atonement is inherently violent (if it is inherently violent)? What is at stake here, theologically speaking? It is tempting to dismiss worries about violence and the atonement with a kind of rhetorical flourish. This sort of response can be found in certain more theologically conservative writers today, and we have already encountered this sort of response when considering penal substitution and, to some extent, satisfaction, in previous chapters. The *rhetorical flourish response* (for so we might call it) goes something like this:

> Crucifixion is an inherently violent act. If the crucifixion of Christ is at the heart of the doctrine of atonement, as a central plank of the way in which Christ's work reconciles us to Godself, then it appears that a central component of God's action in saving fallen human beings involves, or includes, an act of violence. Consequently, any claim that the atonement cannot and must not be an act of violence fails to get off the ground, theologically speaking. For that is not so much an objection against one way of thinking about the atonement as it is an objection to something fundamental to the message of Christianity, namely, that at least a part of the theological meaning of Christ's reconciling work has to do with him dying the terrible death of crucifixion—a ghastly, and torturous way to die, to be sure, but a death requisite for our salvation. In short, remove violence from the atonement, and you effectively remove the atonement from Christian doctrine.[1]

In previous chapters we noted that this sort of attempted rebuttal to the objection against atoning violence is often used in the context of defending doctrines of atonement like satisfaction or penal substitution. The reason is not hard to find. Both these accounts of atonement have at their core ways of

---

[1]It is worth bearing in mind that there does appear to be some biblical support for the notion of atoning violence. See, for example, the comment of the author of Hebrews, who writes that "without the shedding of blood there is no forgiveness" (Heb 9:22).

thinking about the atonement that imply some act of violence. So defending atoning violence, for those who advocate satisfaction and penal substitution doctrines, is just one way of shoring up satisfaction or penal substitution. Similar things could be said, the relevant changes having been made, with respect to traditional ransom views of atonement, the logic of which also appears to require some sort of atoning violence. This is not lost on critics of atoning violence, many of whom take aim at all three of these ways of thinking about the atonement precisely because they appear to require some act of violence in order to make sense.

It might be thought that other models of Christ's reconciling work do not necessarily *require* some act of violence at their core, and so might escape the problem of atoning violence. For instance, the claim that Christ's work is a moral example to us does not necessarily include a justification of his violent death as a requirement for such atonement. It may just be that Christ's death is a consequence of his moral example, rather than a constituent of atonement. This makes a significant difference to what we say about the *nature* of the atoning act, of course, and especially whether it is an act that is, in essence, an act of reconciliation. However, the moral example view of atonement is also subject to criticism with respect to atoning violence, especially from feminist theologians. For it presumes that Christ must be an innocent suffering victim in order for us to be confronted with our own moral failings and moved to change our behavior.[2] So it seems that many of the major historic accounts of atonement are bound up with this worry about atoning violence, even where the view in question may not, on the face of it, appear to be liable to this sort of objection.

Well, then, does the rhetorical flourish response to the problem of atoning violence really address the worry of those authors who have raised the problem in the first place? It does not. It sounds rather impressive when one first encounters it, but a few moments of reflection are sufficient to see that it is, in fact, insufficient. Here is why. Assume, for the sake of argument, that defenders of penal substitution or satisfaction (or, perhaps, some other traditional atonement doctrine) who deploy versions of the rhetorical flourish response

---

[2]A point made very clearly by Joanne Carlson Brown and Rebecca Parker in their classic essay, "For God So Loved the World?" in *Christianity, Patriarchy, and Abuse: A Feminist Critique*, ed. Joanne Carlson Brown and Carole R. Bohn (New York: The Pilgrim Press, 1989).

are right when they say that the crucifixion, a central plank of traditional doctrines of atonement, is an inherently violent act. (It certainly seems that crucifixion is usually a violent act.) Also assume that removing the crucifixion from the Christian doctrine of atonement is tantamount to destroying the very doctrine of atonement itself. What follows from this for the problem of atoning violence? The answer is, nothing at all. It merely begs the question at issue.

Question begging (or to give it its Latin name, *petitio principi*) is a kind of informal fallacy of reasoning where (so it is often said) one person assumes the point at issue is true in responding to her interlocutor. That is approximately right. Put more precisely, it is a fallacy of reasoning where one person includes as a premise in her argument the conclusion at which she is aiming. If the conclusion is the point at issue between the two parties, then the person making the fallacious argument is begging the question at issue between herself and her interlocutor. A common example of this in Christian theological circles is where there is a disagreement about whether the Bible is divinely inspired. If, in response to the question of whether the Bible is divinely inspired Jones says, "Yes, the Bible is divinely inspired because it is written by God," then she is begging the question at issue because she has included as a premise in her reasoning the very point in dispute; that is, whether the Bible is, in fact, divinely inspired. Since the point at issue is *whether* God authored the Bible, claiming the Bible *just is* divinely inspired because God is the author is question-begging.

Apply this reasoning to the rhetorical flourish response. The point at issue is *whether* the atonement is, or must be, inherently violent. Claiming that crucifixion *just is* inherently violent, and that denying the inherent violence of the cross is tantamount to denying a central tenet of Christian doctrine makes two different, though related, mistakes. The first is that it begs the question at issue—for the issue has to do with whether, in fact, the atonement must be inherently violent or not. It is not obvious that the atonement must be inherently violent. Asserting that it just is inherently violent and that such inherent violence is somehow woven into the fabric of the Christian doctrine of atonement is question-begging on a grand scale.

In addition to this, there is a second and closely related problem with the rhetorical flourish response. This is that it conflates the crucifixion with atonement through a subtle sleight of hand. Crucifixion does normally require some act of violence to occur, for nailing someone to a cross normally involves the intention to harm that individual.[3] Yet if the atonement is fundamentally about divine reconciliation with fallen human beings, no harm is intended by it. In fact, quite the opposite is the case. God intends to reconcile us to Godself via the atonement. Even if crucifixion is one central plank of the means of atonement as the advocate of the rhetorical flourish response presumes, some explanation is surely required of how an act that involves violence can also be a component of a larger divine work that precludes violence—an act of divine reconciliation. Rather than address that question, the rhetorical flourish objector conflates crucifixion with atonement in order to place the burden of proof on the critic of atoning violence. But that will not do.

For these reasons, we shall set the rhetorical flourish response to one side as an inadequate and confused response to the problem of atoning violence. Even though it is inadequate, the rhetorical flourish response does indicate a deeper moral issue that we need to consider before attempting a more adequate response to the problem of atoning violence. This is not to do with particular mechanisms for atonement, or even whether the nature of the atonement *must* include some act of violence. Rather, it has to do with the fact that some traditional ways of conceiving the atonement seems to implicate *God* in violence—making of the Deity an abusive, violent being. Joanne Carlson Brown and Rebecca Parker put it bluntly when they write, "Christianity is an abusive theology that glorifies suffering." They go on, "Is it any wonder that there is so much abuse in modern society when the predominant image or theology of the culture is of 'divine child abuse'—God the Father demanding and carrying out the suffering and death of his own son? If Christianity is to be liberating for the oppressed, it must be liberated from this theology." This liberation involves "doing away with the atonement," as they put it.[4] If anything, this is more troubling than the concern about the relationship between atoning violence and traditional atonement models, because it strikes at the very character of God. Does atoning violence implicate God in a way that is morally compromising? Let us examine these issues in

---

[3]Barring things like sadomasochistic acts of crucifixion, or performance art, or acts of penitential mortification that involve crucifixion, which are an annual practice during Easter celebrations in the Philippines in folk Roman Catholicism.

[4]Brown and Parker, "For God So Loved the World?," 26.

more detail. In doing so we will need to ensure that an adequate response to the problem of atoning violence deals with both the fact that the crucifixion of Christ is violent, and yet that atonement is about reconciliation, on the one hand, as well as with the deeper issue of God's involvement in atoning violence on the other hand. A proposed solution that only tackles one of these issues is not an adequate response to the problem.

THREE FURTHER RESPONSES TO THE PROBLEM OF ATONING VIOLENCE

"Divine child abuse" once more. First, a brief recap. As has already been mentioned at the beginning of this chapter, in chapter six we dealt with the question of "divine child abuse," which is one particular version of the problem of atoning violence (one that Brown and Parker mention in their remarks quoted above). We noted in chapter six that the problem of divine "child abuse" is not, in fact, a very deep theological problem for defenders of traditional doctrines of the atonement. Like a superficial cut to the skin that can initially bleed a lot, but that causes no lasting damage, this objection seems at first glance to be deeper and more significant than it is. For it is predicated on a non-Trinitarian understanding of the divine nature and purposes of God. The divine persons of the one Godhead compact together to bring about human salvation by means of their own reconciling work, with the Son voluntarily taking upon himself the punishment, or at least the penal consequences, for human sin. Although this is a work of the entire Trinity—for it is a traditional theological claim that the divine work in creation is always a work of the whole Godhead—the incarnation terminates upon the Son in a particular way. After all, he is the divine person that becomes incarnate. Nevertheless, this is clearly not a case of "divine child abuse"—not even analogously. Nor is it the action of one divine agent against another, for Christianity is inherently monotheistic so that it is metaphysically impossible for the divine persons to be at loggerheads because they are the same divine being, sharing in the same essence.

Even so, dismissing the mistaken view of "divine child abuse" in certain accounts of the atonement, such as penal substitution, does not turn back the deeper issues that the problem of atoning violence raises. In particular, it does not adequately address the issue of the implications for the character of God, which I take to be the most troubling (and most fundamental) aspect of the problem of atoning violence. So we must turn to alternatives. One option involves questioning the assumption that violence must always be morally dubious. Isn't there a place in a properly Christian theology for a notion of *redemptive violence*?

The redemptive violence view. Consider a closely related parallel: *pain*. We usually want to minimize pain, eliminating it where that is possible. We often speak about the problem of pain—C. S. Lewis even wrote a popular book with that title, which was really to do with the problem of evil in some of its familiar guises. But pain is not always a bad thing, and if we lived in a world without any pain at all, it would not be a paradise, but a place of potentially considerable suffering.

For instance, we feel pain when we touch a hot surface like a saucepan heating water on the stovetop. Our instinctive, immediate reaction is to pull our hand away from the source of the pain. This pain reaction causes us discomfort, which can be significant especially if it is associated with a burn or scald. But without pain receptors that alert the brain to the fact that your hand is being burned or scalded by the hot pan you are touching, your body would not react as it did, and you may suffer greater physical privations as a consequence. This is exactly what happens to those who suffer from serious medical conditions like leprosy, which, amongst other things, involves damage to nerve tissue that generate the pain signals relayed to your brain when touching very hot objects like a saucepan heating on the stovetop. As a consequence of this condition, those who suffer from leprosy can often end up causing themselves significant harm because their bodies do not have the same pain reaction that people without leprosy do. Serious nerve damage means that those with leprosy do not quickly or instinctively remove their limbs from harm's way as a result, and suffer the consequences, which can be very severe indeed. So it seems that pain, though something we usually avoid, is not necessarily an evil all things considered. It is, in one important physiological sense, an important way in which your body is able to avoid serious damage, which is an important good that enables you to survive and flourish.

Now, it could be thought that *some* violence is like that. In other words, it could be thought that some violence is a good thing rather than a bad thing, something redemptive rather than destructive, so to speak. Let us call this response to the problem of atoning violence, the *redemptive violence view*.[5] On this way of thinking, the violence involved in hitting someone in anger may be morally reprehensible, but physically restraining someone in order to prevent them from walking into the path of an oncoming vehicle may be both violent, and yet virtuous. Violence does not end with physical actions either. There can be mental actions that are violent. Consider the case of someone who seeks to break another person down psychologically in inter-rogation, or through torture. There may be spiritual acts of violence as well. Think of the Old Testament prophet Balaam being instructed by King Balak to curse the people of Israel (Num 22). A curse would seem to be a good candidate for an act of spiritual violence—calling upon some spiritual higher power in order to cause harm to another—yet in some cases such violence is sanctioned by God as a way of placing limits upon the actions of his people. For example, the way in which Joshua affirms that God will curse those who will not uphold the substance of the covenant relationship he maintains with Israel (Josh 24:19-20), or the way Christ curses the fig tree that does not bear fruit (Mk 11:12-25), or even the way in which Paul curses those who preach another gospel than the one he committed to the Galatian church (Gal 1:8).

The defender of the redemptive violence view maintains that violence is not necessarily physical, and not necessarily always morally reprehensible. There may even be circumstances in which violence is a good thing. But, at the very least, violence can be co-opted by God in order to be redemptive. However, although there are aspects of this response that are helpful, such as the claim that violence need not be merely physical, it seems to me to depend upon a mistaken account of the nature of violence.

Typically, certain actions are thought to be violent because of the *intention* of the person or persons committing the act in question. Thus, hitting someone in anger is usually thought to be morally reprehensible because such an action involves the intention to harm another person by means of physical force. The same is not true of, say, physically forcing someone out of the path of an oncoming vehicle. For in that case, the intention of the person

---

[5]This line of response is elaborated upon by Hans Boersma in his study, *Violence, Hospitality, and the Cross: Reappropriating the Atonement Tradition* (Grand Rapids: Baker Academic, 2004). It is a controversial notion, given that there are many contemporary theologians opposed to the very idea of redemptive violence.

performing the physically forceful action is to protect rather than to harm the other person. Both actions may appear at first glance to be tokens of a similar type of action that is violent in nature. After all, both involve quick and usually painful physical force directed against another person. But there is clearly a difference of intention in physically forceful actions like the two described here, even in cases where we cannot immediately distinguish a difference in the action itself. In the case of hitting another person in anger the intention is to harm, whereas in the case of saving another person from an oncoming vehicle, the intention is to save.

For this reason, it seems to me that it is a mistake to seek to address the problem of atoning violence by claiming that some actions may be both violent and yet not morally reprehensible, and even that some actions may be violent and virtuous, which is what the redemptive violence view implies. It would be even more troubling to apply this way of thinking to God's intention in the atonement, since it suggests that God has an intention to harm Christ in the atonement, even if it is for redemptive purposes. At the very least, such a view instrumentalizes violence, making it a morally permissible means to some greater good end, which is morally troubling when applied to the divine nature. (Does God use wicked means to some greater good? If he does, what does this say about the divine character—that God may use evil to bring about good?[6]) It is not hard to see how such thinking would raise worries about "divine child abuse" in the atonement even if the divine child abuse issue is misplaced for other theological reasons.

The double effect response. Instead of the redemptive violence response to the problem of atoning violence, I propose the following solution, which I can only sketch in outline here. Call it the *double effect response to atoning violence,* or just the double-effect response for short. Our working assumption throughout this book has been that God's intention in the atonement is to reconcile human beings to Godself. This, as I have already stated, is clearly an intention to heal, not to harm. So the divine motivation for atonement cannot be violent if, as I have argued, violence requires an intention to harm.

---

[6]It could be argued that this is just what God does in the case of Job, who suffers because God permits Satan to test him. But the interpretation of these events is not straightforward, and it is not obvious that God is instrumentalizing Job's suffering for some greater good. Compare the apostle Paul's comments in Rom 3:8 that doing evil that good may result is itself a slander against the message of the gospel.

However, in order to bring about this act of reconciliation, God ordains that Christ will be crucified as an act of atonement, or at least, as a central part or aspect of the act of atonement. He ordains the circumstances in which Christ is crucified, including the violence of the Roman soldiers who whip and abuse him, and eventually nail him to the cross. Yet, God does not *intend* the violence of the soldiers. He either foresees their violence and permits it to happen, knowing that they will act in the way that they do. Or, he ordains their violence although he does not intend the violence himself, because it is the violent act of the soldiers, and their intentions that inform their decision to crucify Christ. It is not God who intends that, although God ensures that they do intend that in order to bring about the crucifixion as an aspect of his work of atonement.

This solution to the problem of atoning violence is like the doctrine of double effect as it is often explained in textbooks on medical ethics. The typical example involves a surgeon who is faced with the decision to remove a cancerous mass from the womb of a patient knowing that the procedure to remove the mass will inevitably kill the fetus gestating there. The surgeon does not intend to kill the fetus. She intends to save the patient. Nevertheless, she knows that her action will have the foreseen and inevitable, though unintended, consequence of destroying the fetus. Thus her action in performing this surgical procedure has a double effect: one foreseen and intended, the other foreseen but not intended. Not unsurprisingly, this thought experiment generates important ethical quandaries that clinicians have to address on a regular basis in operating rooms. Hence its popularity as a stock example in medical ethics courses and textbooks.

My suggestion is that something similar obtains in the case of God's act in atonement, the relevant changes having been made. God intends to heal us from our fallen state through reconciliation in Christ. However, in order to bring about this state of affairs a number of related actions that involve violence must happen first. That is, in order to bring about reconciliation with fallen humans, God must first ensure the crucifixion of Christ takes place as one central means to that end. These additional violent acts that contribute to Christ's crucifixion are not intended by God, although they are either foreseen and expected by him, or foreseen and inevitable—depending on whether one thinks God ordains all that comes to pass, or merely foresees but does not determine certain free human actions, including the violent actions that bring about Christ's crucifixion.[7]

This solution also has the benefit of not implicating God in intending violence, which gets at the deeper problem that this raises for the divine character. God intends healing, but in order to bring that about violent human actions are required and foreseen though not intended by God. Moreover, this solution also goes some way towards clarifying how it is that God's action in atonement is of a different order than human action. God is not simply another actor in the great drama of human existence. He is the one who sovereignly brings about what comes to pass, yet without having to compromise his moral character in order to do so.

The double effect response is not without its problems, however. In fact, its greatest strength is also potentially its Achilles' heel, namely, the need to distinguish between what God intends and what God brings about. The double effect response depends upon being able to make this distinction so that God can intend a good outcome (the reconciliation of fallen human beings), but bring this about via some means that includes acts of violence committed by Roman soldiers, though he does not intend the acts of violence himself. Is this a distinction that makes sense? Perhaps. Much depends on what is made of the scope of divine power and knowledge. If one thinks that God foresees but does not determine free human actions then there may be wiggle room sufficient for the purpose. Things are more complicated if it is thought that God brings about all that comes to pass, as is the case in much Reformed theology. For then it looks like God is in some relevant sense causally responsible for human actions, including violent actions like the crucifixion of Christ. And if that is right, then it is difficult to see how God can be in some sense causally responsible for the violent actions of the Roman soldiers who crucified Christ without also being in some important sense morally responsible for their actions as well. After all, he creates and sustains the Roman soldiers and the world in which they nail Christ to the cross, even if God doesn't intend the violent acts they bring about.

---

[7]These are not supposed to be the only logically possible options, but two of the most popular in the literature on the relationship between God's foreknowledge and creaturely freedom. Those wishing to pursue this matter further should consult Linda Zagzebski's article "Foreknowledge and Free Will" in the *Stanford Encyclopedia of Philosophy* online, https://plato.stanford.edu/entries /free-will-foreknowledge.

But perhaps someone who thinks that God ordains all that comes to pass might think God can cause certain events and yet not intend those events as violent acts, although the human person intending them does intend them as violent acts. To see this, let us briefly return to the surgical example of the doctrine of double effect. The surgeon intends to help, not to harm the patient. Yet in order to do so, she must perform a medical procedure that will hurt the patient (the surgery), and, additionally, destroy the fetus. She does not intend to hurt the patient or destroy the fetus. Nevertheless, these are foreseen and inevitable outcomes. She cannot perform the procedure without hurting the patient by wounding her to remove the cancerous mass. And she cannot perform the procedure without destroying the fetus. What is more, we presume there is no alternative open to the surgeon that does not include these two undesirable outcomes as part of the overall act of restoring the patient to full health. Here there is intention to use physical force to bring about injury without the intention to commit violence. The surgeon intends to heal, not to harm. Could God intend something similar? In other words, could God intend to use physical force to bring about injury (to Christ) without also intending violence—without, that is, intending to harm Christ? Perhaps he could. It seems natural to want to deny that God intends to harm Christ. Yet he could bring about a state of affairs in which the Roman soldiers bring about injury to Christ in order to bring about human reconciliation, which is something that God does, indeed, intend. In this way, it might be that those enamored of the view that God ordains all that comes to pass may be able to distinguish between God's intentions and the intentions of those who act violently in crucifying Christ in such a way as to preserve the divine character and yet ensure that what God ordains—the death of Christ for human salvation—is effectually brought about.

I think there is promise in this line of response; however, it is not without difficulties. The problem is, it is not clear that in the case of the atonement God *has to* bring about human reconciliation by means of the violence of crucifixion. That is a matter that would need to be argued for, and I have not offered an argument for that conclusion here. In order to provide a complete account of the double effect response, some such reasoning would need to be forthcoming. There are resources in the tradition for making this claim, such as Anselm's influential idea, expressed in *Cur deus homo*, that God must punish sin either in the person of the sinner in hell, or in the person of some suitable substitute able to offer satisfaction instead. The defender of the double effect response could help him or herself to such reasoning in offering a complete account of the view. That may be one way of meeting this worry about why atonement is necessary in the first place, though there is not the space to pursue that in detail here.

In sum, there are different versions of the double effect response, depending on which view of the relation between divine foreknowledge and human freedom one takes (and I have only sketched two of the most popular responses to that question here). Does the double effect response deal with the two pressing aspects of the problem of atoning violence mentioned earlier at the end of the section on the rhetorical flourish response? There I said that an adequate response to the problem of atoning violence must deal with the fact that the crucifixion of Christ is violent, and yet that atonement is about reconciliation, on the one hand, as well as with the deeper issue of God's involvement in atoning violence on the other hand. Does the double effect response address both of these concerns? I think it does. Although it is not without problems, it does represent one theologically responsible way of tackling the problem of atoning violence that resonates with much in the Christian tradition as well.

CONCLUSION

We have covered a lot of ground in this chapter in order to address a pressing concern raised in recent atonement theology. It is time to take stock as we draw the different threads together. In this chapter we have given some account of the problem of atoning violence. We have seen that it is a problem with different aspects. We have also considered a number of different lines of response to the problem all of which take seriously the Christian tradition, including the biblical witness. The rhetorical flourish response is inadequate; it does not have the resources to address the worry about the divine character that this problem raises. The "divine child abuse" accusation, which we tackled in more detail in chapter six, is only a real theological problem if one denies the doctrine of the Trinity. Nevertheless, it does make clear the seriousness of the problem that atoning violence poses for the character of God. The redemptive violence response makes the mistake of conflating intention and action, so that God ends up coopting violence for his own ends. This is not sufficient to deal with the problem atoning violence poses for the divine character. If anything, it only makes that problem more acute. I have proposed as an alternative the double effect response that distinguishes intention and action, and suggests that God may bring about acts for good ends that include violence, though he does not intend that violence. God could use physical force to bring about injury (to Christ) without also intending violence—without, that is, intending to harm Christ.[8]

With this in place, we may turn in the last two chapters to recent developments in atonement theology. In chapter nine we will consider various ways in which theologians have begun to work on mashup and kaleidoscopic views of the atonement. Then, in the final chapter, I will set out my own constructive account of the atonement, which depends upon the Pauline idea of union with Christ and participation in the divine life.

FURTHER READING

Boersma, Hans. *Violence, Hospitality, and the Cross: Reappropriating the Atonement Tradition*. Grand Rapids: Baker Academic, 2004.

Brown, Joanne Carlson, and Carole R. Bohn, eds. *Christianity, Patriarchy, and Abuse: A Feminist Critique*. New York: The Pilgrim Press, 1989.

Jersak, Brad, and Michael Hardin, eds. *Stricken by God? Nonviolent Identification and the Victory of Christ*. Grand Rapids: Eerdmans, 2007.

Johnson, Adam. *Atonement: A Guide for the Perplexed*. London: T&T Clark, 2015.

Peacore, Linda. *The Role of Women's Experience in Feminist Theologies of Atonement*. Eugene, OR: Pickwick Publications, 2010.

Sanders, John, ed. *Atonement and Violence: A Theological Conversation*. Nashville: Abingdon Press, 2006.

Weaver, J. Denny. *The Nonviolent Atonement*. 2nd ed. Grand Rapids: Eerdmans, 2011.

Zagzebski, Linda. "Foreknowledge and Free Will." *Stanford Encyclopedia of Philosophy*. https://plato.stanford.edu/entries/free-will-foreknowledge.

---

[8]Recently, some Southern Baptist theologians have argued that God does intend to harm Christ in the atonement by punishing him, pouring out his wrath upon Christ. That seems to me to be deeply troubling, and suffers from the same problems as the cosmic divine child abuse objection, namely, it requires a defective doctrine of the Trinity in order to work. Since I think it is impossible for persons of the Trinity to act against one another or to intend to harm one another, this is not a view that can get off the ground, theologically speaking.

9

MASHUP AND KALEIDOSCOPIC
ACCOUNTS OF ATONEMENT

Thus far, we have seen that a number of different models of the atonement have developed over time in the Christian tradition, each of which offers a particular account of how Christ's work reconciles fallen human beings. But in recent years several contributions to the debate have attempted to argue that the different historic accounts of atonement may in fact represent different, and complementary, ways of thinking about the same thing. Thus, Hans Boersma writes "The various atonement theories are not mutually exclusive. It is quite possible to combine elements of the various theories into a coherent whole."[1] Other theologians working on the atonement have attempted to provide a theory about the different models of atonement, arguing that they represent partial and incomplete windows onto the reality of Christ's reconciling work that is greater than any one picture, metaphor, or model. The best, and most accessible example of this latter strategy is the study entitled *Recovering the Scandal of the Cross* by Mark Baker and Joel Green.[2]

In this chapter I want to explore these two ways of trying to provide a composite account of approaches to the atonement. The first view, exemplified by Boersma's comment, we shall call a composite or *mashup account* of the atonement. This is a neologism that is not currently in wide circulation

---

[1]Hans Boersma, *Violence, Hospitality, and the Cross: Reappropriating the Atonement Tradition* (Grand Rapids: Baker Academic, 2004), 115.

[2]Mark D. Baker and Joel B. Green, *Recovering the Scandal of the Cross: Atonement in New Testament and Contemporary Contexts,* 2nd ed. (Downers Grove, IL: IVP Academic, 2011). See also Joel B. Green's contribution to James K. Beilby and Paul R. Eddy, eds. *The Nature of the Atonement: Four Views* (Downers Grove, IL: IVP Academic, 2006), chapter 4.

in the atonement literature, but is a good description of the sort of work in view. I call this sort of approach to the atonement a mashup view because, like mashup novels or mashup music in contemporary culture, those who adopt such an approach take elements of different existing atonement accounts and mash them together into a new, amalgamated whole. Usually this whole privileges certain motifs or ideas above others, subordinating others in the process. But the basic idea is that of the mashup genre: bringing elements from other works together in a new whole composed of the parts cannibalized from elsewhere.

The second sort of approach like this one, exemplified by the work of Baker and Green, seems superficially similar to the mashup accounts of atonement. They call their approach *the kaleidoscopic view*. However, we shall see that on closer inspection this superficial likeness between the kaleidoscopic and mashup views belies some important differences. The most important of these is that kaleidoscopic accounts are not just a mashup of elements from existing atonement doctrines, but a way of thinking about the different historic atonement doctrines. We might say that the kaleidoscopic view of the atonement offers a theory about models of atonement. Defenders of this view are not offering yet another model or doctrine of atonement as such. Instead, the kaleidoscopic approach is a kind of metanarrative about atonement doctrines, that is, a story about how we should think of all the existing accounts of atonement.

To begin with, we shall set out the mashup and kaleidoscopic views, showing how they are similar and yet distinct. Then, in a second section, we will consider some of the problems with these two related approaches to the atonement. In a concluding section I shall offer some reflection on the contribution and significance of this recent turn towards what we might call third-order accounts of the atonement. By a "third-order account," I mean ways of thinking about the atonement that are principally concerned with reflection on existing models or doctrines of atonement that are themselves ways of understanding the biblical material, or about using the parts of other atonement accounts in order to provide some new way of thinking about the reconciling work of Christ as described in Scripture.

MASHUP AND KALEIDOSCOPIC
APPROACHES TO ATONEMENT

Let's start by getting a clearer picture of the two sorts of approaches to the atonement that are the subject of this chapter. We begin with mashup accounts before turning to consider the kaleidoscopic view.

Mashup accounts of the atonement. As I have already indicated, mashup accounts of the atonement cannibalize elements of existing atonement doctrines, reforming them into a new composite whole. Sometimes, the result may be more like a Frankenstein's monster than a particularly appealing account of the reconciling work of Christ. But in the recent atonement literature there have been several sophisticated attempts to provide what I am calling mashup accounts that bear closer scrutiny. A hypothetical example of a mashup view will help to explain how this approach to the atonement works. Armed with this explanation, we can then consider two recent examples in the atonement literature that yield rather different pictures of the reconciling work of Christ. The first of these is the work of the English-Canadian theologian, James I. Packer. The second can be found in the work of the Dutch-Canadian theologian, Hans Boersma.

Mashup accounts of the atonement proceed on the assumption that at least some of the historic accounts of the atonement are compatible with one another. This is not a universally held view, though it is increasingly popular today.[3] For instance, suppose Jones is an Anselmian about the atonement. Because she is an Anselmian, she starts from the assumption that human reconciliation with God must obtain either by the punishment of the sinner in hell, or by some suitable alternative action that provides satisfaction of God's offended honor, generating the requisite merit to atone for the demerit of human sin. As the God-man, Christ acts to bring about just such satisfaction in his work on the cross, which generates the required merit in order to provide atonement for human sin. But recall that on this Anselmian version of satisfaction, Christ is not punished. Punishment is one way God's honor may be

---

[3]Some historic theologians also mashup elements of existing atonement doctrines, like Martin Luther's use of both Christus Victor/ransom language and substitutionary and penal language as well. However, the recent mashup literature is self-consciously borrowing elements from what are perceived to be existing historic models of atonement, just as contemporary mashup literature and mashup music does. That is rather different, I think.

satisfied according to the Anselmian, but Christ's work is not a punishment. How could it be if he is the perfect God-man? Instead, it is a meritorious work that he did not have to perform, but did out of sheer grace and love.

Thus, the Anselmian version of satisfaction is inconsistent with the claim that satisfaction may be provided by Christ being punished in the place of human sinners, or at least, serving the penal consequences that fallen human beings would have to serve without atonement being made. But, as we have seen in previous chapters, this is the claim at the heart of the penal substitution doctrine. So it looks like the Anselmian defender of satisfaction will think that her view of atonement is not consistent with penal substitution because the mechanism of atonement is incommensurate given the logic of the Anselmian argument, set forth so brilliantly in *Cur deus homo*.

Now, of course, someone who did not think that satisfaction and punishment are mutually exclusive categories when applied to the God-man might think that there is no in-principle inconsistency in mashing up the notion of satisfaction with the notion of penal substitution. Then, presumably, the God-man satisfies God *by being punished*. Interestingly, this is how some historic Reformed theologians have thought about the matter, adapting the language of satisfaction to fit their understanding of Christ's work as a penal substitute. My point is just that defenders of the Anselmian version of satisfaction will not be persuaded by such reasoning because they think that these two approaches to the reconciling work of Christ have incommensurate mechanisms for atonement.

Anselmians like Jones are not usually very sympathetic to the ransom view of the atonement either. (Recall that Anselm himself criticizes the view at the beginning of *Cur deus homo* I. 6-7.) And Anselm clearly did not think that Christ's meritorious work was *merely* to provide a moral example to fallen human beings. It would not be difficult to construct an Anselmian version of satisfaction that was inconsistent with the other historic models and doctrines of atonement we have discussed in earlier chapters as well. Even though this is a purely hypothetical example, it makes the point that the central assumption of mashup views of atonement—that at least some of the historic accounts of the atonement are compatible with one another—is not an assumption obvious to everyone. In fact, there are many historic defenders of particular doctrines of atonement who think their own position is the only viable way to think about the reconciling work of Christ, or at least, is superior in its explanatory power to all other competitor views of the reconciling work of Christ.[4]

Without the assumption that at least some of the historic accounts of the atonement are compatible with one another mashup views can make no headway. For, as we have already noted, the very idea of a mashup doctrine involves taking elements from several different historic views of the atonement, and fusing them into a new whole. The mashup theologian need not think that *all* historic doctrines of atonement are compatible with each other, or that elements of *all* these doctrines can be borrowed and retooled to be part of a larger, composite whole. For instance, it might be thought that atoning violence is unacceptable as a central concept in the atonement on the basis of Christ's moral teaching, especially on the Sermon on the Mount. Recently, Mennonite theologians like J. Denny Weaver have been particularly associated with this way of thinking.[5] Someone developing a mashup doctrine that proceeds on this assumption will naturally reject views of the atonement, such as satisfaction or penal substitution, that seem to require a notion of atoning violence. But such a person might like the idea that Christ is a moral example and wish to couple it with the notion that Christ's atonement shows he is victorious over sin, death, and the devil, in order to construct a mashup doctrine on that basis. And this is just what Weaver does, in fact, do.

Another modern attempt to provide something like a mashup account of the atonement is the well-known essay by James I. Packer entitled "What Did the Cross Achieve? The Logic of Penal Substitution."[6] There, Packer sets out what he thinks are the five salient points of penal substitution, which, when he wrote the essay in the early 1970s, was still the prevailing view of the atonement within evangelical circles.[7] Rather than reiterating

---

[4]To take just one example, consider A. A. Hodge's study *The Atonement* (Philadelphia: Presbyterian Board of Publication, 1867), a staunch defense of the superiority of penal substitution over all other historic ways of thinking about the nature of atonement.

[5]See J. Denny Weaver, *The Nonviolent Atonement*, 2nd ed. (Grand Rapids: Eerdmans, 2011).

[6]James I. Packer, "What Did the Cross Achieve? The Logic of Penal Substitution," *Tyndale Bulletin* 25 (1974): 3-45. The essay has been anthologized several times and can be found in the electronic archive of the *Tyndale Bulletin*, housed on the website of Tyndale House at https://legacy.tyndale house.com/tynbul/Library/00_TyndaleBulletin_ByAuthor.htm.

[7]Arguably, penal substitution is still the dominant account of the atonement within global evangelicalism. However, it is no longer the *only* account of atonement espoused by evangelicals. There are good examples of recent evangelical accounts of the atonement that have broadened out what

standard ways of providing an account of penal substitution, Packer opts instead to construct his own "composite" view, which focuses on five motifs as aspects of one biblical-theological model of atonement.[8] These are substitution and retribution; substitution and solidarity; substitution and mystery; substitution and salvation; and substitution and divine love.[9] In commending this particular model of the atonement to his readers he is at pains to point out how it is that the doctrine is a kind of umbrella for most of the other historic conceptions of Christ's reconciling work. He incorporates these other concepts into an expansive vision of penal substitution, one that includes Christ as a moral example, as a ransom for our sin (buying us back at the price of being punished in our place), and as a satisfaction of divine justice.

In one sense the upshot of Packer's essay is not a mashup doctrine, as such, but rather an expanded or more complex way of thinking about penal substitution—what I referred to in chapter six as a kind of "one model to rule them all" approach. Several of the other better-known accounts of the atonement in the history of doctrine are subsumed under the aegis of penal substitution, but only as aspects of penal substitution, not in order to forge a new amalgam from the various parts culled from other accounts of atonement. However, in another sense, his essay could be regarded as a kind of soft-mashup account in as much as he thinks that a number of other historic accounts of the atonement are insufficient as they stand. They need to be grounded in what he takes to be the theologically richer, and more comprehensive account of Christ's reconciling work that penal substitution provides. Yet, importantly, Packer shares with those who defend mashup accounts of atonement the central assumption that at least some of the historic accounts of the atonement are compatible with one another. It is just that, as he sees things, these other historic accounts are partial and faltering attempts to get at a complete truth of the matter that only penal substitution can provide. This is worth noting because Packer's essay has been an important touchstone for many recent defenders of penal substitution.

---

is considered feasible within the doctrinal distinctive of evangelicalism's emphasis on the finished work of Christ on the cross. Hans Boersma, Joel Green, and Mark Baker, three of the other authors discussed in this chapter, are good examples of this recent trend.

[8]Packer, "What Did The Cross Achieve?," 25.

[9]Packer, "What Did The Cross Achieve?," 29.

A second example of a mashup doctrine of atonement, and one that falls more clearly within the parameters we have previously established, is that given by Hans Boersma in his book *Violence, Hospitality, and the Cross*. Boersma's study is an important and careful treatment of the atonement that is as much an attempt to provide a response to criticism about atoning violence (by means of the concept of divine hospitality) as it is a mashup doctrine of atonement in (partial) response to such concerns. However, since we have dealt with the topic of atoning violence in the previous chapter, here we can focus in particular upon Boersma's constructive proposal for atonement theology.

Boersma thinks of all language, atonement language included, as metaphorical in nature. Nevertheless, not all metaphors carry equal weight, especially with respect to the atonement. He focuses on what he takes to be some fundamental metaphors rooted in Scripture and the early church witness, with the notion of hospitality, understood in terms of God's welcome of fallen humanity in Christ's act of reconciliation, playing a central role. This is closely related to a doctrine of recapitulation, found (as we noted in an earlier chapter) in the theology of Irenaeus. As Boersma puts it, "In everything Christ does—and in whatever models we use to describe this—he functions as the representative of Israel and Adam who recapitulates or reconstitutes their life, death, and resurrection."[10] To this Irenaean way of thinking Boersma adds the notion of moral-influence. This is rooted in divine hospitality, for God acts in Christ in order to show us his love as an example for us to emulate. Next, he mixes in the concept of substitution, culled from the Augustinian tradition stemming from the theology of the apostle Paul. Although there are unhelpful ways in which substitutionary language has been used in the history of Christian doctrine (especially in certain versions of penal substitution), it is an important element to a full-orbed understanding of Christ's reconciling work. The final element in Boersma's account is the Christus Victor motif, which he understands to be the goal of atonement doctrine.

Boersma's study is a rich and nourishing treatment of the atonement, and this cameo is no more than the shortest of abstracts, and cannot do it complete justice. Nevertheless, for our purposes even this outline serves to show how his approach is thoroughly grounded in a mashup sensibility. Divine hospitality,

---

[10]Boersma, *Violence, Hospitality, and the Cross*, 19.

revealed in Christ's reconciling work is expressed in the way in which Christ recapitulates Israel and Adam in his own life and work, which seeks to morally influence fallen humans to the good. Christ's atonement is substitutionary in nature, including his taking upon himself the penal consequences for fallen humanity. This enables him to be victorious in his work, triumphing over the powers of darkness. The different elements borrowed from earlier doctrines and repurposed for Boersma's constructive argument yield a complex, multifaceted account of the atonement that is not easily defeated.

The kaleidoscopic view of atonement. Let us now turn to our second account, which looks superficially similar to the mashup approach to atonement doctrines. This is the kaleidoscopic view of the atonement, found in particular in the recent work of Joel Green and Mark Baker. On this way of thinking, the different historic accounts of the atonement, including the different doctrines we have surveyed thus far in previous chapters, are partial pictures of a reality that no single account can adequately explain. As Joel Green puts it in an essay summarizing his position, "The biblical narrative . . . authorizes an expansive range of images and models for comprehending and articulating the atonement."[11] It is important to reiterate here the point made in the introduction to this chapter, namely, that this kaleidoscopic view is not another model of the atonement. Rather, it is a theory about models of atonement, and especially about how they are generated in the different metaphors and images for Christ's reconciling work expressed in the New Testament, and then codified in various atonement doctrines down through the centuries.

We can see this if we compare the kaleidoscopic view with Packer's view. Whereas Packer treats other historic atonement doctrines as insufficient in and of themselves until and unless they are grounded in the more expansive and adequate understanding provided by the model of penal substitution, thereby privileging one doctrine over all the others, the kaleidoscopic view makes no such judgment. In fact, those who adopt the kaleidoscopic view of writers like Baker and Green maintain that no single doctrine of atonement can do the sort of work Packer thinks it can.[12] The reason for this, say Baker

---

[11] Joel B. Green, "Kaleidoscopic View," chap 4 in *The Nature of the Atonement: Four Views*, ed. James K. Beilby and Paul R. Eddy (Downers Grove, IL: IVP Academic, 2004), 170. He is even willing to speak of a "mandate" for developing multiple models of atonement given the New Testament evidence (171).

[12] Baker and Green are also quite critical of penal substitution.

and Green, is that no single doctrine of atonement can provide a comprehensive account of the mechanism by means of which we are reconciled to Christ. Such explanation must ultimately elude our grasp, on the kaleidoscopic account. This sets the kaleidoscopic view apart from other models and doctrines of atonement we have discussed thus far, including mashup views.

The difference can be illustrated like this: Suppose there are three different interpretations of Shakespeare's *The Tempest* written by three different literary critics. The first says *The Tempest* is a summary statement of Shakespeare's work, with Shakespeare himself represented in the principal character of Prospero. A second critic claims that the play is a social commentary on the politics of the time in which it was written. Prospero represents European civilization, whilst Caliban is a figural stand-in for the supposedly "barbarous" nations that European powers claimed to have subdued in the process of colonizing them. The third critic maintains that both these interpretations, whilst interesting, miss something important, namely, the way in which Shakespeare's play prefigures Freudian ways of thinking about the human mind, with Prospero having the rational center, and various other powers and characters representing the mind's attempt to overcome chaos, and subdue primal desires of the Unconscious. Then, along comes a fourth critic. She claims to have a theory about how these different scholars have all come to their interpretations of *The Tempest*. Her theory is not another interpretation of the play. It is a way of thinking about the three different existing interpretations of the play provided by the three literary critics. In other words, the fourth critic is interested in giving kind of metanarrative, or story that explains certain features of the different competing readings of the play given by the three original literary critics.

Put differently, if the first-order creative work is done by Shakespeare in writing *The Tempest*, and a second order work of reflection on the text is undertaken by the three literary critics who proffer three different interpretations of the play, the last critic is more interested in a third order work of reflecting on both the play itself (that is, the first order work of the Bard), and the three interpretations of the play (that is, the second order work of the literary critics), in order to give an account of how these three interpretations relate to one another (as different ways of thinking about the same play), and to *The Tempest* itself. For, of course, the three interpretations may not necessarily be competing ones; they may complement one another.

What Green and Baker are offering is just such a third-order understanding of existing historic accounts of the atonement. Each account is developed in light of a particular biblical motif (ransom, Christ as victor, satisfaction, penal substitution, and so on). Each is fashioned in a particular context and reflects the time and place in which it was crafted (so, for example, satisfaction reflects the medieval feudalism of the society in which Anselm wrote *Cur Deus Homo*; moral influence reflects the optimism of Enlightenment humanism; and so on). And each is a kind of conceptual picture that is incomplete on its own, without being set alongside other pictures provided by other biblical motifs spun out into other models and doctrines of the atonement. Thus, what Baker and Green propose in the kaleidoscopic view of the atonement is an interpretation about other, existing historic interpretations of the atonement—which is to say, a *theory* about models and doctrines of atonement. Put differently, Baker and Green offer a third-order account of the existing second-order "interpretations" of the atonement (i.e., other atonement doctrines and models), which are themselves reflections on what Scripture and tradition say about the reconciling work of Christ.

Understanding that this is what Baker and Green are about is also important for another, related reason. A theory about models and doctrines of atonement such as the kaleidoscopic account is not a recommendation of one way of thinking about the nature of Christ's reconciling work. It is not an argument for a particular view as is true of, say, the satisfaction doctrine or penal substitution. Rather, it is a view about other views. Or, put more carefully, it is a recommendation about how to think about the various historic doctrines and models of the atonement. It is as if Baker and Green are saying, "These different historic models of atonement draw on different metaphors and concepts of atonement found in the Scriptures. But each is incomplete. Each is partial, like the different pieces of a jigsaw puzzle. Only when the different pieces are arranged rightly, and fitted together in the appropriate pattern, can we see the whole picture." This is a novel and illuminating way of thinking about the different historic accounts of the atonement. But just as clearly, it is not itself an account of the atonement. It does not give us anything like a mechanism of atonement, or an explanation of how we should balance out the different pictures, how they should fit together, which pictures are more helpful than others, or even *whether* some pictures are more helpful than others.

So, although this is a proposal that seems ecumenical and irenic in tone, it does not really help us to see what the nature of the atonement is beyond some general sense that by means of the life and particularly the death of Christ on the cross fallen humanity is somehow reconciled to Godself. However, what it does do is help us to see that the different existing accounts of the atonement may all be partial, incomplete "windows" into the reality of Christ's reconciling work. Paradoxically, the kaleidoscopic view relativizes all the existing historic accounts of atonement, making them the product of particular times and cultures. But it does this by making a claim about all atonement doctrines—a claim that, presumably, is not supposed to be relative or culturally contingent. This is a matter to which we shall return as we move to consider problems and objections to the mashup and kaleidoscopic accounts of atonement.

PROBLEMS WITH MASHUP AND KALEIDOSCOPIC APPROACHES TO ATONEMENT

As we come to consider some problems and objections to these two ways of thinking about the atonement, we shall take each view in turn in the same order that we introduced them earlier in the chapter. Having assessed them both, it should be clear that although there are problems with both of these different accounts, they nevertheless do have important things to contribute to the current state of discussion about the nature of the atonement.

Problems with the mashup approach. The first and most obvious concern with the mashup approach (already intimated earlier in the chapter) has to do with the notion that different historic accounts of the atonement are compatible with one another, or that they might be brought together into some larger composite whole. The mashup approach can only make headway if it can show that at least some existing models of atonement complement one another in a way reminiscent of critical realist accounts of truth. According to such critical realism, there is some real truth of the matter independent of human minds, but that our grasp of that truth may be partial, informed by theory, and in need of revision in the light of further data. However, as we have already noted, at least some atonement models appear to be incommensurate with one another—such as the Anselmianism defended by Jones. If that is right, then at least two of the most influential historic doctrines of atonement—that is, satisfaction and penal substitution—will not be compatible with one another and the scope of potential material for mashup doctrines will be that much more limited as a consequence.

However, this presumes a rather narrow conception of "compatibility." At least some of what theologians like Boersma, and, to some extent, Packer, are interested in is motifs and metaphors for atonement that may be brought together in a larger composite whole. For instance, atoning violence, a major preoccupation of Boersma's study, is a motif that applies to both penal substitution and satisfaction, as well as ransom views of atonement, amongst others. Providing a mashup account of atonement that addresses that concern may not necessarily be compatible with particular versions of, say, satisfaction or penal substitution, but it will go a long way to addressing worries raised by those who wish to criticize all those ways of thinking about the atonement that include the notion of atoning violence, satisfaction and penal substitution included. So a mashup doctrine of atonement may not necessarily fold in complete versions of existing doctrines. It might simply adopt motifs or metaphors culled from existing atonement doctrines, using them to construct a new whole.

This brings us to a second concern with mashup accounts of the atonement, having to do with whether a mashup is comprehensive enough. We might put it like this. If a mashup theologian only takes account of some of the historic models, motifs, and metaphors for atonement in her constructive work, then she could be accused of being partial or even of cherry-picking those ways of thinking about the reconciling work of Christ that suit her purposes. If a doctrine of atonement is supposed to provide a comprehensive picture of how Christ's reconciling work saves fallen humanity, then such a mashup view seems inadequate to the task. Perhaps more troubling still, if a mashup doctrine is unable to give some account of all the pictures for atonement in the biblical witness then it would appear to be an insufficient account of Christ's saving work, perhaps even a misleading or seriously skewed account.

This latter point is a real concern for all constructive treatments of the atonement—or indeed, constructive accounts of any other Christian doctrine. Partial, incomplete doctrines of atonement are of very limited value in the grand scheme of things. Yet the starting assumption of mashup accounts that differing models, metaphors, and motifs for the atonement should be brought together in order to provide a more comprehensive way of thinking about Christ's reconciling work is surely right. Whether or not a particular instance of the mashup genre manages to make good on this assumption is another matter, and each such attempt must be judged on its own merits. But what we might call the motivation for mashup approaches does have much to be said for it. It certainly is an improvement upon ways of thinking about the saving work of Christ that simply ignore alternative ways of thinking about the atonement, or set to one side models, metaphors, and motifs that are inconvenient for the particular view being outlined. So a lack of comprehensiveness is not necessarily a problem for the mashup approach as such, though it may be a problem for particular attempts by particular theologians.

We come to our third objection. This has to do with whether mashup accounts are more than the sum of their parts. Suppose you have a coin collection. Intuitively, it seems that there is a thing called "the collection of coins," which is the sum of the total number of coins in your collection. But we usually do not think of that sum as a "thing" over and above the particular coins that it makes up. Instead, we tend to think that the coins are each individual things that you have collected together in one place. The sum of these coins is just the total, the whole, all the coins taken together, so to speak. Or, to put it another way, we typically treat the sum of the coins as no more than a collection of the parts that make it up.

Now, consider a second example. Suppose that you take your coin collection and glue the individual coins together into a statue shaped into a rudimentary human form. It seems to me that in this second case we would agree that the total collection of coins is no longer merely the sum of its constituent members (that is, the individual coins). The particular coins have been formed into some new composite, shaped to look like a human being. The whole in this case is indeed greater than the sum of its parts, for it has formed some new object.

Now, there are philosophical puzzles about such things as wholes and parts (what philosophers call *mereology*) that need not trouble us here. For our purposes, a pre-philosophical way of thinking about the coins will suffice. Let us transpose these two ways of thinking about the coin collection to the mashup accounts of the atonement. Are they no more than a "collection" of bits and pieces culled from other existing accounts of the atonement? That is, are they no more than the collection of coins—simply a sum made up of different parts but nothing more than that? Or, do they compose a new whole, a real thing in addition to the parts that make up this whole, in a way that is more than a mere collection or sum like the statue form of the coins fused together?

It seems to me that much will depend on the particular mashup doctrine in question. But in principle, a mashup account could be either like a collection of parts (and so, no more than the sum of its parts), or like some new composite (and thus, more than the sum of its parts). As with the previous objection, whether or not this is a problem—whether or not a particular mashup doctrine delivers a new composite whole rather than merely the sum of its parts—will depend upon the doctrine in question. Once again, this is not so much a problem for the mashup approach to the atonement in general as it is a problem that may or may not obtain in the case of specific attempts to provide a mashup account of the atonement.

Problems with the kaleidoscopic approach. Let us turn to problems and objections to the kaleidoscopic account. We shall consider three areas of concern. The first of these is that the kaleidoscopic view makes claims about the culturally conditioned nature of historic atonement doctrines without registering the fact that it too is a cultural artifact. If it makes no difference to the truth-value of the kaleidoscopic view that it originates in a particular time and place, then why is that not also true of all the other historic atonement doctrines that it seeks to relativize as in some sense culturally conditioned? In other words, it is not clear what of substance is to be gained simply by pointing out that atonement doctrines, and reflection on atonement doctrines, are both products of particular times and cultures. Necessarily, doctrines are the product of a particular time and culture. But since such a claim is independent of the truth-value of the particular doctrine in question, that turns out not to be a very theologically interesting claim.

A second objection to the kaleidoscopic view is that Green and Baker provide their readers with no means by which to adjudicate between models of atonement. They give no reason to think any one model better than the others, and no place from which to make judgments about the relative merits of different accounts of the work of Christ. As Gregory Boyd remarks in response to an essay by Joel Green on the kaleidoscopic view, "Green denies that any metaphor or set of metaphors can be taken as intrinsically more fundamental than others. There is, then, no normative transcultural, overall framework within which all the variety of New Testament metaphors are to be arranged and properly understood."[13] This is a significant shortcoming of the kaleidoscopic account. For if it has no means by which to discriminate between different models of atonement, no reason for thinking certain models and motifs more basic or fundamental than others, then it is difficult to know whether a given model is more or less helpful than others, or more or less central to the way in which Christians should think about Christ's work.

A third criticism is that the kaleidoscopic view is incomplete or "empty" as an approach to atonement because it says nothing about the nature of atonement or its mechanism. This is simply a consequence of the sort of view the kaleidoscopic account is: it is, as I have labored to explain, a *theory* about atonement doctrines, not a doctrine among doctrines so to speak—a third order reflection on second order interpretations of a doctrine. But if that is right then it should be no surprise that it offers no view of the nature of atonement or the mechanism of atonement. Similarly, to go back to our earlier example of Shakespeare's *The Tempest*, the fourth literary critic who offers a theory about the way in which the three interpretations of the play relate to one another and to the play itself is not attempting to provide another inter-pretation of the play as such. So it would be a category mistake to suggest that something was amiss with the fourth critic's theory about the three interpreta-tions of the play because it did not give another interpretation alongside the other three. Similar things can be said of the kaleidoscopic view, the relevant changes having been made. It is a category mistake to expect a theory about how to think about a given body of interpretative material on a particular text or texts to provide yet another such interpretation. To put it another way, this is to confuse third-order with second-order ways of thinking. Never-theless, the very fact that the kaleidoscopic view is not another atonement model is significant. It means that we should treat it differently from the atonement doctrines, models, and motifs that we have assessed in previous chapters. For it is not giving us a *doctrine* of the atonement at all. Indeed, it cannot give us a doctrine of atonement.

---

[13]Gregory Boyd, "Christus Victor Response [To Joel Green]" in *The Nature of The Atonement*, 187.

THE CONTRIBUTION AND SIGNIFICANCE OF MASHUP AND KALEIDOSCOPIC APPROACHES

A final caveat: it could be argued that the exemplars of mashup and kaleido-scopic views that I have cited would not describe their own views in the way I have. Packer and Boersma do not call their views "mashup" doctrines and Baker and Green do not describe their kaleidoscopic view as a theory about models and doctrines of atonement. Is this tantamount to misrepresenting the views in question? I think not. The reason is that my way of characterizing these views is just a way of drawing out their conceptual implications. I suppose that the apostle Paul would not have characterized the conceptual content of the teaching contained in his epistles as "theology." But that does not mean his work is not theology. It just means he did not refer to it that way. It *is* theology as we understand that discipline today. It might be anachronistic to use a term of Paul that he does not use of himself. But calling his epistles theological is not inappropriate even if it is anachronistic in one, purely his-torical, sense. For this does accurately describe the conceptual content of his letters as we understand them today. Similarly, in explaining how certain views constitute mashup atonement doctrines or theories about atonement doctrines, all I have been attempting to do is get at the conceptual form of those doctrines. That is not an illegitimate exercise and does not involve trying to put words into the mouths of the authors in question. Rather, it involves trying to better understand the views expressed by those authors.

The mashup and kaleidoscopic approaches to the atonement have brought the recent academic work on the reconciling work of Christ into the post-modern age. In the case of mashup views, there is much to be said for attempting to show how different atonement motifs and models may be compatible with one another, and even recombined to form new ways of thinking about the reconciling work of Christ. My own view, set out in the last chapter of this book, could be characterized as a mashup account of sorts in this respect. The kaleidoscopic view has also reminded us that all atonement doctrines are cultural artifacts, and that each such doctrine points beyond itself to a truth greater than any single motif or metaphor. That is an important point as well. Nevertheless, the kaleidoscopic view is not itself another doctrine of atonement, and does not yield a constructive proposal for thinking about the atonement today beyond this insight about other atonement doctrines. As such, its importance is more as a contribution to how we ought to approach thinking about Christ's reconciling work, rather than a positive way of thinking about the nature of that saving work and the mechanism by means of which Christ atones for human sin.

FURTHER READING

Baker, Mark D., and Joel B. Green. "Models of the Atonement." In *Recovering the Scandal of the Cross: Atonement in New Testament and Contemporary Contexts*, 142-65. 2nd ed. Downers Grove, IL: IVP Academic, 2011.

Beilby, James K., and Paul R. Eddy, eds. *The Nature of Atonement: Four Views*. Downers Grove, IL: IVP Academic, 2006.

Boersma, Hans. *Violence, Hospitality, and the Cross: Reappropriating the Atonement Tradition*. Grand Rapids: Baker Academic, 2004.

Green, Joel B. "Kaleidoscopic View." In *The Nature of Atonement: Four Views*, edited by James K. Beilby and Paul R. Eddy, 157-85. Downers Grove, IL: IVP Academic, 2006.

Hodge, A. A. *The Atonement*. Philadelphia: Presbyterian Board of Publication, 1867.

Packer, James I. "What Did the Cross Achieve? The Logic of Penal Substitution." *Tyndale Bulletin* 25 (1974): 3-45.

Tidball, Derek, David Hilborn, Justin Thaker, eds. *The Atonement Debate*. Grand Rapids: Zondervan, 2008.

Weaver, J. Denny. *The Nonviolent Atonement*. 2nd ed. Grand Rapids: Eerdmans, 2011.

10

PARTICIPATION AND ATONEMENT

In previous chapters, we have called attention to the shortcomings of a number of approaches to the atonement. This chapters changes tack, moving from exposition and critique of the views of others, to the theological articulation and defense of one particular approach to the atonement that focuses upon the ideas of participation in the work of Christ and union with Christ. It is what theologians often call a "constructive" account of atonement. That is, it is an attempt to provide a positive account of the doctrine, by way of arguments and reasoning that seek to "construct" a way of thinking about this matter, much as one might construct a bridge from various materials, or construct a painting from the elements of paint, pigment, and canvas.

It is also offered as a model of atonement, with all that entails. It incorporates aspects of earlier accounts of atonement, from the patristic views we dealt with in chapter two to the idea of Christ's work as a vicarious act that can be found in many of the other theologies of atonement that we have encountered in subsequent chapters. It shares a number of intuitions that have surfaced in previous chapters as problems with earlier ways of thinking about Christ's reconciling work. Several of these are fundamental concerns that the model seeks to address, and it is worth making this clear at the outset by considering some of the assumptions that motivate this way of approaching the atonement. Having done this, we shall set out the case for this participatory account of the atonement, which I shall call *the union account*, for reasons that shall become clear in due course. Then we shall consider some objections to this way of thinking. The chapter closes with a conclusion in which I offer some reflections on the contribution of the union account to atonement theology.

THEOLOGICAL ASSUMPTIONS

Recall from previous chapters that there are a number of serious problems attending much traditional atonement theology. The union account attempts to address a number of these issues head on. The first of these worries was that Christ is said to be punished in place of fallen human beings, which we encountered in the model of penal substitution. Since Christ is innocent of sin, it seems that he cannot be punished for sin. Only the guilty can be punished, strictly speaking. Second, and closely related to this, is the worry about the transfer of sin and guilt from Adam and Eve to the rest of the human race. It seems unjust and immoral that I am held responsible for an action performed by ancestors removed from me by many centuries, whose action I could not have condoned or approved. Yet this is just what some traditional atonement theologies presume is the case. This raises a third related issue, which has to do with the fact that such an arrangement, where God ascribes the sin and guilt of Adam and Eve to the rest of the human race, depends upon a kind of moral and legal fiction. God treats us *as if* we are the ones who sinned and are guilty of the action of Adam and Eve, though in fact we are not the ones who sinned and are guilty. Treating a person as if they are sinful or guilty of a crime when they are not is surely another way in which the traditional atonement theology that utilizes such ideas is deeply problematic.

Then there are issues to do with how Christ's work is a reconciling work. It deals with human sin and it also brings us back into communion with God. But what form does such reconciliation take? How are we reconciled to God? In what manner does Christ bring us into communion with God once more? These are also fundamental matters that any account of the nature of the atonement needs to address, including the union account. Scripture speaks of us being united to Christ in very strong language. For instance, in 2 Corinthians 5:21 Paul says, "God made him who had no sin to be sin for us, so that in him we might become the righteousness of God." In 1 Corinthians 6:17 he writes, "Whoever is united with the Lord is one with him in spirit." And in Romans 6:5 he states, "If we have been united with him in a death like his, we will certainly also be united with him in a resurrection like his." The author of Ephesians even compares our union with Christ to the intimate union of a woman and man in marriage, saying that we are members of Christ's body, and that "this is a profound mystery" (Eph 5:29-32).

This union is in some respects a two-way relation because God the Son unites himself to human nature in order to bring about human salvation, and then through his saving work, unites us to himself in Christ by the power of the Holy Spirit. As the writer to the Hebrews puts it, "Since the children have flesh and blood, he too shared in their humanity so that by his death he might break the power of him who holds the power of death—that is, the devil—and free those who all their lives were held in slavery by their fear of death. For surely it is not angels he helps, but Abraham's descendants" (Heb 2:14-16). Similarly, 2 Peter 1:4 speaks of God's "very great and precious promises," that he has given to us "so that through them you may participate in the divine nature, having escaped the corruption in the world caused by evil desires."

This language of a kind of intimate, organic union between the believer and Christ in salvation is something that the patristic writers we encountered in chapter two were striving to express. It is something that the more transactional language of satisfaction or the more legal and forensic language of penal substitution or of the governmental and vicarious penitential accounts of atonement sometimes seem to overlook, or at least downplay. Yet recent work in biblical studies has shown just how important such notions are in the theology of the later New Testament. The biblical scholar Michael J. Gorman sums it up when he writes, "As a fundamental category for understanding Paul, 'participation'—meaning participation in Christ, his crucifixion and resurrection, his story, and/or his present life—is now quite widely accepted." He goes on to say, "For Paul, to be one with Christ is to be one with God; to be like Christ is to be like God; to be in Christ is to be in God. At the very least, this means that for Paul cruciformity—conformity to the crucified Christ—is really theoformity or theosis."[1] The union account of atonement takes this very seriously indeed.

In some ways, the union account may be thought of as an attempt to update central aspects of the way in which patristic theologians like Athanasius and Irenaeus thought about Christ's work. Recall Athanasius's claim that "he, indeed, assumed humanity that we might become God."[2] He thought that

---

[1]Michael J. Gorman, *Inhabiting the Cruciform God: Kenosis, Justification, and Theosis in Paul's Narrative Soteriology* (Grand Rapids: Eerdmans, 2009), 3, 4.
[2]Athanasius, *On the Incarnation*, trans. John Behr (Crestwood, NY: St. Vladimir's Seminary Press, 2006), §54.

Christ acts vicariously on our behalf healing human nature from the inside-out, so to speak—what is sometimes referred to as the doctrine of Christ's vicarious humanity. Standing behind this theological claim is a metaphysical one, to the effect that Christ assumes a universal human nature, and heals it from the inside out so that what he changes with respect to the universal human nature will then affect all other instances of this universal human nature in fallen human beings. This was a widespread assumption in early Christianity, as Benjamin Myers points out. "The view that humanity is essentially one—that there is a universal human nature in which individuals participate—is so widely taken for granted in early Christianity that it is seldom discussed or defended."[3]

But it is difficult to make sense of the idea that somehow Christ's reconciling work changes not just his own human nature, but all other instances of human nature. And it is difficult to know what to make of the claim that he assumes some universal human nature. Normally, we think of a universal in this sense as some property that exists as an abstract object rather like numbers are abstract objects. Just as there may be the universal property of the number two, so there is a universal property of, say, the color blue. Particular things that are two in number, or that are blue in color, are said to be instances of this universal. They instantiate or exemplify the property "two" or "blueness." So Jones's blue shirt exemplifies the property "blue," just as her eyes do, and just as the sky does, and so on. But how can Christ take on the universal human nature? How does one assume an abstract object like that? It is difficult to see how this might be the case. However, there may be another way to get at the theological claim the patristic writers are talking about. It may be that we can get at that claim by substituting a different set of metaphysical ideas to make sense of the theology involved, which draws in important respects on the New Testament material we have already discussed. That is one of the goals of the union account. We might say that it attempts to place the patristic view on a surer metaphysical footing, whilst at the same time taking seriously some of the central claims of later atonement theology, especially the family of views associated with penal substitution. With these assumptions in mind, we can turn to the exposition of the union account.

---

[3]Benjamin Myers, "The Patristic Doctrine of Atonement," in *Locating Atonement: Explorations in Constructive Dogmatics*, ed. Oliver D. Crisp and Fred Sanders (Grand Rapids: Zondervan Academic, 2015), 82.

THE UNION ACCOUNT OF ATONEMENT

Much recent work in biblical and systematic theology emphasizes this Pauline notion of union with Christ. As we have already indicated, it is set out in several places in the New Testament, but a passage that is especially important for our purposes is what is often called the "Adam Christology" of Romans 5:12-19. Here Paul contrasts Adam and his work with Christ and his work, showing that there are important parallels between the two. "Consequently, just as one trespass resulted in condemnation for all people," he says, "so also one righteous act resulted in justification and life for all people. For just as through the disobedience of the one man the many were made sinners, so also through the obedience of the one man the many will be made righteous" (Romans 5:18-19). This passage has been an important source for subsequent theologians who have striven to make sense of how it is that all humanity bears sin from which they need salvation, and how it is that Christ brings about that salvation. An important component of this reasoning has to do with the notion of union or participation. We are united to Adam and somehow participate in his sin, and we are united to Christ and somehow participate in the salvation he provides.

Perhaps this Pauline notion of participation can help provide an account of atonement that has a close relationship to penal substitution and to some of the earlier views of patristic thinkers, yet with a different mechanism of atonement—one that depends on these notions of union and participation. Although I am calling it the *union account of atonement*, it might just as easily be called a *participatory account of atonement*, since both of these notions play significant roles in this approach to the atonement.[4] The central claim of the union account is this: Fallen human beings are somehow really united to Adam so that Adam plus his progeny constitutes an entity, called *fallen humanity*. What is more, those who are believers are also somehow really united to Christ so that they too constitute a real, distinct entity called

---

[4]I have given a more technical version of the union account, set within a broader theological vision of the person and work of Christ in Oliver D. Crisp, *The Word Enfleshed: Exploring the Person and Work of Christ* (Grand Rapids: Baker Academic, 2016). Interested readers are directed there for further elaboration of the view outlined here. Other recent participatory accounts of atonement include Tim Bayne and Greg Restall, "A Participatory Model of the Atonement" in Yugin Nagasawa and Erik J. Wielenberg, eds., *New Waves in Philosophy of Religion* (London: Palsgrave Macmillan, 2009), 150-66, and Robin Collins, "Girard and Atonement: An Incarnational Theory of Mimetic Participation" in Willard M. Swartley, ed., *Violence Renounced: René Girard, Biblical Studies, and Peacemaking* (Telford, PA: Pandora Press, 2000).

redeemed humanity. Fallen and redeemed humanity are, in fact, overlapping entities. A person can be a member of both of these groups. By being united to Adam, I share in his sin; by being united to Christ I share in his righteousness, on analogy with what Paul says in Romans 5:12-19. I am a member of fallen humanity because I am united with Adam, participating in the human race of which he is the putative first member. And I am a member of redeemed humanity because I am united with Christ, participating in the race of redeemed human beings of which he is the first member, being the one who brings about this salvation as the New Adam.

Now, it may be thought that this is merely a metaphor for the way in which we, as members of the human race and descendants of Adam, are said to be united with Christ by his saving work. There are certainly metaphorical elements to this picture. But on my way of thinking it is not merely a metaphor. Rather, my union with Adam in fallen humanity depends on fallen humanity being a *real* composite entity, as real as any other around us from rocks and trees to humans and angels. Similarly, on this view, redeemed humanity is a real composite entity as well. This is important for the purposes of explaining the model, but it is also somewhat counterintuitive at first glance. In order to try to explain how this can be, I shall turn first to examine some helpful comments by the great eighteenth-century theologian Jonathan Edwards, and then to two analogies that will help illuminate these matters, before offering some theological grounding for this approach.

First, let us consider some remarks by Edwards. He says some helpful things that may enable us to begin to get a conceptual grip on this view. In a sermon on justification by faith he writes,

> What is real in the union between Christ and his people, is the foundation of what is legal; that is, it is something really in them, and between them, uniting them, that is the ground of the suitableness of their being accounted as one by the Judge: and if there is any act, or qualification in believers, that is of that uniting nature, that it is meet on that account that the Judge should look upon 'em, and accept 'em as one, no wonder that upon the account of the same act or qualification, he should accept the satisfaction and merits of the one, for the other, as if it were their satisfaction and merits: it necessarily follows, or rather is implied.[5]

---

[5]Jonathan Edwards, "Justification by Faith," in M. X. Lesser, ed. *Sermons and Discourses, 1734-1738: The Works of Jonathan Edwards, Vol. 19* (New Haven, CT: Yale University Press, 2001), 158.

Often Protestant thinkers have believed that we are united to Christ because of what I have called a kind of moral or legal fiction. Recall that on this view, God treats us as if we are just in his sight because of Christ's saving work. He treats Christ as if he were the one guilty of sin in order to punish Christ in our place, and so on. Because of this moral and legal fiction, which is an arrangement brought about by God's command, fallen human beings may be saved. Put in other words, this moral and legal arrangement is the foundation on which a real change in us and in our relationship to God is predicated. On this legal basis God is able to reconcile us to Godself in Christ.

Edwards turns this reasoning on its head. The real change in us and our relationship to God brought about by Christ's reconciling work is not the consequence of some moral and legal arrangement, he claims. Rather, a real change is the foundation of the moral and legal change in our relationship to God. God unites us with Christ so that we participate in his saving work, and, as a consequence of this, he is able to treat us as those justified in his sight. Our real union with Christ in salvation brings about our moral and legal change of status in the sight of God. In a similar manner, the real union of hearts between two lovers is what gives rise to their desire to be legally joined together in matrimony; it is not that they are legally joined together and on that basis find a union of hearts in their marriage.

This sounds marvelous, but it is difficult to see how a fallen human person may be somehow really united to Adam in this entity called fallen humanity, and also really united to Christ in redeemed humanity. Moreover, it is difficult to see how the effects of Adam's sin would be transferred to subsequent fallen human beings on this arrangement. Similarly, it is difficult to see how the benefits of Christ's saving work would be transferred to those fallen human beings he comes to save, given this way of thinking about the atonement.

Here, two analogies will help us to make some further headway. The first of these has to do with Tibbles the cat. Tibbles is sometimes used as an example of mereology, that is, the study of wholes and their parts. Suppose Tibbles is a ginger cat. We say he is a ginger cat because his fur coat is ginger. But although he is a ginger cat, not all of his parts are ginger. His whiskers are not ginger, nor are his teeth, his claws, his bones, or his internal organs—even the fur on his belly isn't entirely ginger. We say he is a ginger cat—by which we mean the *whole cat* is a ginger cat—though we understand that this is not a property of all his parts. So there is a distinction to be made between those properties of a whole thing, and the properties of the parts of that thing, and we need to make sure we are clear about which properties belong to which, in order that we don't confuse what we are speaking about. Similarly, Tibbles's paw isn't Tibbles, nor is his left ear Tibbles; they are parts of Tibbles. Sometimes we do speak about a part as if it were the whole. If you see Tibbles's head framed by a window, you might say "There's that cheeky cat, Tibbles!" even though you can only see a part of him. But you understand that, strictly speaking, the whole and the parts are different and distinct. When you refer to Tibbles through the window, you don't for a moment suppose that the head of the cat that you see is the whole of Tibbles. But the part you do see stands in for the whole of Tibbles, so to speak.

Transpose this way of thinking about wholes and their parts to the union account. Adam and Christ act as the first members of the real composite wholes that stem from them. Adam is the first member of fallen humanity, and Christ is the first member of redeemed humanity. Their actions as first members have implications for all later members of the same entity in a way that the actions of later members of that entity cannot, because they are downstream of the actions of the first members of the entity. In a similar manner, the actions of those who framed the Constitution of the United States shape the nation in a way that no subsequent generation of political policy makers can because they are downstream of that politically foundational event.

What is more, although Adam and Christ are only members or parts of fallen and redeemed humanity respectively, they can stand in for the whole in certain circumstances, like Tibbles's head can stand in for Tibbles when we see him out of the window. So the action of Adam in sinning distributes to all subsequent humans because he stands in for all subsequent humans—not primarily because his primal sin imputed to them, but because they inherit the effects his sin has wrought upon all subsequent human beings as only the first sin of the first human being can. In a similar way, the action of Christ in atonement distributes to all members of redeemed humanity, not primarily because his merit is imputed to them, but because his merit is really communicated to them by the work of the Holy Spirit who unites believers to Christ.

Let us turn to a second analogy, this time focusing on an oak tree. Imagine an acorn that is infected by some chronic disease. It is planted and grows over time into an oak. At each stage of its existence, it bears the marks of the disease introduced to it as an acorn. The sapling, the young tree, and the mature oak are all misshapen by this disease. This disease is like the primal sin that introduces the condition of original sin to human beings in their infancy, through the agency of Adam and Eve. From its introduction to the acorn it spreads to all the later stages of the life of the tree. But suppose a branch that is disease-resistant is grafted into the tree as a young sapling. As the tree grows, the graft infuses health into the parts of the tree immediately around it, killing off the disease in that area whilst the rest of the oak gradually withers away over time. This is like the saving work of Christ that gives life to the tree, and those parts of the tree that grow from it—and of course there are biblical analogs to these organic analogies, including the famous metaphor of vine and branches that is used in John's gospel (Jn 15).

Much more would need to be said if we were attempting to give a complete account of the union view of atonement. However, in light of these two organic examples coupled with what Edwards says in light of the biblical material we touched upon earlier, a picture begins to emerge of an account of Christ's saving work that takes seriously the ideas found in Scripture, and in the patristic witness, as well as much later theology, according to which our participation in Adam's sin, as well as in Christ's work of reconciliation, depends upon us being united with Adam and with Christ, respectively. Just as the parts of Tibbles are united in the one ginger cat, we are united in the one whole that is fallen humanity. We all "share" in Adam's primal sin, which he passes on to subsequent human beings in a way reminiscent of the disease passed on from acorn to oak. Yet if we are also members of redeemed humanity, then we also participate in the benefits of Christ's reconciling work.

However, there is an important asymmetry between the work of these two "Adams." Whereas all of humanity lives chronologically downstream of Adam and Eve as the first humans, so that the effects of their primal sin is passed down the generations to us, the same is not true of Christ. He lives much later than many great saints of the Old Testament. Yet somehow he is said to be a second Adam whose work of reconciliation is able to save those that live before him in time. That seems strange. Yet it is something to which Scripture attests. For instance, in Hebrews 11:13 we read this of the great saints of the Old Testament, "All these people were still living by faith when they died.

They did not receive the things promised; they only saw them and welcomed them from a distance, admitting that they were foreigners and strangers on earth." Later in the same passage we read, "These were all commended for their faith, yet none of them received what had been promised, since God had planned something better for us so that only together with us would they be made perfect" (Heb 11:39-40). God provided something better for us, namely, Christ. The Old Testament saints died in faith in the hope of the things promised them, but without seeing the reality, rather like Moses was shown the Promised Land before he died, in the knowledge that he would not enter it in this life. So Abraham and all the other Old Testament saints are included in the salvation Christ brings, though they only had the hope of salvation. In other words, Christ's saving work is *proleptic*. It is active even before Christ appears in history, so that as the second Adam those who live before him are incorporated in his work of reconciliation, and are included within redeemed humanity.

We often speak proleptically. For instance, in classic gangster movies a character might be heard to say, "He was a dead man before he ever entered McShane's bar." The character wasn't actually a dead man when he entered McShane's bar, but it was as if he was a dead man because the action sealed his fate—he was killed as a result. But in the union account of atonement the proleptic element is much more than a figure of speech. Abraham was *really* a member of redeemed humanity. He was not merely figuratively a member of redeemed humanity before redeemed humanity existed. The difference turns on what Abraham knew, and what was really the case. This is a difference between epistemology (what we know is the case), and ontology (roughly, what actually is the case irrespective of whether we know it or not). Abraham had faith in the hope of salvation. He didn't know Christ. How could he? He lived centuries before Christ appeared. Yet he was actually saved through Christ's work, though this happened many hundreds of years later in time. In a similar way we might say of George Washington, "When he was a child the President was a virtuous boy who couldn't bring himself to tell a lie about chopping down his father's cherry tree with an axe when he was asked about it." Washington wasn't the President when he was cross-questioned by his father about the damaged cherry tree. But we refer to him as such proleptically. For we know now that this boy is the same person who would become the first President of the United States. Similarly, we now know (through Scripture) that Abraham would be included in Christ's work of salvation that was brought about much later in time, though he did not know that.

Well then, how does Christ's work reconcile us to God on this union account of atonement? How are we incorporated into redeemed humanity? Paul in 2 Corinthians speaks of those who are in Christ as new creations. He says that "God made him who had no sin," that is, Christ, "to be sin for us, so that in him we might become the righteousness of God" (2 Cor 5:21). Now, Christ is not guilty of sin. Yet he "becomes sin" for us. I take this to mean he takes upon himself the penal consequences of the other members of redeemed humanity that are guilty of sin (and therefore, also members of fallen humanity) because they are "parts" of the same entity extended across time. By "penal consequences" I mean the hard treatment that would be punishment if it were served upon those who are guilty—that is, fallen human beings—but which is not punishment for Christ. Nevertheless, he takes upon himself the consequences that would befall us without atonement, namely, the harsh treatment we would have received without Christ's intervention.

Yet taking upon himself the penal consequences of the sin of the members of redeemed humanity is only one part of the process. In doing this, he also heals our fallenness. Although this is a process that takes effect over time, it begins at the moment when the saving benefits of Christ's work are applied to us by the secret working of the Holy Spirit. He unites us to Christ, and specifically, applies to us the benefits of Christ's atoning work, so that we may begin the process of growing more like Christ over time. At the moment of reconciliation, we begin the journey of being made more like Christ that continues beyond this life into eternity. We are, on this way of thinking, on a trajectory towards intimate communion with God that continues forevermore. We "become partakers of the divine nature," a process that begins by being united to Christ by the Spirit. It is like a mathematical asymptote in that the human members of redeemed humanity draw ever closer to God in this process, yet without ever becoming God, or losing themselves in God. This way of thinking about the nature of human salvation is often called theosis or divinization, which can sound rather strange and suspicious to many Protestant Christians. However, as Jonathan Edwards puts it, in creating the world God intends for his creatures to be united with himself "in greater and greater nearness and strictness of union with himself, and greater and greater communion and participation with him in his own glory and happiness, in constant progression, throughout all eternity." What is more, God desires an "eternally progressive union and communion with him; so the creature must be viewed as in infinite strict union with himself." This union is like "two lines which seem at the beginning to be separate, but aim finally to meet in one, both being directed to the same center."[6] It is this union that Christ's atoning work makes possible, and that the secret working of the Holy Spirit brings about in the life of the believer and member of redeemed humanity.

Let us summarize the foregoing. As with previous chapters, I shall do this by way of numbered sentences in order to make as clear as possible the shape or logical form of the argument:

1. God brings about an entity comprising Adam (from the fall-onwards) and all of post-fall humanity barring Christ. This is called fallen humanity.

2. Fallen humanity is a real entity that exists across time like the different stages of the life of one tree, from acorn to mature oak.

3. I possess Adam's sin because I am a "part" of fallen humanity along with Adam on analogy with the parts of my body, and the whole of my body.

4. Adam's sin is passed on to the later "parts" of this whole extended across time because he is the first human just as the disease infecting the acorn (the first stage of the life of the oak) affects all the later stages of the life of the oak tree.

5. Christ is the Second Adam. He is the first member of a new humanity, one that is cleansed from sin and reconciled to God.

6. Christ, together with those he comes to save are members of a second real entity, called redeemed humanity.

7. As the hub or intersection between divinity and humanity, Christ is a fitting means by which humans may be reconciled to God. As the

---

[6]Jonathan Edwards, *God's End in Creation* in *Ethical Writings, The Works of Jonathan Edwards Vol. 8*, ed. Paul Ramsey (New Haven, CT: Yale University Press, 1989), 459.

God-human he is able to act on behalf of both God and humanity, communicating between them.

8. Christ has a priority over other "parts" of redeemed humanity although he exists later in time than some of them. For instance, he lives later than Abraham although his work as the Second Adam reconciles Abraham to God (Heb 11:8-16; 39-40).

9. Hence, those living prior to Christ can be proleptically incorporated into Christ's work as the Second Adam.

10. Christ is not guilty of sin; yet he takes on himself the penal consequences of the other members of redeemed humanity that are guilty of sin (and therefore, also members of fallen humanity) because they are "parts" of the same entity extended across time (2 Cor 5:21).

11. Christ's work atones for human sin, removing the obstacle of sin and reconciling members of fallen humanity to God.

12. Through union with Christ by the power of the Holy Spirit, members of redeemed humanity begin a process of transformation into the likeness of God, becoming partakers of the divine nature.

13. This process of transformation goes on forevermore. It is like a mathematical asymptote in that the human members of redeemed humanity draw ever closer to God in this process, yet without ever becoming God, or losing themselves in God.

PROBLEMS WITH THE UNION ACCOUNT OF ATONEMENT

The union account tracks with much of the strong language of union found in the New Testament, and with some of the recent renewed interest in this topic amongst biblical and systematic theologians. It provides a kind of metaphysical backstory to Paul's Adam Christology that does justice to his claims about the real union believers have with Christ because of his reconciling work. In this way, it is able to offer a model of atonement that explains how Christ's work reconciles us to God, and how it is that Christ's union with human nature is a prerequisite to our union with God, one of the most important (perhaps the most important) goals of the atonement.

There are a number of problems with this account, however. The first and most obvious is that it is a non-traditional argument, and some will be concerned that theology should not be about generating novelty but about passing on the faith once delivered to the saints. So, if the union account is a completely new way of thinking about the atonement, we should be suspicious of it. Why has it taken so long for us to uncover this view if it is the right view? What implications does this have for other accounts of the atonement? How are we to understand the union account in light of the views we have encountered in previous chapters?

In one respect, these are worthy concerns. Theological novelty is often in tension with the deposit of the faith once for all entrusted to the saints, as Jude puts it in Jude 3: "I felt compelled to write and urge you to contend for the faith that was once for all entrusted to God's holy people." Yet theological reflection upon that deposit of faith may generate new ways of thinking about the faith, and new insights about the faith, just as someone may have new insights about other texts that have not been seen by previous generations.[7] Our social context, location, and the church and community to which we belong shape our reading of and interaction with Scripture and the Christian tradition in profound ways. What we think about the nature of salvation will be formed by these influences even if we are not aware of it, just as a person wearing rose-tinted spectacles will see a rose-colored world. Each new generation of Christians seeks to appropriate the past, the Christian tradition, and Scripture, in order to make sense of the faith once for all entrusted to the saints. How we do this is different in each generation because our vantage is different, our influences are different, and our place in history and culture is different.

So it is not surprising that the union account reflects these things. After all, it is a model of the atonement, and, as we saw in chapter one, models are simplified descriptions of more complex data. They are also one way of looking at that data, and may not be the only way of doing so. However, in defense of the union account, it should also be apparent that it is steeped in the biblical witness, in new ways in which the theology of Paul is being

---

[7]Consider the way in which priest and theologian Michael Ward has recently shown that C. S. Lewis's *Chronicles of Narnia* are shaped by his fascination with medieval cosmology—the result of which is a very different way of thinking about these familiar children's books. See Michael Ward, *Planet Narnia: The Seven Heavens in the Imagination of C. S. Lewis* (New York: Oxford University Press, 2008).

thought about in contemporary theology, and in previous ways of thinking about the atonement. Its debt to the patristic tradition should be particularly apparent. In many ways, it is an attempt to give an updated and (perhaps) clearer account of some of the core ideas that we noted when we looked at Athanasius and Irenaeus in particular in chapter two. But it is also indebted to later atonement theology as well. It can use language of ransom as part of its explanation of Christ's work of salvation. Moreover, like the satisfaction doctrine, it can speak in terms of Christ's work satisfying God's honor (although the mechanism for atonement is different from satisfaction). But in many ways its emphasis upon the vicarious work of Christ, and upon his work as a substitute bearing the penal consequences for human sin makes it very like penal substitution. Unlike penal substitution, it does not require that Christ is punished as a substitute, strictly speaking. Yet he bears the penal consequences of the sin of those who are members of redeemed humanity. He is able to act on their behalf because they are members of this one entity, redeemed humanity, that exists across time. As in some situations the parts of a thing may stand in for the whole of that thing (like Tibbles's head seen from the window), so also Christ may act on behalf of the whole of redeemed humanity, as the part of that whole authorized to do so by God. Although this is in some respects a new way of thinking about the atonement, it would be more accurate to call it a new way of thinking about some old ideas of the atonement, or a new way of interpreting existing notions about the nature of the atonement. It may not provide all the answers to the atonement, but it does address some of the major concerns we have seen with previous views of Christ's reconciling work, throwing these different parts into a new whole.

A second concern with the union account of atonement has to do with what we can call problems of composition, that is, problems having to do with the wholes and parts invoked by the argument. Put bluntly, how are we to think of these entities called fallen humanity and redeemed humanity? What is their status? In what sense are they *real* things at all? Admittedly, fallen and redeemed humanity are odd things. However, we treat many other sorts of things as wholes even if they are composed of parts fabricated by human beings, such as cars or computers. According to the union account of atonement God generates fallen and redeemed humanity much as he generates the human race as, in a sense, a whole entity that is scattered through time, each of whose members shares in common certain attributes. We are used to the notion that a part of something may stand in for the whole (remember the example of Tibbles through the window). Parts can sometimes act "on behalf" of wholes too. For instance, by means of using my mouth and tongue I can convey what I think about something. Here parts (my mouth and tongue) convey something that is true of the whole human person. The union account takes up the Pauline language about union with Christ and offers a way of understanding how Christ can stand in for the whole of redeemed humanity in atonement just as Adam stands in for the whole of fallen humanity in his original sin.

Third, and in light of this, we can consider whether the union account actually addresses the theological concerns with which we began the chapter, and which we uncovered in thinking about previous attempts to model the atonement. These are the three worries about punishing the innocent, about the transfer of sin and guilt, and about the moral and legal fiction involved in the imputation of sin from Adam to fallen humanity, and from fallen humanity to Christ, as well as the imputation of Christ's righteousness to the redeemed.

Clearly, on this view Christ is not punished. He takes upon himself the penal consequences for the sin of fallen human beings, but that is not the same as punishing an innocent for the sins of the guilty. Next, although Adam's sin is passed onto his progeny, this doesn't necessarily include the idea that the guilt of his sin is transferred as well. And in the case of Christ, he does take upon himself responsibility for the sin of fallen human beings, becoming "sin for us" by his vicarious act of atonement. However, because he is united with the members of redeemed humanity into one organic whole, it is not the case that one individual has transferred to him the sin of another. Rather, as a member of an organic whole of which he is a part, Christ acts. Finally, it should be clear from the foregoing that the union account does not depend on any moral or legal fiction in order to make good on the application of the sin of fallen human beings to Christ, or Christ's act of reconciliation to fallen humanity. As Edwards put it, "The real in the union between Christ and his people, is the foundation of what is legal." It is because we are really united to Christ that he is able to act on our behalf.

CONCLUSION

There is much more that could be said about this view of atonement. It is not necessarily the last word on the matter, for, as we made clear in chapter one, models of atonement are by their nature limited in what they can explain about the reconciling work of Christ. Nevertheless, this view has certain advantages over other traditional views like penal substitution. It doesn't fall foul of the worries about the transfer of sin and guilt, and it doesn't rely on a kind of moral or legal fiction to make good on its theological claims. It also taps into deep theological themes that have been part of the earliest witness in the Christian tradition to the Pauline theology of union with Christ and participation in the life of God. For these reasons, it seems to me to be an approach to the atonement worthy of serious consideration.

FURTHER READING

Bayne, Tim, and Greg Restall, "A Participatory Model of the Atonement." In *New Waves in Philosophy of Religion*, ed. Yugin Nagasawa and Erik J. Wielenberg, 150-66. London: Palsgrave Macmillan, 2009.

Collins, Robin. "Girard and Atonement: An Incarnational Theory of Mimetic Participation." In *Violence Renounced: René Girard, Biblical Studies, and Peacemaking*, ed. Willard M. Swartley, 132-156. Telford, PA: Pandora Press, 2000. Collins has several other versions of papers that contain some of the same basic elements, addressed to different audiences, and located on his institutional homepage: http://home.messiah.edu/~rcollins/

Crisp, Oliver D. *The Word Enfleshed: Exploring the Person and Work of Christ*. Grand Rapids: Baker Academic, 2016.

———. "Sin." In *Christian Dogmatics: Reformed Theology for the Church Catholic*, ed. Michael Allen and Scott R. Swain, 194-215. Grand Rapids: Baker Academic, 2016.

Edwards, Jonathan. "Justification by Faith." In *Sermons and Discourses, 1734-1738: The Works of Jonathan Edwards, Vol. 19*, ed. M. X. Lesser, 144-243. New Haven, CT: Yale University Press, 2001.

Gorman, Michael J. *Inhabiting the Cruciform God: Kenosis, Justification, and Theosis in Paul's Narrative Soteriology*. Grand Rapids: Eerdmans, 2009.

Myers, Benjamin. "The Patristic Doctrine of Atonement." In *Locating Atonement: Explorations in Constructive Dogmatics*, ed. Oliver D. Crisp and Fred Sanders, 71-88. Grand Rapids: Zondervan Academic, 2015.

Tanner, Kathryn. *Christ the Key*. Cambridge: Cambridge University Press, 2010.

GLOSSARY OF TERMS

atonement: The English word for the reconciling work of Christ, meaning *at-one-ment.*

commercial view (of atonement): The way in which Anselm's doctrine of satisfaction is sometimes described in older textbooks of theology. This is because Anselm's view presumes a kind of transaction between the Father and the Son in the atonement—hence, a kind of commercial view of the atonement.

critical realism: The idea that there is some real truth of the matter independent of human minds, but that our grasp of that truth may be partial, informed by theory, and in need of revision in light of further data.

doctrine: A comprehensive account of a particular teaching about a given theological topic held by some community of Christians, or some particular denomination.

expiation: The way in which atonement does away with the power of sin in fallen human beings.

governmental view (of atonement): *See* penal non-substitution.

kaleidoscopic view (of atonement): The notion, associated with the work of Joel Green and Mark Baker in particular, that no one atonement model is sufficient; the multiplicity of atonement models each provide a "window" into the truth of Christ's reconciling work that no single account can adequately express.

mashup view (of atonement): The attempt to take elements of different existing atonement accounts and "mash" them together into a new, composite whole. Usually this whole privileges certain motifs or ideas above others. The basic idea is that of the mashup genre in literature and music: bringing elements from other works together in a new whole composed of the parts cannibalized from elsewhere. An example is the work of Hans Boersma.

mechanism (of atonement): The means by which Christ's work actually reconciles fallen human beings to Godself. All atonement models include a mechanism or account of how this comes about.

model (of atonement): A simplified description of more complex data that attempts to give a "picture" of the data that approximates to the truth of the matter, e.g., the model of an atom in a physics textbook, or the penal substitution model of atonement.

moral exemplar: The idea that Christ's life and death in particular are a moral example of divine love toward fallen human beings that should elicit a response of love in us, and an appropriate change of character as well.

non-penal substitution: The view according to which the atonement is substitutionary in nature, so that Christ stands in our place, but not as a penal substitute. Instead, he offers up an act of perfect penitence or apology on behalf of fallen humanity. This view is sometimes called *vicarious penitence.*

penal non-substitution: The view according to which Christ's reconciling work is penal in nature (having to do with God's moral law), but is not a substitutionary work, strictly speaking. He does not stand in our place taking upon himself our punishment. Instead, he is a penal example, or deterrent. God treats Christ harshly so that his moral law is upheld, and so that he can offer fallen humanity salvation. This view is often called the *governmental view.*

penal substitution: The view according to which Christ stands in our place, taking on himself the punishment that is due to fallen human beings, being punished for them so that God does not have to punish them. The idea is that God's retributive justice must be exercised, and punishment must be handed out. But a suitable penal substitute may be able to take that punishment in place of the guilty. A weaker form of the doctrine only requires that Christ take upon himself the penal consequences of human sin, not the actual punishment for it.

propitiation: The sacrifice of atonement by means of which God is said to be appeased.

ransom view (of atonement): The view according to which Christ pays the price of his life in order to purchase fallen human beings. Often this is illustrated by means of a story where Christ pays the devil a price to buy humanity that have sold themselves into his dominion through sin. However, this story and the notion of ransom are distinct.

reconciliation: Another word for the way in which Christ's atoning work brings us back into right relationship with God.

redemption: The purchase price of something that must be paid in order to buy it back. In the atonement, this is the purchase price of fallen humanity paid by Christ in the atonement.

satisfaction: The view according to which Christ's work is not a substitution, strictly speaking, but a work of supererogation, or an act above and beyond the call of duty, by means of which he generates an infinite merit that can be offered so as to satisfy God, who has been dishonored by the sin of human beings.

supererogatory: A moral action that is above and beyond the call of duty.

theory (of atonement): A theory is some overarching conceptual framework or system of ideas based on general principles independent of those that require explanation, such as a "theory of education," or the "theory of evolution." Accounts of the atonement are not really theories in that sense.

theosis: The doctrine of salvation according to which human beings are destined to be united to God through Christ by the power of the Holy Spirit, thereby participating in the divine life. Often this union is described in terms of a union of natures, not of essence. The idea is that humans are on a trajectory into God, so to speak, becoming ever more like him, but never losing themselves "in" him, like a drop of water in an ocean, nor ever becoming fused with him. This is a widespread doctrine taught in the early church fathers, by some medieval theologians, and by a number of Protestant thinkers too, such as John Calvin, (arguably) Martin Luther, and Jonathan Edwards.

transformative experience: An experience that brings about significant transformation that one could not necessarily anticipate prior to undergoing that experience. A view developed in recent philosophy by L. A. Paul.

union account (of atonement): The view (based on Pauline language of "participation" in Christ, e.g., in Rom 5:12-19) according to which fallen human beings are somehow really united to Christ through his atonement. We somehow really participate in the reconciling work of Christ and his saving benefits, being made "one" with him.

BIBLIOGRAPHY

Abelard, Peter. *Commentary on the Epistle to the Romans*. Fathers of the Church Medieval Continuations Series. Translated by Stephen R. Cartwright. Washington, DC: Catholic University of America Press, 2011.

Anselm of Canterbury. *Cur deus homo*. In *Anselm: Basic Writing*, translated by Thomas Williams, 237-326. Indianapolis: Hackett, 2007.

Athanasius. *On the Incarnation*. Translated by John Behr. Crestwood, NY: St. Vladimir's Seminary Press, 2006.

Augustine. *Confessions*. Translated by Thomas Williams. Indianapolis: Hackett, 2019.

———. *Sermons on the Liturgical Seasons*. Fathers of the Church Patristic Series, translated by Mary Sarah Muldowney. Washington, DC: The Catholic University of America Press, 1984.

Aulén, Gustaf. *Christus Victor: An Historical Study of the Three Main Types of the Idea of Atonement*. London: SPCK, 1931.

Baker, Mark D., and Joel B. Green. *Recovering the Scandal of the Cross: Atonement in New Testament and Contemporary Contexts*. 2nd edition. Downers Grove, IL: IVP Academic, 2011.

Bayne, Tim, and Greg Restall, "A Participatory Model of the Atonement." In *New Waves in Philosophy of Religion*, edited by Yugin Nagasawa and Erik J. Wielenberg, 150-166. London: Palsgrave Macmillan, 2009.

Beilby, James K., and Paul R. Eddy, eds. *The Nature of Atonement: Four Views*. Downers Grove, IL: IVP Academic, 2006.

Berkhof, Louis. *Systematic Theology*. 1939. Reprint, Edinburgh: Banner of Truth, 1988.

Boersma, Hans. *Violence, Hospitality, and the Cross: Reappropriating the Atonement Tradition*. Grand Rapids: Baker Academic, 2004.

Brown, David. "Anselm on the Atonement." In *The Cambridge Companion to Anselm of Canterbury*, edited by Brian Davies and Brian Leftow, 279-302. Cambridge: Cambridge University Press, 2004.

Brown, Joanna Carlson, and Rebecca Parker, "For God So Loved the World?" In *Christianity, Patriarchy, and Abuse: A Feminist Critique*, edited by Joanne Carlson Brown and Carole R. Bohn, 1-30. New York: The Pilgrim Press, 1989.

Calvin, John. *Institutes of the Christian Religion*. Edited by John T. McNeil. Translated by Ford Lewis Battles. 1559. Reprint, Philadelphia: Westminster Press, 1960.

Campbell, John McLeod. *The Nature of the Atonement*. 1856. Reprint, Grand Rapids: Eerdmans, 1996.

Collins, Robin. "Girard and Atonement: An Incarnational Theory of Mimetic Participation." In *Violence Renounced: René Girard, Biblical Studies, and Peacemaking*, edited by Willard M. Swartley, 132-156. Telford, PA: Pandora Press, 2000.

Craig, William Lane. *The Atonement*. Cambridge Elements. Cambridge: Cambridge University Press, 2018.

Crisp, Oliver D. *The Word Enfleshed: Exploring the Person and Work of Christ*. Grand Rapids: Baker Academic, 2016.

———. *Saving Calvinism: Expanding the Reformed Tradition*. Downers Grove, IL: IVP Academic, 2016.

———. "Methodological Issues in Approaching the Atonement." In *T&T Clark Companion to Atonement*, edited by Adam J. Johnson, 315-34. London: Bloomsbury T&T Clark, 2017.

———. "The Logic of Penal Substitution Revisited" in Derek Tidball, David Holborn, and Justin Thacker, eds. *The Atonement Debate*, 208-227.

———. "John McLeod Campbell and Non-penal substitution." In *Retrieving Doctrine: Essays in Reformed Theology*, 92-115. Downers Grove, IL: IVP Academic, 2011.

———. "Penal Non-substitution." In *A Reader in Philosophical Theology*, edited by Oliver Crisp, 299-327. London: T&T Clark, 2009.

———. "Sin." In *Christian Dogmatics: Reformed Theology for the Church Catholic*, edited by Michael Allen and Scott R. Swain, 194-215. Grand Rapids: Baker Academic, 2016.

Edwards, Jonathan. "Justification by Faith" In *Sermons and Discourses, 1734-1738: The Works of Jonathan Edwards*, vol. 19, edited by M. X. Lesser, 144-243. New Haven, CT: Yale University Press, 2001.

———. *The Works of Jonathan Edwards, Vol. II*. Edited by Edward Hickman. 1834. Reprint, Edinburgh: Banner of Truth, 1974.

Evans, G. R. *Anselm*. Outstanding Christian Thinkers. London: Bloomsbury, 2005.

Finlan, Stephen. *Options on Atonement in Christian Theology*. Liturgical Press, 2007.

Forsyth, P. T. *The Cruciality of the Cross*. London: Hodder and Stoughton, 1910.

Franks, R. S. *The Work of Christ*. 2nd ed. London: Thomas Nelson, 1962.

Gathercole, Simon. *Defending Substitution: An Essay on Atonement in Paul*. Grand Rapids: Baker Academic, 2015.

Gomes, Alan W. "De Jesu Christo Servatore: Faustus Socinus on the Satisfaction of Christ." *Westminster Theological Journal* 55 (1993): 209-31.

Gorman, Michael J. *Inhabiting the Cruciform God: Kenosis, Justification, and Theosis in Paul's Narrative Soteriology*. Grand Rapids: Eerdmans, 2009.

Grensted, L. W. *A Short History of the Doctrine of Atonement*. Manchester: University of Manchester Press, 1920.

Grotius, Hugo. *A Defense of the Catholic Faith Concerning the Satisfaction of Christ Against Faustus Socinus*. Translated by Frank Hugh Foster. 1617. Reprint, Andover: Warren F. Draper, 1889.

Gunton, Colin E. *The Actuality of Atonement: A Study of Metaphor, Rationality and the Christian Tradition*. London: T&T Clark, 1988.

Hick, John. *An Interpretation of Religion: Human Responses to the Transcendent*. 2nd ed. 1989. Reprint, London: Macmillan, 2004.

———. *The Metaphor of God Incarnate*. 2nd ed. 1993. Reprint, Louisville, KY: Westminster John Knox Press, 2005.

Hodge, A. A. *The Atonement*. Philadelphia: Presbyterian Board of Publication, 1867.

Holmes, Stephen R. "Penal Substitution." In *T&T Clark Companion to Atonement*, edited by Adam J. Johnson, 295-314. London: Bloomsbury, 2017.

Irenaeus. *On the Apostolic Preaching*. Translated by John Behr. Crestwood, NY: St. Vladimir's Seminary Press, 1997.

———. *Against Heresies*. In vol. 1 of *The Ante-Nicene Fathers*. Series 1. Edited by Philip Schaff and Henry Wace. Edinburgh: T&T Clark, 1885.

Jeffery, Steve, Michael Ovey, and Andrew Sach, *Pierced for Our Transgressions: Rediscovering the Glory of Penal Substitution*. Wheaton, IL: Crossway, 2007.

Jersak, Brad, and Michael Hardin, eds. *Stricken by God? Nonviolent Identification and the Victory of Christ*. Grand Rapids: Eerdmans, 2007.

John of Damascus. *On The Orthodox Faith*. In vol. 9 of *The Nicene and Post-Nicene Fathers*. Series 2. Edited by Philip Schaff and Henry Wace. Edinburgh: T&T Clark, 1898.

Johnson, Adam. *Atonement: A Guide for the Perplexed*. London: T&T Clark, 2015.

Lewis, David. "Do We Believe in Penal Substitution?" *Philosophical Papers* 26, no. 3 (1997): 203-9.

McEwan, Ian. *Atonement*. New York: Anchor Books, 2003.

McGrath, Alister E. "The Moral Theory of the Atonement: An Historical and Theological Critique." *Scottish Journal of Theology* 38 (1985): 205-20.

McIntyre, John. *St. Anselm and His Critics: A Re-Interpretation of the Cur Deus Homo.* Edinburgh: Oliver & Boyd, 1954.

Miley, John. *The Atonement in Christ.* New York: Philips and Hunt, 1879.

Mozley, J. K. *The Doctrine of the Atonement.* New York: Charles Scribner's Sons, 1916.

Myers, Benjamin. "The Patristic Doctrine of Atonement." In *Locating Atonement: Explorations in Constructive Dogmatics,* edited by Oliver D. Crisp and Fred Sanders, 71-88. Grand Rapids: Zondervan Academic, 2015.

Van Neiuwenhove, Rik. *An Introduction to Medieval Theology.* Cambridge: Cambridge University Press, 2012.

Niebuhr, H. Richard. *The Kingdom of God in America.* 1932. Reprint, Middletown, CT: Wesleyan University Press, 1988.

Gregory of Nyssa. *The Great Catechism.* In vol. 5 of *The Nicene and Post-Nicene Fathers.* Series 2. Edited by Philip Schaff and Henry Wace. Edinburgh: T&T Clark, 1892.

Packer, James I. "What Did the Cross Achieve? The Logic of Penal Substitution," *Tyndale Bulletin* 25 (1974): 3-45.

Paul, L. A. *Transformative Experience.* Oxford: Oxford University Press, 2014.

Peacore, Linda. *The Role of Women's Experience in Feminist Theologies of Atonement.* Eugene, OR: Pickwick Publications, 2010.

Plantinga, Richard J., Thomas R. Thompson, and Matthew D. Lundberg. *An Introduction to Christian Theology.* Cambridge: Cambridge University Press, 2010.

Pugh, Ben. *Atonement Theories: A Way Through the Maze.* Eugene, OR: Cascade Books, 2014.

Purves, Andrew. *Exploring Christology and Atonement: Conversations with John McLeod Campbell, H. R. Mackintosh and T. F. Torrance.* Downers Grove, IL: IVP Academic, 2015.

Quinn, Philip. "Abelard on Atonement: Nothing Unintelligible, Arbitrary, Illogical, or Immoral About It." In *A Reader in Philosophical Theology,* edited by Oliver D. Crisp, 335-53. London: Bloomsbury, 2009.

Rashdall, Hastings. *The Idea of Atonement in Christian Theology, Being the Bampton Lectures for 1915.* London: Macmillan and Co., 1919.

Ray, Darby Kathleen. *Deceiving the Devil: Atonement, Abuse, and Ransom.* Cleveland, OH: Pilgrim Press, 1988.

Ritschl, Abrecht. *The Christian Doctrine of Justification and Reconciliation.* 2nd ed. Translated by H. R. MacIntosh and A. B. Macaulay. Edinburgh: T&T Clark, 1902.

Romanides, John S. *The Ancestral Sin.* Ridgewood, NJ: Zephyr, 2002.

Rutledge, Fleming. *The Crucifixion: Understanding the Death of Jesus Christ.* Grand Rapids: Eerdmans, 2015.

Sanders, John, ed. *Atonement and Violence: A Theological Conversation.* Nashville: Abingdon Press, 2006.

Schleiermacher, Friedrich. *The Christian Faith.* Edited by H. R. MacIntosh and J. R. Stewart. Edinburgh: T&T Clark, 1928.

Socinus, Faustus. *De Jesu Christo Servatore, Part III.* Translated by Alan W. Gomes. PhD dissertation, Fuller Theological Seminary, 1990.

Stump, Eleonore. *Atonement.* Oxford Studies in Analytic Theology. Oxford: Oxford University Press, 2018.

Sweeney, Eileen C. *Anselm of Canterbury and the Desire for the Word.* Washington, DC: Catholic University of America Press, 2012.

Swinburne, Richard. *Responsibility and Atonement.* Oxford: Oxford University Press, 1989.

Tanner, Kathryn. *Christ the Key.* Cambridge: Cambridge University Press, 2010.

———. *Jesus, Humanity and the Trinity: A Brief Systematic Theology.* Minneapolis: Fortress Press, 2001.

Tertullian. *On Repentance.* In vol. 3 of *The Ante-Nicene Fathers,* edited by Alexander Roberts and James Donaldson, 657-668. New York: Charles Scribner's Sons, 1905.

Thurow, Joshua. "Communal Substitutionary Atonement." *Journal of Analytic Theology* 3 (2015): 47-69.

Tidball, Derek, David Hilborn, and Justin Thaker, eds. *The Atonement Debate.* Grand Rapids: Zondervan, 2008.

Visser, Sandra, and Thomas Williams. *Anselm.* Great Medieval Thinkers Series. Oxford: Oxford University Press, 2010.

Ward, Michael. *Planet Narnia: The Seven Heavens in the Imagination of C. S. Lewis.* New York: Oxford University Press, 2008.

Weaver, J. Denny. *The Nonviolent Atonement.* 2nd ed. 2001. Reprint, Grand Rapids: Eerdmans, 2011.

Weingart, Richard E. *The Logic of Divine Love: A Critical Analysis of the Soteriology of Peter Abailard.* Oxford: Oxford University Press, 1970.

Williams, Garry J. "Penal Substitution: A Response to Recent Criticisms." *Journal of the Evangelical Theological Society* 50/1 (2007): 71-86.

Williams, Thomas. "Sin, Grace, and Redemption." In *The Cambridge Companion to Abelard,* edited by Jeffrey E. Brower and Kevin Guilfoy, 258-78. Cambridge: Cambridge University Press, 2004.

Zagzebski, Linda. "Foreknowledge and Free Will." *Stanford Encyclopedia of Philosophy.* https://plato.stanford.edu/entries/free-will-foreknowledge.

GENERAL INDEX

SCRIPTURE INDEX

Finding the Textbook You Need

The IVP Academic Textbook Selector
is an online tool for instantly finding the IVP books
suitable for over 250 courses across 24 disciplines.

ivpacademic.com